THE CULTURE OF LABOURISM

THE CULTURE OF LABOURISM
The East End Between the Wars

JOHN   MARRIOTT

EDINBURGH UNIVERSITY PRESS

Edinburgh University Press
22 George Square, Edinburgh

Distributed in North America
by Columbia University Press
    New York

Set in Linotron Palatino
by Koinonia Ltd, Bury, and
printed in Great Britain by
Robert Hartnoll Ltd, Bodmin

British Library Cataloguing
    in Publication Data
Marriott, John
    The culture of Labourism: West
Ham between the wars.
    1. London. Political parties:
Labour party. Great Britain, history
    I. Title
    324.24107

ISBN 0 7486 0248 8 (cased)

CONTENTS

ACKNOWLEDGEMENTS

Few books are the product of single, individual labour. This one certainly isn't, and it gives me pleasure to be able to acknowledge those who have contributed in one way or another. It was made possible by my colleagues in the Cultural Studies department at the Polytechnic of East London; in particular, Sally Alexander, Catherine Hall, Alan O'Shea, Ken Parker, Bill Schwarz and Winifred Stokes. They recognised that since the polytechnic was located in an area of enormous historical significance it would be worth undertaking research better to understand that history, persuaded the polytechnic authorities that the research should be financed, and during the research were to provide constant critical support and encouragement despite their own demanding commitments. Thanks also to Jerry White and Dan Weinbren for some highly enjoyable evenings spent discussing a mutual love of London history.

Howard Bloch and Jill Davis in the London Borough of Newham, Local Studies Library have given me free access to its records, and provided a most conducive environment in which to work. Here also I have continued to benefit from the extensive knowledge of Frank Sainsbury, ex-borough librarian of West Ham. Other librarians and archivists have been hospitable. Sean Bamford at the NUR, Peter Carter at the GMBATU and Eddie Durkin at the TGWU allowed me access to unions records, David Webb at the Bishopsgate Institute helped with its outstanding collection of London cooperative material, as did Steven Bird at the Labour Party with the party archive, and Joyce Motyka, Administration Officer, Cooperative Women's Guild. The library of the London School of Economics and Political Science was, as always, invaluable.

Nor is this book the product of single-mindedness. No matter how large a part of my life it has occupied over the past two years or so, Billie Holiday and John Coltrane were never far away. But most I owe to my family. From my early fanciful ideas of becoming a historian, and in spite of the inevitable emotional and financial assault courses, Frances, Georgia, Keir and Sergei have been a constant source of good-humoured support and encouragement.

John Marriott

ABBREVIATIONS

ASCJ	Associated Society of Carpenters and Joiners
ASLEF	Associated Society of Locomotive Engineers and Footplatemen
ASRS	Associated Society of Railway Servants
AUCE	Amalgamated Union of Cooperative Employees
BSP	British Socialist Party
CP	Communist Party
CU	Cooperative Union
CWS	Cooperative Wholesale Society
DWRGLU	Dock, Water, Riverside and General Labourers' Union
FGRA	Forest Gate Ratepayers' Association
GER	Great Eastern Railway
GWGLU	Gasworkers and General Labourers' Union
ILP	Independent Labour Party
LCC	London County Council
LDCU	London District Council of the Unemployed
LLP	London Labour Party
LMS	London, Midland and Scottish
LNER	London and North Eastern Railway
MEA	Municipal Employees Association
NAUL	National Amalgamated Union of Labour
NFDDSS	National Federation of Discharged and Disabled Soldiers and Sailors
NSP	National Socialist Party
NUGW	National Union of General Workers
NUM	National Union of Mineworkers
NUR	National Union of Railwaymen
NUWM	National Unemployed Workers Movement
RILU	Red International of Labour Unions
SCS	Stratford Cooperative Society
SDF	Social Democratic Federation
SDP	Social Democratic Party
SE	*Stratford Express*

TGWU	Transport and General Workers' Union
TUC	Trades Union Congress
UBWU	United Building Workers' Union
WCG	Women's Cooperative Guild
WHBG	West Ham Board of Guardians
WHMA	West Ham Municipal Alliance
WHTC	West Ham Trades Council

1

PERSPECTIVES: LABOURISM AND WEST HAM

> There is a place called Canning Town and further out,
> Silvertown, where the pleasant meadows are at their
> pleasantist; doubtless they were once slums and wretched
> enough. (William Morris *News from nowhere*, 1890.)

Some seventeen years ago I moved with my young family to West Ham from Ealing. Considerable though the distance was across the metropolis, I sensed that the cultural and historical boundaries we traversed were of far greater significance. Not that the destination was a familiar one. At the time West Ham was little more to me than a name, most directly associated with a football team that had a reputation for style and steadfast support in spite of limited success on the field. As a borough, it no longer existed. A rather strained merger with adjacent East Ham in 1965 had created the London Borough of Newham. But cultures and histories are not defined by administrative boundaries, and I soon recognised that in quite tangible ways something of West Ham survived in the indigenous population – now rapidly declining and ageing – and in the language.

Any romanticised impressions I may have had of the East End were quickly tempered if not dispelled by the striking images of endemic poverty and a sclerotic political culture. Protracted industrial decline since the 1920s, accelerated in the postwar period by the closure of the docks, had produced all the symptoms of a depressed inner-city area which, according to a government survey using a range of socioeconomic indicators, was the second most deprived urban borough in the country (Department of the Environment 1983). The south in particular was enveloped in a pall of neglect. Streets which once throbbed with dock and factory workers and their families were now deserted. To walk through Silvertown and Custom House was to walk through ghost towns.

Politically, the area was dominated by the Labour Party. For as long as anyone could remember the council had been overwhelmingly Labour, and all the MPs came from the ranks of the party. So secure was this control, I was told, that if a monkey in a red jacket was put up as a candidate it would be elected. Yet popular political interest was low, and the council was rarely perceived to represent adequately the interests of local people. A study of political participation in four London boroughs over the years 1968-74 revealed that in Newham decisions were taken at informal caucus meetings of the Labour group (Chamberlayne 1978). There was little discussion of policy either within the majority or with community representatives. Councillors, most of whom had strong local roots and had been in power for many years, came to believe they had a permanent mandate and readily resisted any challenge to their authority. Demands from local groups for increased participation in the processes of decision making concerning housing and welfare were seen as politically inspired and met with hostility. Democratic councillors, it was argued, should not be usurped by pressure groups. The prevailing ethos was one of 'benevolent neglect'.

This political landscape stood in some contrast to what I understood to be the quite exceptional role played by West Ham in the historical development of the Labour Party and the trade union and cooperative movements. Around the Stratford locomotive works a powerful cooperative movement had grown in the last third of the nineteenth century, and from the Beckton gasworks in 1889 new unionism had sprung. Both movements were to retain a considerable presence in West Ham, and influence pioneering efforts to develop labour representation. The first independent labour MP, Keir Hardie, was elected from West Ham South in 1892, and the first labour council assumed control of municipal affairs in 1898. It was a contrast that I found intriguing, and when given the opportunity embarked on research to explore further its nature and consequences.

As is so often the case with such ventures the programme was overambitious; by the time I completed the initial research I had reached no further than 1910 (Marriott 1984). At least I had a firmer grasp of the industrial development of West Ham and the distinct political culture it had witnessed, particularly during the 1890s. Now I felt in a position to explore the fate of this culture, and thereby the roots of the contemporary political landscape. The single most significant feature in this landscape was the Labour Party. Formed nationally in 1900 it had played no role in pioneering local labour representation; not until the early interwar years did it emerge with quite remarkable rapidity as the dominant political force in West Ham. It was to these crucial years, therefore, that I turned attention in an endeavour to understand not the triumphal march of the party as such, but rather the broader cultural structures that laid the foundations for its success.

This study is concerned ostensibly with the political development of West Ham in the early interwar years but, I hope, not merely that. Rather I wish to use the experience of West Ham as a means to examine the nature of working-class political intervention. The success of the Labour Party in West Ham was part of a national movement that culminated in the assumption of parliamentary power in 1924 and the emergence of the party in a recognisably modern form. And West Ham was not the only predominantly working-class area that gave rise to a political authority seemingly remote from popular allegiance. Indeed, at a national level the party has never been able to command active and continued support from a large majority of the working-class electorate.

The triumphs and failures of the party cannot be seen solely in terms of its own policy, strategy and organisational forms. It was nurtured by a tradition of working-class involvement in politics which exhibited strong continuities well into this century. I choose to define this tradition as labourism, and attempt to locate the Labour Party within it. In so doing I depart somewhat from studies of working-class involvement in the formal political sphere during the twentieth century. To justify such an approach it is necessary to take a theoretical detour. Those readers who have an aversion to such are advised to pass quickly by the next two sections, and move to the discussion of West Ham which provides the historical context for what is to follow.

1.1 The boundaries of labourism

To begin by defining the object of inquiry is good practice, not least because it can serve to resolve ambiguities in common use and provide a snapshot of the landscape to be charted. Had I access to a neat and sound definition of labourism I would use it; sadly I do not. Instead I have to start by describing something of the unease I feel about its use and study within the literature, and gradually move toward a position from which I can either offer a definition of labourism or construct boundaries within which it exists and operates.

There is a tendency, especially since the publication of Miliband's *Parliamentary socialism* (1961), to equate labourism with the history and practice of Labour within the parliamentary sphere. At no place in this influential tradition is labourism defined, but it is evident that the term refers almost exclusively to the political orthodoxy dictating the course of labour representation in parliament. And for good reason; the Labour Party, after all, has for most of this century been the most obvious and visible manifestation of working-class political activity. The consequence is, however, that much of the subsequent work on labourism has directed attention to the nature of the party, as if the two were coterminous. Indeed, it is often difficult to imagine the existence of labourism beyond the boundaries of the party.

In a characteristically elegant analysis, Nairn (1965) traces the origins of the party in Victorian trades unionism. Profoundly subordinate, and remote from the few voices of intellectual protest, trade unions could provide no effective challenge to bourgeois hegemony; rather they were firmly embedded in the mystical pragmatism, rationalism, evolutionism and nationalism of the Victorian epoch. This trade unionism came eventually to believe in the need for parliamentary representation to safeguard its interests, and from the start determined the course of political intervention.

Thus the mental horizons of labourism (by which Nairn refers to the tradition of independent working-class representation) were severely circumscribed. Even those currents that attached themselves to the drift of labourism, and with which they often had an uneasy relationship, were pathologically infected by the same bourgeois traditions. It was utilitarianism that provided the administrative rationality of Fabianism, and an impotent protestantism the spirituality of the Independent Labour Party. Both denied struggle for power as an agent of social change, but accepted the necessity of evolution, the logical consequence of which was belief in the centrality of parliamentarianism.

Similar arguments appear in Forester (1976), Haseler (1980) and Panitch (1986). Here there is a shared concern to distance the history of the Labour Party from that of socialism. Because of the wholesale integration of the theory and practice of the party into the national cultural formation, at no time did it promote its working-class constituency as an agent of social change. Instinctive acceptance of a corporate identity for this constituency forced the party into an integrative role on two distinct but related fronts. The working class represented by the party was encouraged to assume separate but non-antagonistic relations with other social classes, while the party itself became increasingly enmeshed in the parliamentary system, denying the worth or validity of extra-parliamentary struggle.

It is in the light of such that we can begin to understand the inception and growth of the Labour Party. The party was not the product of a distinct working-class movement informed by a corpus of political theory, but emerged as a pragmatic response to new challenges, and subsequently developed through political expedience. From the outset its commitment to Labour representation was characterised by an incipient logic of empiricism, evolutionism, compromise and defence.

In the period between its formation and the outbreak of the first world war the party made limited progress. Membership remained low, constituency organisation was primitive, its parliamentary presence was small, and much of the intellectual leadership was disillusioned. Sharing a common cultural and spiritual heritage with a section of the older and more firmly entrenched Liberal Party, Labour simply had not been able to capture sufficient support from the working-class electorate.

The precise nature of the impact of the first world war on the fortunes of the Labour Party remains open to debate. In the standard account of the party's growth into a modern political organisation over the period 1910-24, McKibbin (1974) concludes that the war was not of first importance to its ultimate rise to power:

> Everything points to Labour's enduring *ante-bellum* character: continuity of leadership and personnel, effective continuity of policy, and, above all, continuity of organization. The Labour Party … remained as it had been before 1914 – propagandist and evangelical. (p240.)

The rise of Labour was intrinsically related to the eclipse of the Liberal

Party. Whatever the reasons for the latter, Labour was able to fill the political vacuum created, not as an automatic or natural beneficiary, but because of the electoral advances gained from growth of the trade unions.

Other writers prompt us to question aspects of McKibbin's thesis, in particular, its extraordinary neglect of the war. For Nairn (1965) the war *made* the modern Labour Party. Experience of wartime administration persuaded Labour leaders that they had a responsible role to play in a new economic system which had successfully revealed the inadequacies of *laissez faire* capitalism, while among the working-class electorate a sense of the potential of a new social order in the postwar period took root. These arguments tend to be supported by a detailed study of the impact of the war on East London (Bush 1978), and the more recent work of Waites (1987) in which he demonstrates that during the war the working class was able temporarily to reappropriate nationalist sentiment, articulating it with an assertive, class-conscious resistance to perceived excesses of capitalist exploitation.

In the immediate postwar period the Labour Party, strengthened by more efficient constituency organisation, a new constitution and programme, and a confident trade union movement, was able to mobilise this heightened working-class consciousness among an enlarged electorate. By 1924 the party was recognisably the party of today (McKibbin 1974 p236), and in a position to take power for the first time.

This body of work is familiar enough. Although disputes continue over detail, there remains a persuasive logic to its arguments, paralleling that which it accords to the growth of the party. However, as explanations of the nature of political intervention or development of the party they are at best partial, not least because problems over the boundaries of labourism and its location within working-class culture are not addressed. The putative identity of labourism and the Labour Party is questionable, and, given a powerfully argued case for seeing the party as an integral part of the national culture, rather surprising. In fact, the party emerged out of working-class experience; more specifically, it was itself *part* of a political response to that experience. This political response is what I refer to as labourism.

In this conception labourism predated the party, for it was during the second half of the nineteenth century that it emerged as an identifiable political culture within the working class (Saville 1973). The moment was significant. By this time chartism had been dismantled; with it went the first, and arguably last voice of mass working-class opposition to the state, and Britain entered into a relatively stable period of economic progress within a successfully reconstructed hegemony. Given these conditions it was virtually inevitable that nascent labourism would be inflected and conditioned by bourgeois thought, and subsequently remain impervious, even hostile, to other traditions, most notably Marxism.

Furthermore, labourism has a universe wider than labour representation, although at this stage in the discussion its boundaries remain ill-defined. Labourism influenced working-class intervention in the formal political sphere through the Labour Party, but it also reached into trade unionism and determined attitudes to alternative bodies of political thought such as toryism, Marxism and fascism. Perhaps of greater significance, labourism influenced abstinence from the formal political sphere.

To provide clarification I wish to return to Nairn, for whom labourism is the 'second best socialism' inherited and subsequently cultivated by the party. Diverse elements of middle-class Fabianism and left-wing protestant militancy were encompassed in a way that subordinated those socialist currents capable of expressing the most dynamic working-class interests. Now it is perfectly legitimate to draw the boundaries of labourism in this way, but the matter becomes troublesome when these are located within wider structures. Labourism emerged as the 'natural, effective instrument of adaptation of a working-class movement to a society which itself ... leaned instinctively and wholeheartedly toward the past' (Nairn p160). The movement was in essence moderate trade unionism, which became the nucleus of labourism and from the start exerted total authority over the Labour Party: the party was 'trade unionism translated onto the political plane' (ibid. p169).

The shift toward formal politics was qualitatively novel, and presented to the working class a potentially valuable opportunity of engaging in new forms of hegemonic struggle to remodel society. But the relation of labourism to the working class was passive; it accepted as given the position of the class and its organisations in an historically-evolved bourgeois society. This is the 'central defect' of labourism:

> The political potential of the working class is not realized when the political movement founded on it accepts as determinant the structures and outlook already created by the workers in their struggle as a subordinate class. These structures cannot *really* determine the form and content of a political movement – hence, as the entire story of Labourism so clearly demonstrates, when political parties embrace this basis they finish by being determined by quite different factors. That is, by the pressures of bourgeois society outside the proletariat by paralysing conventions and myths. (ibid. p172-3.)

Thus labourism, now representative of working-class rather than trade-union struggle, is actually determined by forces outside that class. The model constructed by Nairn resembles a series of concentric circles. At its centre stands labourism coterminous with the Labour Party, from which we move out successively to trade unionism, the working class and finally bourgeois society. Within this model forces of determination are centripetal and linear; all forms can be dismissed ultimately as the products of bourgeois ideology.

The historical record suggests, however, that at every interface the relationship between levels cannot be seen in this way; rather the potential for each level to exercise autonomy has to be recognised. Take, for example, the relationship between trade unions and the Labour Party. The party was established by the 1900 delegate conference dominated numerically by trade unionists, but the initiative and motive force behind the resolution was a socialist one accepted only hesitatingly by the tradition of radical Liberalism belatedly recognising the need for state action to preserve and promote trade union advances. It was, characteristically, a compromise. And although trade unions continued to dominate membership of the party, provide most of its funds and in many areas the nuclei of constituency organisation, the relationship between the two was often a troubled one. Trade unions never had total authority. Most of the leadership and active workers of the party, for example, were schooled in the ILP or Fabianism, quite outside the union movement – a point Nairn concedes in his discussion of the specific nature of hegemonic control exercised by the unions. Because they lacked the capacity for complete cultural and political hegemony, he argues, not all elements in the movement were assimilated. Active hegemony in effect operated only on the moderate right wing of Labour, that 'intellectual group most congenial to the majority of Trade Union leaders' (ibid. p181).

Tensions in the relationship between trade unions and the Labour Party arise from their different locations within bourgeois society. Neither are totally assimilated; in practice there is a process of constant negotiation. Within this trade unions, because of their location at the point of production, have a greater potential for oppositional action than an integrative Labour Party:

> Although the party's ideological history facilitates its ability to act as an integrative party, it faces an inhibiting structural constraint in its association with trade unions. While the party ideology does not see capital and labour as permanently antagonistic forces and therefore promotes policies which integrate the demands of both these classes, the trade unions, by virtue of their very functions in industry, cannot accept this position without strain. (Panitch 1986 p74.)

Without accepting the necessarily and inevitably more integrative role of the party, I believe the argument is a valid one; we cannot assume an easy identity between labourism and trade unionism. The boundaries of labourism and its location within the working class need to be re examined. Rather than seeing labourism within the narrow confines of a trade union dominated political intervention at the level of the state, I wish to consider it as a political culture within working-class experience at all levels, which cannot be reduced to a bourgeois ethos, and which has as a major component (but only a component) the Labour Party. A degree of refinement is offered by Forester (1976 p36) in distinguishing between the typologies of labourism and socialism:

LABOURIST	SOCIALIST
passive	active
reflexive	educative
empirical	ideological

pragmatic	principled
evolutionary	revolutionary
practical	intellectual
'ethic of responsibility'	'ethic of ultimate ends'.

Such a conception of labourism incorporates all non-marxist elements, including those within the Labour Party that had specifically middle-class origins and allegiances. Given the working-class location of labourism, further refinement is necessary.

The opposition between Marxism and 'labour socialism' is one of the central concerns of Macintyre's useful study of Marxism in Britain (1980). He defines labour socialism as the 'political perspective of Labour activists of the period' (p47). It was that of an articulate minority within the party which had a complex relationship with the class upon which it depended and which it claimed to represent. As an ideology, labour socialism shared many of the features of labourism. It was empirical, evolutionary and pragmatic. At the same time, however, labour socialism was more coherent and critical than labourism. MacDonald, Glasier and others did attempt to develop an organic view of society which denied justice to its working class, and provide guidance on how it might be transformed in order better to integrate the class into a corporate whole.

This is crucial in distinguishing labourism, for while the thrust of labour socialism was toward integration of the working class as a means of overcoming genuine grievances, labourism accepted instinctively a separate working-class identity (ibid. p57). This identity was rarely seen in terms of antagonistic class relationships, but could provide an untheorised sense of other oppositional social groups and an unsympathetic state.

This delineation of labourism is ideal-typical; in practice it could exhibit contradictory tendencies. But its emphasis on working-class culture, and distinction from labour socialism and the tradition of parliamentary representation, is a potentially productive one. Given this, two questions arise: at what level does labourism operate? and what elements of working-class experience impinge on it?

1.2 The culture of labourism

As long as historical studies of labourism were concerned with formal political involvement of the working class in the Labour Party, it was likely that the national level would dominate. Thus most effort has been devoted to exploration of the party's national figures, its role in the parliamentary sphere, the evolution of constitutional, policy and organisational forms, relationships with trade union and cooperative leaders, and parliamentary elections (see, for example, the contents pages of Cole 1948b, Miliband 1961 and McKibbin 1974).

Implicit in these works is the belief that national developments were unproblematically reflected at the local level, that the national was simply an aggregate of the local: 'There is a sense in which the achievements and failings of Labourism at the national level are mirrored at the local level, a sense in which constituency Labour parties are a microcosm of the national Labour Party' (Forester 1976 p71). Theoretically and empirically this emphasis is misplaced.

Working-class politics is located in a wider material, cultural and social universe, and has no meaning outside that universe. Moreover, for the vast majority of the working class, certainly for the period with which this study is concerned, the universe was strongly bounded by local factors. The growing literature on local labour parties is a belated recognition of this; nowhere is the point made more forcibly than in Savage's (1987) study of labour politics in Preston from 1880 to 1940.

In the elaborate theoretical edifice constructed by Savage, it is accepted that development of the Labour Party was related to changes in the 'national polity' (p10), and that over time 'nationalization' of politics produced more uniform patterns of working-class political activity (p187). These do not provide evidence, however, of the efficacy of the national, rather of the convergence of the local in different parts of the country. It is in the locality (defined in physical terms) and not at the national or regional level that practical working-class politics are developed (p40). Politics have their bases in perceived interests of the working class, but their form and direction are mediated by capacities for action, and these are determined by local social structures (p62). More specifically, the rise of the Labour Party in Preston was based to a large extent on the ways in which forms of skill structured certain capacities for political action, in which gender solidarity affected political forms, and in which the social structure determined class alliances (pp40–1).

Empirically, the advance of the Labour Party was very uneven. Overall, gains of the war and the immediate postwar period were not consolidated. Raised expectations of an inevitable triumph as the party continued to expand were never fully realised, even in areas with a strong industrial base (Howard 1983 p73). Statistical aggregates suggesting an inexorable logic to Labour's advance in the 1920s disguise considerable reversals in certain localities and unexpected increases in others (Savage 1987 Ch8). A complex interplay of industrial structure, patterns of social relations, efficacy of constituency organisation, trade union strength and national development determined the achievement of local parties, and hence an understanding of the political dimensions of working-class action over this period has in large measure to incorporate the locality.

Even similar patterns of advance belie major variations in local circumstances. In both East London and the adjacent West Ham, the Labour Party made rapid and considerable gains at local and national elections. The temptation is to see this as part of a general dynamic conditioned by similar wartime experiences, party organisations and social structures; but historically the areas contrasted strongly, and West Ham lay outside the influence of Morrison's London Labour Party (p29 below).

To focus discussion on the culture of labourism I wish to examine in a little more detail Savage's (1987) study of working-class politics in Preston.

Situated within a tradition of sociological inquiry into working-class attitudes and behaviour, it is a theoretically sophisticated attempt to account for the dynamics of political change in a particular locality. Drawing on the work of Lockwood and Goldthorpe, he conceptualises the relationship between the political strategies and working-class interests and capacities in a potentially productive manner.

Underlying the analysis is a belief that particular forms of strategy arise out of a recognition by working-class members of a need to reduce the material insecurity immanent in the forced commodification of labour – 'people engage in various forms of action because it is in their interests to do so' (ibid. p7). The potentially damaging essentialism and determinism of this approach is deflected by an argument that there is no inevitability in these forms. Class location in itself guarantees nothing; politics are 'undetermined' by interests. Rather, practical forms are conditioned by local social structures through the provision of specific *capacities* for action. Thus structures facilitate 'mutualist' struggle in which workers aim to establish alternative and independent markets for production and distribution, 'economistic' struggle to increase job security within extant relations of production, and 'statist' struggle to promote interests through enlisting the aid of the state principally through legislative enactment. As examples of these Savage cites friendly societies (mutualist), trade unions and collective bargaining (economistic), and schemes of direct labour (statist).

Local social structures are characterised by particular configurations of skill, by gender relations and by communal bonding. As these change, so do capacities for different forms of political action, with profound consequences for the Labour Party. In 1920s Preston, for example, electoral support for the party increased, not out of sympathy with the defeat of the general strike, but rather because, with a loosening of the hold of trade unions and mobilisation of female and neighbourhood support, the party turned to 'consumer-oriented statist policies' (ibid. p179).

To be theoretically consistent, increases in electoral support for the party need to be related to changes in the local social structure. And so they are, but not linearly and unproblematically. Parties, it is argued, are 'forced to latch on to various capacities in order to generate support'. They have, therefore,

> to operate among the capacities and struggles which exist outside themselves: while they are crucially important in forming these into a programme they cannot create practical policies themselves for these arise from people's practical negotiation of their immediate environment. (ibid. p190.)

Sadly, the crucial insight into the ability of parties to articulate political programmes is not explored in the main body of Savage's work. Intimately linked to this question is that of 'practical negotiation'. People do not negotiate in a direct and immediate way with material conditions; the negotiation is structured through consciousness. At an individual or party level discourses not only mediate between material conditions and their interpretation but can organise experience itself. It follows that in order to understand the efficacy of political parties or the ways in which political forms relate to everyday experience, account must be taken of the appropriate political discourses. This takes us into the realm of language.

Advances in structuralism have had a belated impact on British historiography. Where its influence has been felt, productive new lines of inquiry have been opened. Stedman Jones' (1982) re-examination of chartism, for example, argues that its political form cannot be understood as a simplistic response to the putative material experience of a class, nor can its political language be seen as an expression of that experience. Chartism articulated experience within a complex rhetoric that interpellated radical working-class support at a national level. Recognition of the way in which this rhetoric drew upon previous discourses and defined the nature of authority relationships provides a more secure interpretation of the chronology of chartism's rise and subsequent demise than can accounts describing it as merely an expression of acute social and economic deprivation.

If this approach tends to proximate to idealism in seeing linguistic forms as closed, self-referential systems without any manifest acknowledgement that they are located in distinct socio-economic structures, this is not to deny its potential in interpreting political forms. The collection of essays edited by Joyce (1987) is an important contribution to the history of work, not only for the satisfying ways in which it challenges orthodoxy about the social and political role of work, but also for its advocacy of the need to rethink work as a social construct. The labour process, it is argued, cannot be seen merely as an economic process attendant upon capitalist rationality and imposed on the workforce; it is embedded in social and cultural practices, and without an understanding of this apparatus, particularly the meanings attached to work, it is difficult to account for the specific form of change, for the relationships between 'work' and 'leisure', and for the significance of skill and social relations at the point of production.

Individual essays demonstrate the extent to which the constituent discourses of work have to be located beyond the economic sphere. Gray's (1987) study demonstrates that around factory reform from 1830 inherent contradictions of liberal ideology were renegotiated. As a consequence the moral and legal boundaries of liberal economics, at first fluid, became more settled from the 1840s when a discourse of reform and moral improvement framed economic and Benthamite languages with a moralised and rationalised social commitment. McClelland (1987), on the other hand, shows how discourses upon the nature of work were condensed from a range of social commentators, and incorporated not only arguments about the underlying system of economic relations, but also those about individuality and morality. How workers understood work, therefore, was not based on a simple perception of its demands, but was refracted through available discourses on the nature of the wider society.

Savage stands outside this tradition. He denies the salience of language, indeed of culture, to an understanding of political change. It is, he argues, almost impossible to gain access to the nature of working-class consciousness in the past; secondly, political practice is more strongly related to strategy and tactics than to views of society; and thirdly overarching concepts such as culture presuppose internal coherence.

This reasoning is suspect. It is possible to investigate working-class consciousness through those records that survive (admittedly relatively few) and oral testimony. In any case, methodological difficulties should not dictate epistemology. Without an understanding of consciousness, of the linguistic appropriation of experience, the link between structure and action tends to be conceived in mechanistic terms. As an alternative, therefore, I devote considerable attention to the discourses of labourism, and their role in securing hegemony over working-class political activity.

This is not to evade questions of strategy and tactics, merely to place them in an appropriate context. Too much emphasis in previous work has been directed to the role of strategy in explaining the fortunes of the Labour Party. Organisation was important to the success of the party in the interwar years, but efficient constituency organisation in itself did not guarantee popular support, or poor organisation forfeit it. Furthermore, such administrative histories tend to adhere to whig interpretations in which the ascent of the party is seen unproblematically as a concomitant of the rise of labour and the evolution of more efficient organisational forms. The dramatic advance of Labour in the interwar years, for example, is attributed to Morrison's success in organising the London Labour Party (p28 below). It is a neat and convenient equation, but one which fails to appreciate that both electoral gains and the growing strength of the London Labour Party were due to more fundamental structural and cultural shifts in the metropolitan working class. Labourism is not to be understood merely in its institutions and strategies; it emerged from and is rooted within lived social and material relationships.

Because these relationships rarely form a coherent totality, political cultures themselves, including labourism, are replete with internal contradictions and inconsistencies. The articulation of elements within an ideology, however, is a dynamic process; contradictions may be resolved, but also new ones created. As a consequence, even if cultures do not form unified wholes, they adapt to change and have the power to effect it.

These are some of the issues that inform my approach to labourism. I use as a vehicle the experience of West Ham in the interwar period. West Ham was an area adjacent to East London where formal politics during the 1920s came to be dominated by the Labour Party to an extent experienced in few other areas of the country. The historical legacy of this hegemony continues to have a profound influence on the contemporary political landscape. Chapter 2 attempts to demonstrate the specific appeal of formal labourism by examining the construction of political discourses around the working class. Against this, the principal opposition in the form of the Municipal

Alliance espoused narrow sectional interests, and gradually lost support as Labour consolidated electoral power.

Chapter 3 explores the position of trade unions within labourism, questioning the nature of the relationship between unions and the party. Shifts in activity are identified, and the consequences for labour representation examined. It was within this sphere that militant challenges to labourism arose and were subsequently dismantled.

But the most concerted challenge was manifest in struggles waged by the unemployed around the poor law. The politics of these struggles are analysed in Chapter 4. Their effectiveness in forcing the guardians to sustain 'liberal' scales of relief is not in doubt, for the state was eventually forced to intervene and supersede the guardians in an unprecedented assault on local representational democracy. But the inherent political weaknesses of the struggles, the chronic inability to attract support from other sections of labour, and the social composition of the unemployed led directly to a collapse of militancy after state intervention.

Finally, despite the strength of the Labour Party and its eventual domination of local politics in West Ham, its ability to mobilise the electorate was limited. Polls (as one surrogate of political activity) were consistently low, and at no time was there popular representation amongst the leadership. The political machinery was controlled by a relatively small number of members of the South West Ham branch of the National Socialist Party, an organisation occupying an increasingly right-wing presence within the party. To explore this, Chapter 5 attempts to locate formal labourism within wider aspects of popular culture, work and the home, and speculates on the relevance of alternative political traditions to an understanding of the contemporary basis of Labour Party support.

As a preliminary to this, it is necessary to describe something of the historical background to interwar West Ham.

1.3 The development of West Ham

The industrialisation of West Ham was remarkable (Marriott 1984, 1988, 1989). Within fifty years West Ham was transformed from an essentially agricultural economy with a few nucleated settlements to the industrial heartland of south-east England. It is unlikely that such vigour was ever witnessed elsewhere, certainly not in the British experience of industrialisation. Population change (Table 1.1) suggests something of its scale and chronology.

Situated as it was in the corner of rural Essex, immediately adjacent to the sprawling East End of London, West Ham was subject to diverse influences; in the final analysis, however, its growth cannot be seen as integral to either of its neighbours. From the start and in the course of its development, industrial development was distinctive, not least because its rapid phase from 1870 onwards coincided with a prolonged agricultural depression in the eastern counties and a collapse of staple industries in East London.

Table 1.1 *Population of West Ham, 1851–1931*

1851	18,817	1901	267,358
1861	38,331	1911	289,030
1871	62,919	1921	300,860
1881	128,953	1931	294,278
1891	204,903		

Source: *Census of population*, relevant years.

A concentration of so-called noxious and offensive trades in West Ham has led to speculation that industrialisation was promoted by weak legislative control. Manufacturers, it is argued, sought refuge in West Ham from East London vestries determined to sanitise their parishes. Evidence for this, however, is scant. Few vestries had the will to enforce legislation, especially when economic interests were jeopardised. We need rather to consider its industrial transformation in the context of the development of a communications infrastructure.

The River Lea forming the eastern boundary of the metropolis provided good communication, ample supplies of water, and motive power for the mills, distilleries and calico industries that had settled in West Ham previously, and was to continue in that role. Of greater lasting significance, however, was the construction in 1839 of the Eastern Counties railway line from London to Norwich via Stratford, Colchester and Ipswich. Soon after this was complete a spur line from Stratford to wharves at Bow Creek, extended to North Woolwich, was added. This line effectively opened up the southern reaches of West Ham which until then had been deserted marshland, and focused attention on Stratford as a centre of railway activity.

Within five years the same railway contractors responsible for the spur line were actively pursuing plans to build a new dock system in the area. Alternative accommodation in the metropolitan area for a new breed of large steamships had become a matter of some urgency. The natural projection of the land along the Thames conferred distinct advantages on West Ham as a site for the new docks. By 1855 the Victoria Dock was complete. A cost of £900,000, generally recognised to be remarkably low, was made possible by cheap labour, innovatory techniques and a favourable terrain.

Despite the establishment of a communications infrastructure (Figure 1.1) it was another fifteen years before West Ham embarked on the phase of rapid growth. Excess land acquired for construction of the docks was not released, and the area remained remote in the minds of manufacturers. The docks themselves did not promote local industrial growth until William Cory installed a battery of hydraulic cranes to unload seaborne coal, thereby guaranteeing abundant, relatively cheap supplies for local industries. By 1875, 55 per cent of all coal shipped to London was unloaded at the Victoria Dock.

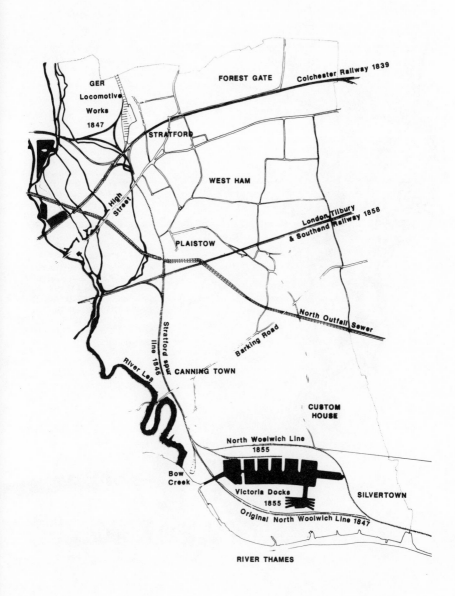

FIGURE 1.1 *The communications infrastructure of West Ham, 1860*

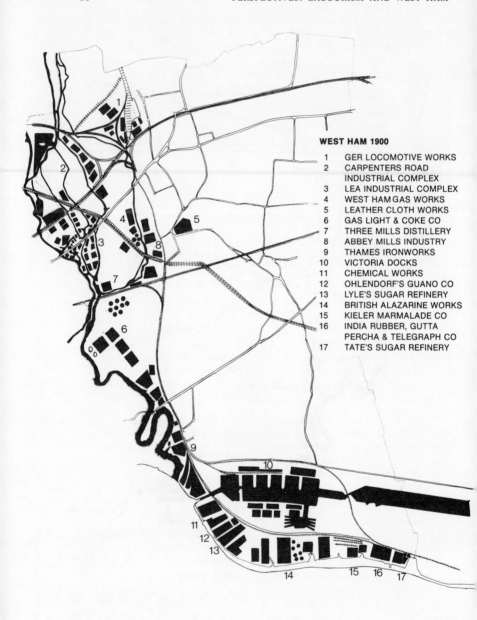

WEST HAM 1900

1   GER LOCOMOTIVE WORKS
2   CARPENTERS ROAD
    INDUSTRIAL COMPLEX
3   LEA INDUSTRIAL COMPLEX
4   WEST HAM GAS WORKS
5   LEATHER CLOTH WORKS
6   GAS LIGHT & COKE CO
7   THREE MILLS DISTILLERY
8   ABBEY MILLS INDUSTRY
9   THAMES IRONWORKS
10 VICTORIA DOCKS
11 CHEMICAL WORKS
12 OHLENDORF'S GUANO CO
13 LYLE'S SUGAR REFINERY
14 BRITISH ALAZARINE WORKS
15 KIELER MARMALADE CO
16 INDIA RUBBER, GUTTA
    PERCHA & TELEGRAPH CO
17 TATE'S SUGAR REFINERY

FIGURE 1.2 *Industrial settlement in West ham, 1900*

This was instrumental in the siting of the giant Gas Light & Coke Company works at Beckton and the expansion of the Thames Ironworks and Shipbuilding Co. Together these firms gave birth to Canning Town, where the vast majority of their workforces resided, and spawned numerous subsidiary industries (Figure 1.2). New firms relying on the import of seaborne raw materials and export of heavy finished goods were attracted to locationally advantaged sites on the Thames waterfront. The Albert Dock was constructed in 1881; extending from the Victoria Dock it completed a water channel across the whole of the southern promontory.

Industrial expansion also occurred in the north. Soon after completion of the network of lines around Stratford, work started on a massive locomotive plant. By the end of the century the Stratford locomotive works occupied a site of twenty-two acres and employed 7000 people. The Leathercloth works and the numerous smaller scale chemical firms around the Lea also continued to expand, although size and density of settlement never quite matched that of the south.

The considerable locational advantages possessed by West Ham which gave rise to its extraordinary growth were to become fetters on the ability of its industry to adapt to a transformed economic environment in the twentieth century. So rapid had been the settlement and subsequent expansion that by the outbreak of the first world war few suitable sites remained to attract new industry. Furthermore, established firms continued to benefit from their location (Figure 1.2). The communications infrastructure was extended and, following pioneering development of the electricity supply by West Ham corporation, motive power became available at rates cheaper than in any other metropolitan area. Under these circumstances firms were content to remain. By 1924 industry and population reached a peak; at that time the population of West Ham was exceeded only by those of London, Birmingham, Liverpool, Manchester, Sheffield, Leeds and Bristol. But the barriers to new industry and a reluctance or inability of established firms to adapt laid the foundations of stagnation and protracted decline which has continued to the present.

Empirical evidence on the mature economy of the interwar years demonstrates the abiding legacy of its nineteenth-century development. Proportionately high levels of employment were to be found in chemicals, shipbuilding, food and drink, transport and the docks, retail distribution, and the public services of gas, water and electricity. Low levels existed in vehicles, banking and insurance, and public administration (Table 1.2).

It was an industrial structure weighted heavily toward the use of semiskilled and unskilled labour. From the early stages of industrialisation the demand for unskilled labour was exceeded only by the supply; as an occupational category it remained dominant. Labourers were found in the docks, railways, factories and domestic spheres, many of them employed on a casual basis. Attracted by the prospect of work during industrial expansion they migrated in their tens of thousands from the environs of East London and the eastern counties, both of which were suffering the

TABLE 1.2 *Employed^a unemployed (per cent), and location quotients^b for West Ham, Greater London and England & Wales in selected industries, 1931*

INDUSTRIAL HEADING	WEST HAM			GREATER LONDON			ENGLAND & WALES	
	Empld	Unempld	LQ	Empld	Unempld	LQ	Empld	Unempld
CHEMICAL	5,992	11.7	5.6	56,832	6.9	1.7	147,512	14.2
METALS	11,434	18.9	0.9	306,850	11.3	0.8	1,761,800	19.4
Engineering	2,992	11.3	1.1	72,754	11.0	0.8	380,750	18.6
Electrical installation	2,081	18.6	1.2	85,818	11.2	1.6	234,940	12.4
Vehicles	1,168	8.6	0.5	56,936	10.0	0.8	326,288	14.6
Shipbuilding	1,479	41.0	1.7	6,691	31.4	0.3	118,096	41.2
CLOTHING	7,773	4.2	1.4	238,461	5.6	1.4	777,767	6.6
FOOD, DRINK	11,704	11.2	2.9	145,133	8.7	1.1	558,972	9.3
WOODWORKING	2,499	13.3	1.4	80,105	14.6	1.5	238,803	13.4
PAPER, PRINT	4,824	6.3	1.6	161,623	6.8	1.7	411,121	7.5
BUILDING	6,152	20.9	1.0	232,211	15.7	1.2	846,793	16.9
GAS, WATER & ELECTRICITY	2,864	9.9	1.9	64,582	4.4	1.4	209,707	8.0
TRANSPORT	16,693	15.4	2.0	304,244	8.2	1.2	1,152,028	10.6
Railway	3,745	3.8	1.1	100,228	2.8	0.9	477,961	3.7
Road	3,868	8.7	1.3	124,882	7.3	1.3	414,508	9.0
Water	4,379	29.0	4.7	33,392	19.7	1.2	127,901	29.4
Docks	4,082	14.3	5.2	33,151	14.2	1.4	108,268	15.7
COMMERCE	23,693	7.7	1.2	820,773	6.3	1.3	2,769,366	6.8
Distribution	22,329	8.0	1.2	726,393	6.4	1.3	2,531,467	7.2
Bank, insurance	1,364	3.4	0.8	94,380	1.9	1.8	237,899	2.8
PUBLIC ADMINISTRATION	7,438	11.8	0.7	343,122	4.0	1.1	1,378,059	6.7
Local government	5,256	14.6	0.9	176,104	5.6	0.9	826,742	9.3
PERSONAL SERVICE	9,377	11.0	0.6	582,907	6.8	1.1	2,245,716	7.3
OTHERS	11,563	17.7		429,816	14.2		4,188,926	17.4
TOTAL	122,006	12.6		3,766,659	8.5		16,686,570	11.5

Source: 1931 *Census*, Industry Tables.

Notes: ^a Excluding unemployed.

^b location quotient is a measure of the degree of concentration of an industrial employment in a region. For transport, as an example, it is calculated as:

numbers employed in transport in West Ham as a percentage of all industries in West Ham

numbers employed in transport in England & Wales as a percentage of all industries in England & Wales effects of economic recession.

Large-scale migration from East End boroughs began in the 1870s. Forced by a combination of decline in staple industries and a crisis in housing, the exodus across the River Lea to an urban environment not altogether dissimilar to the one the migrants had inhabited, particularly around the docks, reached a climax in the 1880s. It was during this period that the boroughs of Bethnal Green, Stepney, Mile End and Poplar witnessed a net loss of population for the first time. Migration from the eastern counties, while on a smaller scale, was forced by no less desperate circumstances. Dominated by an economy based on cereal crops, the region had been plunged into recession by a series of poor harvests in the 1830s. Pressure to migrate, however, was mitigated by the restricted physical and mental universe occupied by rural labour; cognitively, the move to a distant urban environment was enormous. But the widespread adoption of agricultural technology and scientific farm management – Essex was in the forefront – increased the body of displaced labour and the compulsion to migrate. Completion of the eastern counties railway network removed the last barrier; now labour was prepared to move rather than tolerate chronic want.

1.4 Patterns of social and political settlement

The settlement pattern of this migrant population in West Ham was determined by its industrial topography. Given that the vast majority of workers – labourers in particular – had to live close to their actual or potential place of employment, the social composition of the locality reflected its industry. And in spite of considerable growth the composition of residential settlement was remarkably stable over time. Localities adjacent to industrial concentrations such as Canning Town, Silvertown, and the Lea complex at Stratford had the highest proportions of unskilled labour, and, as a concomitant, the deepest social distress. Numbers of semiskilled and skilled workers were also high, especially around the Stratford locomotive works, Thames Ironworks and chemical factories in the south. Not surprisingly an inverse relationship existed between the proportion of labourers and that of lower professionals. The latter were concentrated quite markedly in Stratford and Forest Gate within easy reach of the main railway line into the city.

As industrialisation reached maturity the previously isolated settlements expanded and merged, and communications improved, but the social topography of the nineteenth century remained. A template had been forged which was subject to only minor modifications over time. We can gain some idea of this from data included in the household survey cards compiled in 1929-30 for the *New survey of London life and labour* (see Appendix 1). Such is the wealth of information that analysis could easily become a complex statistical exercise. I am concerned here merely to reconstruct a broad outline of the borough's socio-economic character. Table 1.3 shows the class composition of the four areas of West Ham.

TABLE 1.3 *Employed (number and percentage) in the areas of West Ham,
classified by occupational group, 1929–30*

	Skilled manual	Semi-skilled manual	Un-skilled manual	Retail	Clerical	Other	Total
Canning Town	1795	5384	24347	2765	1698	871	36860
	4.9	14.6	66.0	7.5	4.6	2.4	100
Plaistow	1746	4511	12756	2668	2765	1405	25851
	6.8	17.5	49.3	10.3	10.7	5.4	100
Stratford	2183	5869	15617	2474	2668	1065	29876
	7.2	19.6	52.3	8.3	8.9	3.6	100
Forest Gate	1164	2231	4705	1601	2765	2035[a]	14501
	8.0	15.4	32.5	11.0	19.1	14.0	100
Total	6888	17995	57425	9508	9896	5376	107088
	6.4	16.8	53.6	8.9	9.2	5.0	99.9

Source: Household survey cards, *New survey of London life and labour*.
Notes: [a] Includes 1455 professionals.

TABLE 1.4 *Birthplaces of manual workers (per cent) living in West Ham, 1929–30*

		West Ham	East London	London	Other
	m	41.4	20.3	11.3	27.0
Skilled					
	f	—	—	—	—
	m	51.2	18.6	11.0	19.3
Semiskilled					
	f	76.9	15.4	3.8	3.9
	m	62.2	16.2	9.3	12.3
Unskilled					
	f	68.4	16.1	8.0	7.5

Source: As for Table 1.3.

This tends to confirm the persistence of unskilled labour in the
workforce; had unemployed been included (see Chapter 4) the dominance
would be even more evident. In every area it remained the largest category,
although distribution was heavily skewed toward Canning Town. Here
over half the total workforce was unskilled, and here resided nearly half
the borough's pool of unskilled labour. Levels of skilled and semiskilled
labour were relatively low; together they exceeded those in retail and
clerical occupations, but not by much.

Most unskilled labourers were part of the indigenous working-class
culture inherited from the nineteenth century. 62.2 per cent of male and
68.4 per cent of female unskilled workers were born in West Ham, only 12.3
per cent and 7.5 per cent respectively originated from outside the metropolitan area (Table 1.4).

As with most occupational groups males were dominant, although the
degree of domination tended to increase with skill level and with the
incidence of unskilled labour (Table 1.5). Such figures say much about

TABLE 1.5 *Percentage of males in occupational groups, by area, West Ham, 1929–30*

	Skilled manual	Semiskd manual	Unskd manual	Retail	Clerical
Canning Town	100	90.1	68.9	68.4	71.4
Plaistow	100	91.4	63.9	65.5	49.1
Stratford	100	96.7	58.7	66.7	65.5
Forest Gate	100	89.1	63.9	69.7	49.1

Source: As for Table 1.3.

TABLE 1.6 *Average ages of male and female workers in occupational groups, West Ham, 1929–30*

	Skilled manual	Semiskilled manual	Unskilled manual	Retail	Clerical
Male	39	39	33	32	28
Female	—	23	25	26	22

Source: As for Table 1.3.

TABLE 1.7 *Workplaces (per cent) of West Ham residents, by area, 1929–30*

Area	West Ham	East London	Other London	Other
Canning Town	63.0	16.1	15.8	5.1
Plaistow	52.0	15.1	24.2	8.7
Stratford	58.2	19.7	18.2	3.9
Forest Gate	57.4	13.3	24.3	4.9

Source: As for Table 1.3

ways in which female employment was determined by economic and cultural constraints. In a population of working age where females outnumbered males, only 29,000 women compared with 65,815 men were employed in the above groups. Female work was heavily weighted, as we might expect, toward unskilled manual, shop and office work, traditional areas of female employment. Ages of female workers were consistently below their male counterparts (Table 1.6).

Marriage remained an effective barrier to further work for women largely through the operation of domestic ideologies enshrined in employment practice and male culture. In general, married women could find paid employment only when the family income was insufficient or in a family business such as a shop. This may explain their slightly higher ages in unskilled manual and retail occupations.

Strong historical continuities in residence were certainly due the persistence of local patterns of employment. Table 1.7 shows recorded workplaces of West Ham residents.

TABLE 1.8 Average weekly earnings (£.s.d) by occupational group and gender, West Ham, 1929–30

	Skilled manual	Semi-skilled manual	Unskilled manual	Retail	Clerical
Male	3.12.6	3.2.6	2.5.0	2.10.0	2.9.0
Female	—	1.14.6	1.1.6	1.4.6	1.16.6

Source: As for Table 1.3

A large majority of residents in all areas of the borough worked locally or within easy reach of East London. There was a distinct occupational dimension to this. Approximately 58 per cent of manual workers were employed in West Ham, compared with 74 per cent in local shops and only 33 per cent in clerical jobs.

The strong tendency for manual workers to live close to their workplace is further demonstrated by data on some of the larger local firms. Of the 6111 recorded as working in the Royal docks, 5093 (83.3 per cent) lived in Canning Town or Plaistow. Similarly, 4414 West Ham residents worked at Tate & Lyle's sugar refineries, 4171 (94.5 per cent) of whom lived in Canning Town or Plaistow, while of the 3880 employed at the LNER locomotive works, 3444 (88.8 per cent) lived in Stratford or Forest Gate. Occupational structures of these firms also conform to the social topography of the areas in which they were located. Thus the workforces of Tate & Lyle and the docks had respectively 71.9 per cent and 59.8 per cent unskilled labour, compared to 31.1 per cent at the LNER.

There was also a broad uniformity in the hours worked by those in manual occupations both across gender and geographical area. Unskilled labour averaged forty-six hours per week, semiskilled and skilled forty-seven. These figures do not take into account irregular employment, and so those for unskilled labour in particular have to be treated with caution. Many labourers were employed on a casual basis, having only intermittent work; these, if included, would reduce the average. Clerical workers averaged forty-five hours per week, while retail workers averaged fifty-five reflecting the extremely long working week of many shop assistants.

Finally, let us consider wages. There were no significant differences in wage levels across the borough, but across occupational group and gender the contrasts were striking (Table 1.8).

Wages for unskilled labour were the lowest, being significantly below even shop workers who are generally recognised to be among the most intensely exploited (except that their hours were much longer). In all groups, female wage rates were a fraction of the corresponding male rates – except in clerical work, where women could expect to receive less than half that of men.

Estimates of the scale and depth of poverty in a population are fraught with methodological difficulties (see the discussion in *New survey*, III,

Ch.V). The *New survey* took as its poverty line an income of 38–40 shillings per week for a family of two adults and two children aged ten and four. On this basis we can say that the vast majority of families with an unskilled manual worker as sole earner were at best only marginally above that line. That is, where unskilled labour prevailed there was chronic want and deprivation.

The picture of the working population of West Ham emerging from these data is one dominated by unskilled male manual workers. Wage rates were consistently low; these, associated with the devastating consequences of endemic casualism, plunged the majority into a life of want and destitution. In part because of the geographic isolation of the borough, in part because of the necessity of living near the workplace, this population was rooted in the locality, producing a fierce sense of self identity and exclusion. The relatively small number of women employed were concentrated on unskilled manual, shop and office work, and could command rates less than half those of men in the same occupational groups.

This socioeconomic profile was not distributed uniformly. Unskilled labour was concentrated in Canning Town next to the industrial concerns sited by the Thames, although large numbers were found also in Plaistow and Stratford, finding employment in the locomotive works and the numerous medium-sized chemical and manufacturing firms in the Lea industrial complex. Proportionately and absolutely more retail and clerical workers lived in the north of the borough, making use of the good transport facilities to the shops and offices of the metropolis. Forest Gate in particular had a high population of clerical and professional workers.

Industrial expansion had brought no prosperity to the majority of the population. The occupational structure of West Ham in the interwar years was still dominated by unskilled labour, amongst which the ravages of casualism had persisted, even intensified (see Chapter 4). And as long as casualism persisted there was little that local agencies could do to break the downward spiral of underemployment, overcrowding and deprivation. As the *New survey* was forced to conclude:

> The southern area (Canning Town) is the abode of workers at the docks, gas works and sugar refineries, marmalade and rubber factories: there is also a fleeting population of seafaring men of various races who help to provide a livelihood for the keepers of numerous common lodging houses... Poverty and overcrowding are characteristic of the greater part of the Canning Town and Silvertown areas, which make up what is perhaps the largest part of unbroken depression in East London. (*New survey*, 1932 III, p409.)

During the phase of rapid growth this impoverished and entrenched population gave birth to a distinct political culture. Details of this are described at appropriate stages in this book, so here a brief outline will suffice.

The transformation effected by industrialisation undermined the basis of the rural economy in West Ham and so established new contours of class relationships. The landed gentry abandoned the parish, selling off their land to speculative developers. They were replaced by a local bourgeoisie and petit bourgeoisie associated with the ascendant manufacturing and commercial sectors, while rural labour gave way to industrial labour. Over the ensuing twenty years the last vestiges of a rural economy were erased, while the considerable physical presence of an industrial proletariat, much of it working in large plants, became increasingly apparent. And yet until the outbreak of widescale industrial unrest in the late 1880s, this class remained passive.

The numerically dominant stratum of unskilled labour encompassed and eventually unified two distinct traditions which were related to the origins of their members, namely, rural labour from the depressed eastern counties and the casual poor from East London. Rural labour had internalised deferential attitudes toward authority and a fatalistic acceptance of its conditions during a protracted history of custom and dependence, but at times in the nineteenth century had demonstrated radical resistance to the imposition of capitalist rationalisation. Reductions in wages and employment had provoked acts ranging from isolated arson and cattle maiming to collective wage riots. Later, as capitalist work relations and practices were successfully implemented, rural labour organised a national union; but it was built upon unsure foundations and, significantly, Essex witnessed its crushing defeat in 1874 at the hands of local farmers. Thus the rural culture brought by migrant labour to West Ham during rapid growth was fatalistic and ideologically subordinate.

Casual labour from East London had shown little evidence of an ability to construct and maintain stable forms of resistance (this is taken up in Chapter 5). The exigencies of survival in a shifting and precarious labour market, containing its own ideological practices, undermined any sense of loyalty to and tradition of organisation. Resistance was volatile, at times anarchist in nature; spontaneous riots against bread prices or unemployment were short lived, providing the poor with a temporary release of tension and an opportunity to express hostility to respectability and the law. Attempts to harness the numerical strength of the casual poor had foundered on the rocks of seeming apathy.

Neither of these cultures could have provided an effective basis to challenge hegemonic authority in West Ham; both were effectively foreclosed within dominant ideological discourses. Most significant were those around the operation of the poor law. Earlier in the century the select vestry in West Ham had implemented measures to deal with a perceived crisis in relief which were singularly effective in reducing relief and reasserting authoritarian values. Administration was placed on a sounder financial footing, its distribution made visible and public. Protests were countered by claims of the objective necessity of maintaining financial security. Thus the discourse of relief was transformed by the select vestry. By exercising the articulating principle of rationalisation it constructed a unified discourse, deeply embedded in social practice, that reconstituted the poor as subordinate, shamed and obligated. Administrative reforms brought about by the 1834 Poor Law Amendment Act merely consolidated the already established authority in West Ham.

The seeming unconscious and 'objective' basis of poor relief preempted challenges to the poor law from the only section of the population likely to do so, namely, the poor. So effective was hegemony around the poor law that it continued throughout the preindustrial period and the period of rapid growth. Not until the 1920s was struggle again witnessed on the terrain of poor relief, this time with dramatic consequences (Chapter 4).

Unlike casual labour, skilled workers were heir to a tradition of militancy. They had displayed a radical, organised resistance to both industrial capital and the state in the first half of the nineteenth century. But with the defeat of chartism and a period of stabilisation during which skilled labour consolidated its privileged economic position, the ideology of skilled workers unified increasingly around a discourse of possessive individualism, self help and respectability inscribed within extant relations of production. The structural basis of skilled labour had been effectively dismantled by the collapse of staple industries in East London, particularly after the downfall of the Overend Gurney financial empire in 1866. Within West Ham, on the other hand, the large workforces of the Stratford locomotive works, the Thames Ironworks, Beckton gasworks and others provided skilled workers with an opportunity to rebuild. Reconstituted, however, within new ideological discourses, skilled labour proved unwilling or unable to acknowledge its radical lineage and act accordingly. Friendly societies and the cooperative movement testified to the accommodation.

It was during this period of political passivity that the middle class and petit bourgeoisie, with the tacit approval of the local industrial bourgeoisie, cemented an alliance in the movement toward incorporation of West Ham. The attendant promotion of civic identity secured the alliance around a complex discourse articulating notions of localism, utilitarianism, paternalism and individualism into a unified whole that came subsequently to lead working-class opinion when it mounted its most concerted opposition.

This opposition was initiated and had its structural base in the industrial sphere, more specifically, in the gas industry where a growing number of semiskilled workers suffered from intensification of work during the 1880s. It drew upon a general concern to reduce the working day; then, with renewed confidence, attempts were made to extend the struggle by forcing a closed shop. The counteroffensive launched by the industrial bourgeoisie with the aid of the state, however, exposed the fragility of the position of semiskilled workers; despite their strategic position in the production process, without support of skilled sections they could not halt production. Defeated on the industrial terrain, they turned their attention to local politics; in particular, labour representation and municipal activity.

In its conception the development was novel in seeking to transcend barriers between industrial and political struggles. Moves toward incorporation had demonstrated that the local state possessed a degree of autonomy and power, which could be mobilised to provide sorely needed basic amenities for the local population and to intervene in the labour market. This shift led to the return in 1892 of Keir Hardie as the first independent labour MP, and in 1898 of the first labour council in British electoral history. Although the victory of Keir Hardie owed much to historical contingency and of the labour council to traditional Liberal support, the assertion of working-class identity was instrumental.

On assumption of power labour attempted to implement a programme of progressive reform but in pursuit of this adopted methods that were seen by opponents to be an open challenge to representative democracy. Fearing the introduction of caucus politics as the first stage toward installation of a socialist regime, disaffected Liberals were drawn into the camp of the Tories; together they formed the Municipal Alliance, and by skilful reassertion of discourses of municipal activity embodied in incorporation assimilated the challenge of labour and took power in 1900.

From then until the suspension of elections during the first world war the Labour Party (as it now was) and Municipal Alliance fought with roughly equal strength for municipal control, and indirectly for parliamentary seats, although for most of the time the Alliance retained power. In the immediate postwar period the Labour Party experienced rapid ascent to a position of unchallenged authority which has to the present never been relinquished. The nature, lineages and reasons for this success – and its ultimate failure – are the concerns of this study.

2

THE ASCENT OF THE LABOUR PARTY

When socialists in the north grew dispirited I would say to them 'When you die you shall go to West Ham'. (Philip Snowden at an ILP meeting in West Ham, 1902.)

Class war and self-interest are taking the place of Cooperation and the Common Good. Words are taking on new meanings. (West Ham Municipal Alliance. 1923.)

2.1 The metropolitan experience

In November 1919, West Ham held its first municipal election for six years. Labour Party candidates won in seven of the nine wards contested, thus gaining four seats and a comfortable majority on the council. This majority was increased in subsequent elections, and the Labour Party came to command a seemingly unassailable authority over local politics that lasted until 1965, when the borough amalgamated with East Ham into Newham, and thereafter.

The ascent of the Labour Party in West Ham during the early interwar years can be thought coterminous with its emergence from political obscurity to power in the metropolis as a whole, but there are considerable theoretical and empirical problems in the equation that challenge any such identification.

The significance of Labour's advance has long been recognised. As early as 1924 Herbert Morrison (who else?) pointed to the four-fold increase in the Labour vote over six years, and offered an explanation of the previous poor record:

Ten years ago London was the despair of the Labour movement. The provincials regarded us as a gassy, protesting, quarrelsome, cantankerous crowd, very good at cursing the enemy and cursing ourselves, but no good at effective fighting against the well organised political parties. Even the propaganda of the London Labour and Socialist movement, said the provincials, served to provide votes for the Liberal Party machine for the simple reason that London Labour had no organisation that could reap the result of its own propaganda. (*London News*, December 1924.)

But now things were different:

> This change – approaching a political revolution – has been achieved
> by hard work, constructive education methods and sound organisa-
> tion from the polling districts upwards. Had we followed the advice
> of our so-called revolutionary counsellors, this substantial move
> toward a political revolution would not have taken place to anything
> like the extent shown by the figures. This is further indication of the
> fact that the so-called revolutionary tactician has in general a reac-
> tionary effect. (ibid.)

The ten years that had witnessed this transformation were precisely
those occupied by Morrison as secretary of the newly-formed London
Labour Party (LLP). The calculus on which he based his explanation was,
therefore, a neat and self-fulfilling testimony to the record of the LLP; and
yet it is one that has survived intact. Paul Thompson (1967) sees the
triumph of Labour as a constructive coalescence of the mature proletarian
class consciousness which emerged with the displacement of small-scale
production and an effective LLP, while Julia Bush (1978), concentrating on
the experience of East London, argues that during the first world war
socialist activity and the growing confidence and strength of the trades
unions enabled the LLP to establish a solid base which it exploited to the full
when hostilities ceased.

More recently, and critically, Jim Gillespie (1984), while not denying the
significance of the LLP, points to the need to break with the implicit teleol-
ogy of these explanations. The equation linking trades unionism with
Labour's advance cannot be applied to London; not only were unions
weak, but in the interwar period suffered setbacks as the depression
deepened. The success of Morrison's project derived not from the cementing of working-class allegiance to Labour through the unions, but in
filling the political vacuum created by the downturn of political and
industrial militancy in the immediate postwar period. This he effected by
intervention in the local state on ground cleared by the trades boards, the
attempted decasualisation of dock labour, and the use of local authority
workforces to promote more radical demands on the national state for
solutions to crises experienced in local economies.

Thus Gillespie proceeds carefully to examine structural conditions
underpinning changes in East London industry and the interventionist
strategy of the LLP. While acknowledging the importance of contemporary
political debates, however, little is said on how these local crises were
perceived and demands articulated. The contention that 'unemployment
dominated every municipal election at least until 1937, and lay at the heart
of discussions within the LLP' is difficult to reconcile with the detailed
programmes promoted by the LLP in London County Council (LCC) or local
elections (see, for example, *Labour News*, February and April 1925). The
work on political discourses around welfare, housing, unemployment and
other issues of local concern articulated by Labour as well as its opponents
remains to be done.

Empirically, the problem of seeing Labour's rise in West Ham as part of the metropolitan experience is that the borough was administratively separate. The direct influence of the LLP extended only as far as the metropolitan boundary at Bethnal Green; the West Ham Labour Party was autonomous. Furthermore, the industrial and political history of the borough was distinct (p13-26 above). Rapid industrial growth in the latter half of the nineteenth century promoted a political culture that can only with caution be described as radical. The election of Keir Hardie in 1892 owed more to historical contingency than to a heightened class consciousness among the electorate. And the labour council – in reality a fragile and temporary alliance of Social Democratic Federation (SDF), Independent Labour Party (ILP), christian socialist, Irish nationalist and independent members – elected on a platform little different from that of progressives on the LCC, was never able to challenge effectively the accepted boundaries of municipal activity.

Morrison's epitaph on London Labour before the war, therefore, is not one that can be applied to West Ham. Labour may not have been able to maintain control of the municipal sphere for a prolonged period, but it had built a strong tradition of formal political activity which was to form the basis of hegemonic power in the interwar years.

2.2 War and the 1918 election

The Labour Party emerged from the war with renewed strength and confidence. Its leaders had retained a distance from the perceived excesses of militancy that began to surface and gain momentum after 1917 when opposition to the war mounted and hopeful eyes turned to Russia (for good accounts of this period see Cole 1969 and Miliband 1973). The 1918 constitution rebuilt the party machine, creating a centralised, national body out of a loose federation of affiliated organisations, so laying the foundation for an effective election machine, while its political commitment was enshrined in *Labour and the new social order*, a manifesto that was sufficiently ambiguous to attract people with quite different conceptions of the role of the party in heralding socialism, and yet seemed to many to offer a new beginning.

But the road to 1918 had been a troubled one. Attitudes toward active participation in the war opened deep fissures in the movement which, at the extreme, were never healed. Common action on issues at a local level seemed threatened, but at no time did the war seriously compromise the determination of labour leaders to defend living conditions; in many instances the struggle was intensified, although not to the point of sabotaging the war effort.

Patriotism was pervasive in West Ham. Deeply embedded in the local population and the majority of the labour leadership, it influenced political strategy on all important issues (see Bush 1984 for most of the next two paragraphs). A campaign led by the War Emergency Workers National Committee to secure increased labour representation on poor law and distress committees attracted support from pro- and antiwar factions. Will Thorne – MP, trade unionist and patriot – declared that the patriotism of West Ham socialists would not prevent them from taking a strong political stance on relief questions (*SE* 15 August 14). As part of the same struggle against destitution, meetings were organised to protest at increasing food prices and profiteering ; a large attendance at Canning Town Public Hall heard Sylvia Pankhurst and resolved to campaign for government price controls and votes for women (*SE* 27 February 15). Occasionally, such campaigns took more militant forms. A wave of brief, unofficial strikes for higher wages was organised by large workforces at the Victoria and Albert Docks and West Ham council (pp81-2). But there was a limit beyond which the furtherance of working-class interests conflicted with the national interest; few were prepared to advance there in the first two years of the war.

Although a mass antiwar movement failed to materialise, significant bodies of socialist thought within the British Socialist Party (BSP), Independent Labour Party (ILP) and Herald League were mobilised against conscription. The West Ham Trades Council resolved that conscription was a serious threat to the labour movement, and summoned Thorne to explain his support for it at the 1916 Labour Party conference (*East Ham Echo* 12 February 16). Even Thorne's branch of the BSP expressed disquiet (BSP, South West Ham branch, *Minutes* 28 January 16).

Such incidents were symptomatic of tensions within the socialist movement that were to have long-term consequences. The experience of the BSP was particularly significant. West Ham had two branches. Even before the outbreak of war relations between them were strained. A visit to the North branch to discuss political tactics reported that the

> position was serious, and that any chance of arriving at an agreement had been alienated by bad management. Comrade Stokes said that if we took no action the Progressive Party would. Comrade Shreeve also said that if the North West Ham branch was impossible to work with, we as citizens living under present conditions were bound to take action. (ibid. 12 March 14.)

A complete split was also threatened when the North branch voted to withdraw from the BSP if it affiliated to the Labour Party (ibid. 4 August 14). But this merely delayed for a while the inevitable. At the 1915 BSP National Conference, the branch moved that the conference:

> calls upon the working class to concentrate upon the greater war at hand, namely, the class war. The relentless struggle of the workers against unemployment and hunger in times of peace as in times of war makes it vital for them to organise for the overthrow of the capitalist system and for the establishment of the Socialist Commonwealth. (*Justice* 4 March 15.)

South West Ham branch, on the other hand, was the only East London branch to support prowar resolutions of the Central branch. A majority of the 1916 conference called for action to end the war, immediately provoking Hyndman and his supporters, including Jack Jones (soon to become Labour MP for Silvertown) and Thorne to depart and set up the National Socialist Party (NSP). The South branch subsequently voted to affiliate, and for the remainder of the war continued to campaign on a platform of 'Victory abroad; Welfare at home' for adequate pensions, food supplies and relief, especially for families of servicemen. The North branch, small and isolated in comparison, concentrated on propaganda and education work, helped at one meeting by John MacLean who spoke on the organisation of economic classes (BSP, NWH branch, *Minutes* 12 August 17). In cooperation with local branches of the ILP, the trades council and Plebs League, a series of weekly classes on Marxism was held at Stratford at which average attendance was over 80 (Bush 1978 p128).

The Russian revolution gave renewed confidence to socialist organisations, but did little to ease tensions between pro- and antiwar factions. While Thorne hoped that Russia would now turn to the war with increased resolve, the North branch moved to the 1918 BSP conference

that this conference congratulates our Bolshevik comrades of Russia on their splendid efforts to bring about a general peace, and their unflinching opposition to the brigands of international capital, though we deplore the fact that their efforts to stir the workers of all the belligerents to revolutionary action has not so far met with success, yet we promise to do all in our power to awaken the proletariat of this country to class consciousness so that a speedy end may overtake the tyranny of capital. (BSP, NWH branch, *Minutes* 20 January 18.)

Just over a year later head office of the NSP called on branches for special propaganda 'To kill bolshevism' (NSP, SWH branch, *Minutes* 14 March 19). But the tide was temporarily turning against the prowar lobby. The combined efforts of ILP and BSP members at a West Ham Trades Council and Central Labour Party conference on the selection of parliamentary candidates defeated Will Thorne; D J Davis (ILP), B Gardner (ILP), J Edwards (BSP) and J Jones (NSP) were nominated (ibid.13 January 18). It was a notable victory for the pacifists, particularly since Thorne was established as the senior labour figure through a continuous involvement in local politics over nearly thirty years, and had represented West Ham South since 1906. Following pressure from the NSP and Lansbury, the National Labour Party urged West Ham Trades Council not to run a candidate against Thorne at Plaistow. More significant, however, was the very real threat to Labour unity posed by the determination of Thorne and Jones to stand as NSP candidates, and the resignation from the Labour group on West Ham council of eight key figures, including Thorne, Jones, Godbold and Thomas Kirk (*SE* 9 February 18). Kirk complained of the

perpetual insults that every decent labour man has endured through standing up for his country in the hour of her crisis from men who have foisted themselves on the Labour movement by wirepulling tactics. These men have no industrial history and owe their presence

there to men like Will Thorne, Jack Jones, etc., who in the past gave
labour the footing that it has attained... To be associated with them
you must be either a square-headed German or a bearded Bolshevik.
I have resigned membership of the West Ham Town Council Labour
Group and in future will answer to the West Ham Branch of the
National Union of Railwaymen. (*SE* 19 January 18.)

Thorne also turned to his union in a decisive move (p78). The trades
council acceded, and left him with a clear run. Jones, however, would have
to stand against Davis. In the ensuing campaign, Thorne, Jones and their
supporters exploited populist rhetoric on the war. Mansfield claimed that
Thorne had consistently acted in accord with the

sentiments of the majority of people in the borough... He was
prepared to stand out and fight on their own, and let the people of
West Ham say who should represent them. He knew what those
pacifists were: they were partly, if not absolutely, pro-German. He
was sure this was not the general view. He knew what the boys were
fighting for, and was sure that the public would give a right judge-
ment when the proper time came. (*SE* 26 January 18.)

Pacifists in the ILP and BSP, Jones argued, had done more harm to the
working-class movement than could have been inflicted by the Municipal
Alliance. If democratic unity inside the movement was impossible, the
only course was to appeal to the democracy of the borough (*SE* 19 January
18). The trump card, however, was union support. Thorne and Jones were
senior officers of the National Union of General Workers (NUGW), which
declared its commitment to overthrowing German aggression and to the
candidature of Thorne (*SE* 26 January 18); meanwhile the massive Stratford branch of the NUR congratulated Kirk on his 'loyal support for our
valued representative Alderman Will Thorne M.P.' (*SE* 2 February 18).

Thorne appeared in khaki as Hon. Colonel of the 1st Essex Volunteers,
spoke at large pro-ally demonstrations of no peace until the defeat of the
Habsburgs, and refused cooperation with German socialists, while the
dockers' leader Ben Tillett railed against German atrocities and pacifist
blacklegs (*SE* 20 July 18). At a NSP rally in Stratford, Thorne claimed that '90
per cent of the organised workers were behind them'. Jones referred to
'cranks – long-haired men and short-haired women' who formed the
(British) Socialist Party, and explained that the title of NSP better represented the time and circumstances than SDF because 'social democrat was
associated with Germany and Germanic thought, and during the present
war the action of most of the social democrats of Germany had made the
term stink in the nostrils of most people' (*SE* 1 June 18).

This populist, anti-intellectual hostility was also extended to the new
constitution of the Labour Party. In a letter to the local press Kirk expressed
criticism of the party's stance on peace by negotiation, and the disastrous
consequences of adopting the new constitution:

Carpetbagger political adventurers have joined. Railwaymen were
going to object to funds being used to further the political careers of

such men. Socialism was not pacifism, neither was it Fabianism with its 'superior person' bureaucratic tyranny and government by experts policy. The bolsheviks they had with them, trying to nobble the Labour Party, were men without a country – mere cosmopolitans, half-baked visionaries without a mission... The workers' control of industry would follow naturally upon the realisation of their industrial and political power. Let them see to it that their power is used effectively in the coming elections for the establishment of a bona-fide working-class party, and above all let them beware of the intriguing politics and hypocritical middle class friends of Germany. (ibid.)

Here are the principal themes of the populist discourse wielded by the labour leadership of West Ham in the dying hours of the war that was to inform much of the course of politics in the ensuing years. It was an aggressive assertion of a predominantly male, working-class integrity against incursions from middle-class intellectuals and foreign influence. It was nationalist and virulently anticommunist. On the relationship between industrial and political power, however, it was less clear, reflecting general unease between the two spheres of working-class activity (Chapter 3 below). Political power was to be secured through the commonsensical and practical consolidation of union power at the workplace, and the use of the ballot, not through pursuit of transient revolutionary ideals imported from other countries. But precisely how this power was to be used to reach what appears to be the ultimate goal of workers' control is not conceptualised.

There was little that was new. Indeed, its constituent elements characterised and were inherited from the tradition of labourism that emerged in the second half of the nineteenth century (Saville 1973). This tradition drew on diverse influences. Chartism, although defeated, endowed sections of the working class with a sense of class identity that may have lacked a vision of the totality of class relationships, but was sufficiently powerful to define broad boundaries of interest. Thus a class consciousness perceiving class relationships as antagonistic, to be dismantled through political struggle, informed few working-class activities; rather a sense of an undefined 'us' against an unknown 'them' pervaded. This identity was overwhelmingly defensive, for it was asserted, particularly in the industrial sphere, only when threatened by attempts to abolish traditional rights, customs and practices. And even if the defence took militant forms, its boundaries were defined by extant relations of production.

Working-class consciousness was also moulded by attempts of the Conservative Party after extension of the franchise in 1867 to construct working-class interests as their own (p57). The identity was forged as by articulating 'the people' as 'the nation', the delineation of which excluded all non-English. At the height of imperial power, exclusivity was rigidly applied.

So, themes of nationalism, self-identity, industrial power, anti-intellectualism and xenophobia had all featured in working-class rhetoric, but in the postwar period they derived particular effectivity by being reworked into a unified discourse of labourism. Against it, socialist currents within the ILP and BSP seemed defenceless. W Ward, ILP and NUR, attempted to counter the charges made by labourists at a meeting of the newly-formed West Ham Labour Party:

> A lot of misapprehension was abroad among a large section of the people as to the aims and objects of the National Labour Party. A lot of people ran away with the idea that they were Pacifists, but so far as he was concerned that was not true. What they had said was at the end of the war they aimed at a safe and lasting peace, and to obtain that they demanded a setting up of a League of Nations. (*SE* 28 September 18.)

D J Davis, ILP and councillor, shifted attention to the more positive aspects of the party's programme:

> The Labour Party were leaving no stone unturned and had published 'The New Social Order'. There it was laid down clearly and definitely not only what they aimed at, but how they were going to secure it... The Labour Party had an ideal, and it was the only party which had one and told the people how to achieve it... He prophesied that there was no man or woman big enough to stand forever in the way of the Labour Party achieving their aims. The war was apparently in the way, but that was more as a result of misunderstanding than anything else. (ibid.)

There was a small attendance. At an election meeting B Gardner, ILP and councillor, argued for a redistribution of wealth in the period of reconstruction and warned of the dangers of placing trust in Lloyd George (*SE* 30 November 18)

Meanwhile the BSP was being driven into obscurity. It faced hostility from Labour leaders, and never succeeded in gaining an electoral or industrial base. The majority of its relatively small membership was in retail or professional occupations, and included a confectioner, draper, dentist, Socialist Sunday School worker and a transport manager. Two had been imprisoned for espionage for the duration of the war (Enever, tape). Following a ballot in favour of affiliation to the Labour Party, Edwards withdrew his candidature at Stratford, and later resigned from the BSP (BSP, NWH branch, *Minutes* 1 September 18). More resignations followed. On 22 December a vote of 6-2 favoured dissolution of the branch (ibid. December 18). All members were to join the local Communist Party, which in ensuing years became a rather more effective instrument of political influence, particularly on the West Ham Trades Council (p106) and amongst the unemployed (p142).

Coalition candidates at Stratford, Upton and Silvertown fought on the war record of Lloyd George and the necessity of reparations, often in language that echoed the sentiments of the NSP. Lt Col Carthew in Silvertown spoke of the cheap talk about this League of Nations... They would be in favour of it if it could be worked out in a practical form: but it did not mean they were going to give up the freedom of the seas. Nor did it mean that Germany and the countries associated with her would be let in until they had purged their crimes. (*SE* 23 November 18.)

The subsequent election witnessed easy victories for coalition candidates in the north of the borough. Lyle defeated Masterman at Stratford; Wild defeated Gardner at Upton, gaining nearly three times as many votes. At Silvertown, Jones, the unofficial Labour candidate, beat Carthew, Davis coming a poor third, while at Plaistow Thorne inflicted a crushing defeat on Lupton. At a victory rally Thorne stated that all four seats could have been won for Labour if they had fought as pro-ally candidates (*SE* 1 January 19). Mansfield saw this as the foundation for a

solid Labour Party in the House of Commons – not the faddists or theorists, but practical, hard-headed industrial workers who understand the workers' aims and desires. Electors in various parts of the country had cleared out some of the cranks who were prostitutes in the Labour movement in order to get into the House of Commons. (ibid.)

2.3 Labour's populism

But the war was over, and the Labour Party nationally entered into one of the most critical and confused periods of its history. Within the next two years resolutions would be sought and reached on fundamental political issues such as the legitimacy of constitutional action, a programme of social and parliamentary advance, and the relationship of the party to both trade unions and socialist organisations (Cole 1969). These resolutions, for the most part the outcome of pragmatic adaptation of a moderate collectivism enshrined in *Labour and the new social order*, and the implementation of constitutional change, were to lay the foundations of a mass party able to command the loyalty of large sections of the enfranchised working class. And it was around the locality that loyalty was built.

Something of the complexity of this process is evident from the experience of West Ham. Most striking in the immediate postwar period was the alacrity with which official Labour leaders discarded the patriotic card. Cessation of hostilities reduced its political weight, but so effective had it been in the 1918 election and so important was the ex-servicemen's vote, that it could have been played a while longer. Some local Labour figures, notably Herbert Rumsey (MM, DCM), used their service record against opponents, but the central drive was toward Labour unity and social reform.

Early in 1919 Thorne reported back from a meeting between local ILP and NSP branches:

He met Alderman Davis and discussed the advisability of the members on the council coming together again in order that they would be unanimous in open council, especially now that Labour is in the majority. (NSP, SWH branch, *Minutes* 30 March 19.)

The South West Ham branch subsequently decided to affiliate to the Central Labour Party in West Ham 'to work amicably in the coming election' (ibid. 10 August 19). This new mood of reconciliation was prompted by a recognition that Labour had an unprecedented opportunity to recover from damage inflicted by divisions during the war and strengthen its position in the struggle against socialist currents:

> The need for sound social democratic education was never greater than it was today and there was never a better opportunity for the building up of a strong National Socialist Party. In the war period Anarchists of all shades and colours were allowed free hold, with the results they saw before them. An educated democracy would never for a moment be influenced by the ill-balanced ideas of the direct actionists. (SE 23 August 19.)

The programme cementing this unity was taken piecemeal from the Labour manifesto. At this stage it lacked coherence, but was made directly relevant to local conditions. Housing, public health and education featured strongly. In his maiden speech in parliament, Jones referred to the consequences of living in 'one of the poorest districts of East London, where the housing problem was of a very intense character' (SE 15 March 19). Thorne later spoke of the potential of concerted action around such issues:

> In days gone by there had been little differences between the members of the party on the war policy, but the war was now over and they wanted to unite all their forces... One of the most important questions they had to consider was that of public health, including housing. Education was also a big question and a lot of money would have to be spent on it. (SE 25 October 19.)

Simultaneously, Jack Wood, soon to be returned unopposed in the forthcoming municipal election, told the West Ham Trades Council that 'he was more delighted to have a place on (the) united Labour Party platform than to have a seat on the council' (ibid). Other candidates spoke of the need to rid West Ham of its slums and provide its children with the opportunity to reach university.

A by-election in March 1919 gave Labour a clear majority of two on the council; but this was overshadowed by the election in November, the first for six years, when Labour won eight of the nine wards contested, so gaining four seats. It was a sweeping victory, giving Labour effective control of thirty of the forty-eight seats on the council (SE 8 November 19)

Election material published by different candidates demonstrates the diversity of Labour's appeal. J T Scoulding in Hudsons Ward spoke of housing, 'the immediate necessity of which is only too apparent and has been continually kept in the front of the Labour Party's demands on the West Ham Council', education 'free from the elementary school to the university thus give our class equality of opportunity', and municipal employment, 'the local authority being model employers and setting the standard for the rest of the community in respect to wages and conditions of employment' (Election leaflets, 1919). He added that he, unlike his opponents, did not apply for exemption from military service – actions speak louder than words'. Rumsey in West Ham Ward used the same programme, but also issued a leaflet giving details of how he won the DCM, concluding 'Do your bit by voting for the man who has done his bit for you'.

J Wood in the Custom House and Silvertown Ward expressed the need to administer effectively the 1918 Education Act, 1918 Maternity Act, and the 1919 Housing and Town Planning Act: 'In a period of reconstruction only a majority of conscious Socialist and labour men and women on the council will have the determination to make West Ham a healthier, cleaner, more sanitary town to live in'. This went to the very heart of an ideal that, although lacking cohesion, was encapsulated in Labour's programme and no other. W R Hughes, an Oxford settlement worker and independent councillor, sensed this:

> It is difficult at any time to represent a large body of one's fellows; in these critical days of reconstruction it is harder than ever. We want big changes and we want them quickly, but we cannot see clearly enough how to set to work. We hold, at the bottom of our hearts, the same ideals of justice and brotherhood, and it is this common aspiration that I should like to express and represent. It is because I feel that the impulse that is behind the work of the Labour Party is mainly the same longing for the time when man [sic] will be able to live in free and equal comradeship that I find myself in line with that party. (ibid.)

Such an ideal, shorn here of a class dimension, resonated with the belief of a majority of the working-class voters in West Ham after the war that the Labour Party was the only party able to represent their interests, overcome their frustrations and grievances, and provide the means through which their hopes could be realised. In some respects the platform of the rate-payer-based, antisocialist Municipal Alliance resembled that of Labour. A Symes in High Street Ward, for example, pointed to the 'vast problems to be faced by the Borough – houses for the working classes, road improve-ments, removal of slums, tram system improved', but then went to the heart of the matter:

> I view with alarm the increase in rates. I am a strong advocate of the strictest economy, and feel that spending money extravagantly means still higher rates and higher rents, which manufacturers, shopkeepers and the whole of the electors are unable to bear.(ibid.)

Claims to represent the legitimate interests of the community as a whole in a non-political, non-party mandate were integral elements of the Alli-ance programme. As a counter to the determinedly working-class basis of Labour's populism, it sought to unite 'forces working for good govern-ment of the borough, and to combat the policy of the extremists who seek to create a privileged section of the community at the expense of the rest' (Municipal Alliance, nd). In practice, it was the Alliance that represented privilege, and was generally recognised to do so (p65-7). Its strength lay in the relatively wealthy wards north of the borough – Forest Gate, Upton and

Park – where the local bourgeoisie and petit bourgeoisie were concentrated. The different class basis of Alliance and Labour is suggested by occupations of their candidates:

WARD	MUNICIPAL ALLIANCE	LABOUR PARTY
New Town	Bate: iron and steel worker	Groves: coach builder
Forest Gate	Ward: managing printer	Mann: railway foreman
High Street	Symes: builder	Reed: fitter's labourer
Broadway	Flaxman: manufacturing chemist	Anderson: accountant
Park	Bulling: claims inspector	–
Upton	Ridgwell: postmaster	Digby: warehouseman
West Ham	Bolger: retired pay clerk	Rumsey: printer's assistant
Plaistow	Wybrew: manager	Hughes: settlement worker
Hudsons	Harding: gentleman	Scoulding: union organiser
Canning Town	Allpress: minister	Gardner: clerk
Tidal Basin	–	Kerrison: voluntary worker
Custom House & Silvertown	–	Wood: glass bottle maker

Too much should not be made of this. Names of occupations are notoriously ambiguous. More important, the relation between class location and political allegiance is not linear and unproblematical. The surprise is not that an accountant stands for Labour while an iron and steel worker is an Alliance candidate, but rather that the class basis of the two sets of candidates is so distinct. Were the backgrounds of candidates examined, the contrast would be even more striking. Edith Kerrison, for example, described as a spinster on the election notice, was a former nurse, member of the ILP, and had devoted years to the improvement of maternity welfare in the poorest parts of the borough (p50). Almost all the other Labour candidates had long and notable records in the union movement. Scoulding, for example, had been a member of the Amalgamated Society of Watermen, Lightermen, and Bargemen since 1895, London organiser since 1911, and district secretary of the Transport Workers Federation since 1912. The same argument applies with even greater force to the parliamentary candidates – Jones, Thorne, Davis and Gardner.

Labour activists were rooted in particular localities and political traditions, and these were to provide the basis for labourist hegemony in the formal political arena of West Ham throughout the interwar period. Far from seeing the ascent of Labour in the immediate postwar period as a spontaneous response to frustrated hopes and deteriorating social conditions, it was rather a resolution or convergence of deeper currents at a specific historical conjuncture. And it was this convergence that engendered a tradition among the working-class electorate of voting Labour; Labour came to be identified with working-class interests as it had never been before. Of these currents, by far the most important were trade unionism and cooperation: trade unionism demands separate treatment (Chapter 3 below), here I wish to turn to the cooperative movement.

2.4 Cooperation enters politics

By the end of the nineteenth century an important cooperative movement was established in West Ham. Founded in 1860 by a group of railwaymen at the Eastern Counties Railway works at Stratford, it had progressed steadily, in part through amalgamation with smaller societies at Canning Town in 1882, Plaistow in 1883 and Beckton in 1892, all of which centred on colonies of skilled and semiskilled labour (Marriott 1984). By 1903 Stratford Cooperative Society (SCS) had a membership of 12,914: the Royal Arsenal Cooperative Society (21,788) apart, it was the only one in the metropolitan area that could rival the strength of traditional strongholds of cooperation in the north.

This expansion, however, was to be overtaken dramatically in the next decades. At the outbreak of war, membership was 34,209, in 1918 it was 44,068; soon after the formation of the London Cooperative Society (LCS) in 1920 by amalgamation with Edmonton there were 100,020 members, and at the end of the interior period after further amalgamations, notably with the West London Society, there were 794,637. With sales of over £16m and 18,840 employees, it was the largest society in the world (LCS 1941), and Alf Barnes, president of the LCS since its inception, had achieved his dream of a unified London cooperative movement.

Exceptional though such growth was, cooperation expanded in most other areas of the country. It had been recognised for some time that only through rationalisation into larger productive and distributive units could the movement overcome the damaging rivalries among societies in the same neighbourhood, and through economies of scale promote further growth. But it was not until the twentieth century that these policies proved effective. The interwar years witnessed an increase in national membership from 4,131,000 in 1919 to 8,716,000 in 1940, while the number of societies fell from 1357 to 1065. In 1920, only London and Leeds had societies with average memberships of over 90,000. By 1940, London had 817,053, Arsenal had 332,567, and six others in the north and midlands had over 90,000 (Bonner 1970).

From the outset cooperation was a political movement. Having intellectual origins in Owenite socialism, pioneer cooperators saw control of distribution as a means toward the abolition of capitalism, or in minimal terms, a major shift in the balance of power and wealth. Although objectives came to be redefined, compromising the original radicalism, attitudes toward representational politics remained firm. Formal political involvement was considered unnecessary, even harmful, since cooperation successfully embraced a wide range of political opinion (Greening 1914). Evidence that Liberals had used the movement to pursue policies favourable to their party had confirmed to many that cooperation should be neutral (Bailey 1948).

As the nineteenth century closed significant sections of cooperative thought turned to representation, largely as a response to the experience of local government and particularly the trade unions:

> The trade unionists have learnt the lesson; they have taken it to heart. They know that only through the legislature of the nation can the battle for common justice be effectively fought and permanent well-being for the people obtained. Hence their determined entrance into the political arena. Having done this... what was more natural than for them to invite the sister institution, with its professedly similar aims, to join them? It is a pity, therefore, that some cooperators have attributed motives for this invitation. (Hines 1911.)

A resolution was passed at the 1897 Congress that 'the time has arrived for the direct representation of the cooperative movement in Parliament'. This enthusiasm, inspired by Scottish sections, was short lived, and nothing came of the move, but it did signal a phase of agitation over representation that was to culminate in formal acceptance of the principle at the 1917 Congress.

Experience of cooperation during the war set the final seal. The movement had grown in a climate of free enterprise, and while it remained relatively small it did not appear to threaten the capitalist market or private business. But in the years preceding the outbreak of war it had become by far the largest single retailer. War exacerbated the tensions (Maguire 1987). The state was forced to assume some measure of control over distribution of food and levels of profits, and thus intervene in the market. This was in part a response to an upsurge in militant opposition to food shortages and profiteering which was simultaneously driving many trade unionists into cooperation. But it was also apparent that by taking control of the food supply the government had a powerful weapon against the movement – one that it used without hesitation. Between 1914 and 1916 the government discriminated blatantly against cooperation. Inadequate army contract work was given; societies were treated unfairly by military tribunals, on many of which sat rival local shopkeepers; the Cooperative Union was deliberately ignored in government discussions on imports and rationing; and the restricted distribution of goods, based on prewar levels, took no account of increasing membership of the societies (Webb and Webb 1922). Such action created bitter resentment. A meeting of the scs early in 1917 called for the dismissal of Lord Devonport, the first Food Controller, who had made his fortune in wholesale grocery and was vehemently opposed to cooperation:

> This meeting strongly condemns the regulations of the Food Controller, which favour the rich who are not in danger of being without food, make it possible for the wealthy to provide unscrupulous

profiteers to defraud the nation by government sanction i.e. the fixing of prices for potatoes and other edibles, and therefore calls for Lord Devonport's removal from office. (SCS 1917.)

Potentially more damaging to cooperation, however, were proposals to impose a profits tax on cooperative revenue. The Excess Profits Duty was widely regarded as a concession to mounting concern over profiteering (Maguire 1987), but the decision to levy it on societies posed fundamental questions about the nature of the cooperative enterprise. Since cooperation was mutual trading – a genuine alternative to traditional retailing which existed to generate profit – the act of levying a profits tax challenged the integrity and identity of the movement, endowing it with the same status as private trading. Following as it did two years of bitterness caused by the government's political intervention in food distribution, the tax provoked an immediate and direct response from large sections of the movement. The scs submitted a resolution to the cooperative congress:

That in view of the many matters of vital interest to the Cooperative Movement, such as the excess profits duty, the threatened income tax on dividends, the state control of wheat, sugar, coal, etc., which must come before Parliament in the immediate future, this Congress hereby instructs the Central Board to consider ways and means of ensuring the adequate representation of cooperative knowledge and opinion in Parliament. (SCS *Magazine* 1917.)

In the period leading up to congress the campaign for political representation gathered momentum. None put the case more forcibly than the Parliamentary Correspondent of *Cooperative News:*

Cooperators cannot expect to protect themselves against the threatened attack of the opposing forces without carefully preparing a united plan of campaign, in the same way that the Labour Party has mobilised its battalions... The Labour Party has become a power in the land owing to its having at its back a large mass of the voting strength of the country. Until the cooperative electorate is similarly organised we shall remain in a state of political impotency. Our political weakness is our opponents' strength. (*Cooperative News* 6 January 17.)

By the eve of congress the vote seemed a foregone conclusion:

The voices of the old guard will be raised against this striking new departure, but they will be raised in vain. The old fulminations against political alliances will be heard, and the old predictions of financial disaster will be trotted out; the old yarns about schemes of interested but impecunious politicians who desire to insert their capacious hands into our money chests will be ventilated; we shall, in fact, be inundated by all the old bosh which has so long confused the issues and blocked the way to advance in the direction of cooperative representation. But this time they will be of no avail. (ibid. 28 April 17.)

And so it was. Congress voted 1979 to 201 for a resolution calling on the cooperative movement to secure direct representation in parliament and on local administrative bodies. The Cooperative Party was thus established. Stratford cooperators lost little time in implementing the decision. At a special meeting of the SCS a rule change empowered the society to use 1 per cent of net profits for 'any contingency that may arise in connection with the business of the Society' including political representation. 1 per cent was also allocated to the education fund (SCS 10 November 17). A Parliamentary and Local Government Advisory Committee was also set up with a brief to 'consider and recommend to the General Committee what, in their opinion, is necessary for the purpose of effectively carrying into effect the resolution passed at the Swansea Congress'. Some had a clear idea of what was required and successfully moved that

> in so far as Cooperation is fundamentally opposed to the existing economic basis of society, this meeting of Stratford Cooperators consider it desirable, in order to fully organise and obtain the best results from their political acts, that the advisory committee be instructed to enter into negotiations and act in conjunction with the Trades Council and Labour Represention Committees in the area covered by this Society's operations. (ibid.)

Coincident with unprecedented growth in local cooperation, then, was a move toward overt political involvement along lines of interest broadly similar to those of Labour. But before the alliance could be cemented a number of problems had to be resolved, not least of which was residual opposition within the society to its recent shift in direction. This opposition – a minority, but a significant one – cohered around disaffected Liberal cooperators, some of whom occupied influential positions in the society and were active in the Municipal Alliance. One such member, J C Carroll, convened the Cooperative Reform Committee. At its first public meeting, attended by over 100 members, anger was voiced at the action of the socialist majority on the management committee in rushing the society into all the dangers of party politics (SE 5 January 18). A Flocks, elected chair, explained that

> he had for sometime been anxious as to where the society was drifting. He referred in indignant terms to the action of less than 50 members (largely socialist) in voting that the society should be represented in Parliament and on local bodies only by those who choose to go through the Labour party, whilst all members were called upon to pay the cost. (ibid.)

And in language identical to that used in the Municipal Alliance critique of the Labour council declared that their object was to

> see that the society returned to sane management, and elected only business men who would look after the society's interests first, and seeing that the present majority favoured representation by socialists only, they should be fought one by one as they appeared for re-election, until the confidence of the membership, at present abused and outraged, was restored, and the society stood for co-operation pure and simple. (ibid.)

The Reform Committee set its sights on the quarterly meeting later that month. Large advertisements were placed in the local press appealing to members to 'roll up in your thousands … and vote "Cooperation for Cooperators". No cooperation money for party politics. No doubtful experiments with other people's savings' (*SE* 5 January 18). The committee had considerable success in elections at the meeting, securing all three contested seats on the General Committee and, more importantly, ousting Alf Barnes from the presidency in a close vote. But it lost the crucial vote. Flocks moved that the resolution authorising the Advisory Committee to negotiate with local Labour councils be rescinded. Replying for the General Committee, Barnes argued that this would alienate the movement from organised labour. In the subsequent vote, the motion was defeated 314–243 (*SE* 2 February 18).

The other major problem faced by political cooperation was the establishment of a practical working relationship with the Labour Party and trade unions. The pressures to affiliate to the Labour Party were obvious. Affiliation would secure the alliance, provide the means to a united front during elections, and, as far as the party was concerned, increase much needed revenue. Some attempts were made by political parties to annexe the cooperative representation movement, acts that were exploited by J C Carroll in a circular stating that resolutions in support of the Labour Party were being forwarded, together with proposals to finance political work by increasing contributions (see interviews with S F Perry, Secretary of the Cooperative Representation Committee in *Cooperative News* 29 March 19, 5 April 19).

However committed the cooperative movement was to political involvement, there remained a powerful independence, and this proved decisive. The first national conference of the Cooperative Party set the agenda. Barnes spoke for the majority:

> the movement had to discuss the ultimate and logical outcome of political action or it would be adding to confusion. He would never have supported cooperative politics had he thought that it would develop a Cooperative Party, pure and simple, antagonistic to the main democratic Labour movement. He supported the alliance because to take the cooperative movement into the Labour Party wholly would not help the Labour Party: and it was necessary to build up a political consciousness in the movement so that cooperative ideals could be translated by political machinery. (ibid. 25 September 20.)

The conference resolved to support an alliance, within which local committees would be free to draft municipal programmes and choose candidates. This formed the basis of an informal but generally close working relationship between the cooperative movement and the Labour Party (and via this with the trade unions) until a national agreement in 1927 formalised it.

A programme for the Cooperative Party was formulated at the

conference soon after its formation. The programme declared a commitment to safeguarding the interests of cooperation, to ensuring that 'process of production, distribution and exchange, including the land, ... be directed by the state in the interests of the whole community', to the elimination of profiteering, and the provision of adequate housing and education for the people (SCS 10 November 17). So close was it to *Labour and the new social order* in terms of its content and timing, a certain duplicity is suspected. But whatever the mechanism of its conception, it meant that Labour and cooperation would enter future elections on a mutually beneficial and supportive programme of social and political reform.

Ten cooperative candidates ran at the 1918 general election, only one of whom was successful. S. F Perry saw the exercise not as a disappointment but as an heartening indicator of future progress:

> In the last general election it was encouraging to find where contest had taken place that enthusiasm for cooperative representation had been considerably increased, and in addition the opportunity of bringing before the general public the benefits of cooperation has resulted in a very material addition to the cooperative forces in the district. All round the feeling has been that by developing political representation, cooperation has increased its hold on the general public and is daily attracting new adherents to its principles. (*Cooperative News* 29 March 19.)

Here was the desired nexus between popular politics and popular culture, between politics and trade. Political consciousness of the public would be enhanced by recognition of the benefits of cooperation, then of the need for cooperative representation. As the cooperative movement expanded, so would widen the net of an electorate committed to cooperation or, in the absence of cooperative candidates, to Labour.

No candidates were proposed by the advisory committee of the scs for the forthcoming election. A decision to contest a parliamentary seat 'if a favourable opportunity should occur' and to grant £250 as expenses was taken in October, but it came too late (scs *Quarterly report* 28 October 18). Speaking against the movement C Hughes argued that by passing this they would 'be voting for pacifism, and there would be no patriotic Stratford society after that' (*SE* 3 August 18). In the following local elections, however, the committee – now the Stratford and District Local Cooperative Representation Council – selected six candidates for urban councils and boards of guardians. Five were successful, three being elected unopposed (ibid. 8 April 19).

Later in the year the committee sponsored four candidates in council elections. In spite of local cooperative strength there was none in West Ham because of potential conflict with the West Ham Trades Council and Labour Representation Committee, which at the time controlled selection of Labour candidates. Instead two were put forward in East Ham and two in Southend. They worked closely with local Labour parties, and hopes were high. Election addresses proposed reform in housing, education, public health, direct labour, and municipal milk and coal supplies (scs *Magazine* November 19); they were indistinguishable from those of Labour candidates. But the elections, in areas less propitious than West Ham, returned only McGiff, in East Ham.

Active steps were also taken to strengthen links with local trade unions. Joint advisory committees of cooperators and unionists were established under the slogan 'Every cooperator a trades unionist: every trades unionist a cooperator'. By October 1919, the *Stratford Cooperative Magazine* could report that:

> Many trades unions are banking their new funds with the C.W.S. bank and cooperative societies are uniting with trades councils in trial propaganda campaigns. Special efforts should be made to distribute literature among the members of local trades union branches. Several pamphlets issued recently by the Publications Department of the Cooperative Union are eminently suitable for this purpose (1) 'United action: Trades unionists and cooperators combine to meet the capitalist menace', (2) 'Cooperation and Labour unrest', (3) 'Cooperators and reconstruction'.

These discussions were given a sense of urgency by the bitter railway strike of October 1919. Anticipating industrial action the West Ham Trades Council established a committee to confer with the scs on the best means of guaranteeing adequate supplies of food in the Stratford stores for the families of strikers (*SE* 4 October 19). The scs was to play a crucial role in this and future strike action. Barnes considered it as integral to cooperative politics:

> The capitalist class are concentrated and centred in the government of this country today to an extent they never were before; they are using the House of Commons for the purpose of defeating the working class organisations of this country, and the cooperative movement realised when the government set out to challenge the N.U.R. it was their duty as a cooperative organisation to go to the aid of the N.U.R. I am pleased to say that Stratford gave the lead to other societies... There was a general recognition that throughout the cooperative movement and the trades union movement they had got to become more closely welded together to safeguard their common interests. (scs *Magazine* December 19.)

The initial decision at congress to enter the formal political arena was taken to defend the trading interests of cooperation against incursions by the state, and when sponsored candidates were elected to parliament they tended to work within the brief by monitoring legislation. At a local level, particular societies identified these interests unambiguously with those of organised labour within both the Labour Party and the trade union movement. Figures like Barnes used a language of class politics unacceptable to substantial bodies of cooperative opinion, but it accorded precisely with that of Labour in the interwar period and engendered powerful alliances in spite of cooperation's formal independence. These alliances

consolidated the identification of Labour with the working-class electorate. Within the cooperative movement consumers were reconstituted as
political subjects, for members were encouraged to view cooperation not
merely as 'grocers shops and savings banks', but as a viable political
movement acting in the interests of the working class against capitalism.
It is in this context that the dramatic growth of cooperation assumes its full
import.

It was largely under the influence of Barnes that the scs entered into
discussions with the Edmonton Society on amalgamation soon after he
was re-elected as president of the scs in January 1919. Amalgamations
were part of cooperative rationalisation in a drive to improve trading, but
for Barnes this one had a distinct political dimension. On 3 March 1919 he
presented a paper to a conference of management committees of London
societies, on the basis of which it agreed to the principles of amalgamation
(Barnes nd, 1940). Fearing the loss of democratic control, however, two
groups were recommended – south London, and east, north and west
London. Amalgamation between Stratford and Edmonton, therefore, was
the first step in a protracted and complex process. Barnes subsequently
presented the case to a meeting convened by the Education Committee of
the scs. In response to criticism that scs would be damaged by amalgamation with the smaller and less successful Edmonton Society, he argued
that the scs

> did not belong to Stratford, but to the cooperative movement as a
> whole... He was firmly convinced that it was only by consolidating
> working class effort to meet capitalist effort that they would win
> through to salvation... People had been forced to combine for their
> own salvation. The cooperative movement had been going through
> the same process, and every week was being confronted by the same
> forces which had compelled trade unionists to consolidate their
> forces. (SE 30 August 19.)

The subsequent general meeting voted 397-227 for amalgamation,
below the necessary two-thirds majority (SE 6 September 19). Undeterred,
Barnes launched an extensive publicity campaign amongst members. He
had the full support of the general committee which, after a rout of reform
candidates, was now dominated by socialists, many of whom, like Barnes,
were in the ILP. Early in 1920 another special meeting voted 705-170 in
favour of amalgamation, and the London Cooperative Society (LCS) was
established (SE 17 April 20). The West London Society was later incorporated in September 1921.

2.5 The Women's Cooperative Guild and the female vote

Within the broad cooperative movement existed the Women's Cooperative Guild, an organisation that was to exert an influence over the political
alignment of working-class women in the interwar period quite disproportionate to its numerical size. Founded in 1883, its relationship to the
cooperative movement was from the start problematic. Male hostility to

the notion that women could assume active roles within the social and political spheres of the movement in part prompted the guild, but it also endowed a jealously-guarded independence that enabled the guild to work outside the political boundaries of accepted cooperative practice. Apart from a nominal annual grant from the Cooperative Union the guild remained self-governing and self-financing (for good general accounts see Llewellyn Davies 1904, Sharp 1933, and Gaffin and Thoms 1983).

The guild shared a common intellectual heritage with the main cooperative movement in Owenite and Christian socialisms, articulated around a particular conception of consumer power. The image of 'basket power' possessed by women cooperators was a formidable and persistent one, and the guild applied itself to the task of arousing women to a sense of this leverage. In realising such power, it was argued, cooperators as consumers pursued the same general objectives as trade unionists in their role as producers. The path to radicalisation, therefore, progressed from an initial attraction to the 'divvy' to an appreciation of wider cooperative ideals.

The guild, untrammelled by the weight of conservatism, was in the vanguard of cooperative thought and action. Its platform comprised issues of direct interest and concern to women, and which were of deep political significance, as Eleanor Barton, General Secretary 1925-37, recognised:

> There has never been a time when women were not interested in politics... Are not politics bound up with all that a woman is most concerned with – housing, food prices, the education of her children, the health of her family? Cooperative Guild women, however, have been more than interested in politics. They have made it their business to gain real knowledge in the political sphere, because they belong to a great consumers' organisation with the definite purpose in view of production for use rather than for profit, and of the development of a higher and nobler system of society. Cooperative women have realised that if the principle 'Each for all and all for each' is good in their shopping, it is equally good in production, in education, and in the affairs of the nation and of the world. (Barton nd, 1931.)

Few recognised the importance of campaigning on issues relevant to the quotidian experience of women better than Margaret Llewellyn Davies. It was during her time as General Secretary from 1889 to 1921 that the guild emerged as a national force. When she took office the guild had 1800 members in 51 branches; when she retired there were over 51,000 in 1077 branches. With this transformation came administrative change and consolidation of a coherent political agenda. There were times when her preoccupation with 'basket power', with the sovereignty of the consumer seemed part of a conception of political change that was both reformist and restricted, not least because it failed to challenge domestic discourses of women's roles; but such attention has to be seen in the context of a commitment to conceptions of political radicalisation based on personal development. After thirty years of active involvement, her vision of cooperation remained undimmed:

> the abolition of profit making and democratic control mark out cooperation as nothing less than a revolution, so fundamental, vital, and transforming is the change it is effecting in the economic structure of society... We are working for no patchwork modifications, for no 'reconciliation of capital and labour', for no 'infusion of a better spirit' into old industrial forms. We are laying the foundation of a new industrial civilization. (Llewellyn Davies 1922.)

The guild provided working-class women with an opportunity not only to escape domestic confines and meet informally in local branches, but to engage with social and political issues far removed from traditional religious and philanthropic pursuits. Thus, in addition to the teas and social evenings organised to promote 'friendliness and a sense of brotherhood [sic] so much part of the cooperative creed' (ibid 1904 p34), branches began to campaign actively on 'conditions of women workers, public health, cooperation and the poor, housing, land and free trade'. On being granted freedom of the guild in 1922 Llewellyn Davies singled out three campaigns, all of which came in the second half of her term of office when the guild was emerging as an influential body and could build upon the experience of the earlier struggles – the attempt to bring cooperation within the reach of the poorest, minimum wages for women employees in cooperative societies, and reforms in married women's lives, in particular the inclusion of maternity benefit in the 1911 National Insurance Act (Gaffin and Thoms 1983).

The guild could not have achieved this in isolation. In the 1890s it embarked on a series of campaigns to promote closer relationships with trade unions. Joint meetings were held in East London to publicise the benefits of cooperative shopping. Important labour figures such as Tom McCarthy, Sidney Webb and Clementina Black spoke of the use of buyer power to improve working conditions, and handbills were distributed exposing the damage inflicted by sweated trades (Llewellyn Davies 1904). During the 1894 coal strike more practical forms of work were undertaken. Guild members took in children from strikers' families, gave clothing, helped on relief committees and distributed flour tickets.

Simultaneously, close links were formed with the Women's Trade Union League to promote trade unionism, and launch inquiries under the auspices of the Women's Industrial Council into conditions of female employment. Both the guild and the league were later represented on the wartime Standing Joint Committee of Women's Industrial Organisations (Gaffin and Thoms 1983 p60). The guild also contributed regularly to investigations undertaken by the Labour Department of the Board of Trade into female labour. This work intensified in the course of the war, as a result of which the guild formed a close working relationship with the Women's Labour League, laying the foundation for greatly increased involvement of women in local Labour parties (Cole 1948b p141).

Of equal importance in its long-term consequences was the promotion of female representation on public bodies. The so-called citizenship campaign was launched in 1894 when members were urged to work for the return of women as poor law guardians. Not coincidentally, the number of women guardians increased in that year from 169 to 877 (Clifford 1895). Such successes gave the guild confidence to pursue representation in other areas:

> Guild women have fully recognized what useful and important citizens' work can and should be done by working women. However much ignorant opposition there may have been at first to women taking part in public life, there are comparatively few cooperative men or women who would now oppose women being poor law guardians or members of educational communities. The Guild is now advocating that further steps should be taken, namely, that women should be made eligible for seats on town councils. (WCG 1904.)

From there it was but a small step to parliamentary representation:

> Some of our members may not have got beyond the idea that women should only exercise the rights and duties of citizens locally… They should be amongst the easiest to convert to more enlightened views. Guild members are not content with the position in the cooperative world which may be summed up in the saying of the man 'My wife and I are one, and I am that one'. (ibid.)

In 1907 local cooperative branches were petitioned to forward a resolution to congress in support of the women's franchise. Ten did, but the resolution was rejected on the grounds that it was 'political'.

In the first decade of this century membership of the guild more than doubled. There were nearly 26,000 women in 521 branches, and the guild was a considerable force in cooperative, local and national politics. Its success in securing provision in the 1911 National Insurance Act for maternity benefits to be paid directly to the mother was both the culmination of work in maternity and infant welfare, and the springboard for new campaigns. Margaret Bondfield joined the guild in 1911 and with Llewellyn Davies assumed a critical role in reform of health and maternity policy. A circular from Llewellyn Davies dated 15 August 1914 urged branches to approach public health committees with demands for:

1 Medical advice for the mother before and after childbirth.
2 Doctor or midwife at confinement.
3 Dinners for expectant or nursing mothers.
4 Milk for mothers and young children.
5 Dinners for children under school age where provision cannot satisfactorily be made at home. (Llewellyn Davies 1914, published by WCG.)

Such demands were given urgency by the publication in 1915 of *Maternity: letters from working women* which described experiences of motherhood in harrowing terms; they were also to set the agenda for the 1918 Maternity and Child Welfare Act and interwar policy.

Locally, the guild was actively building support. Within the scs area branches existed at Stratford, Canning Town, East Ham, Walthamstow, Ilford, Barking and Southend. But it was during the war that real expansion occurred as branches turned with renewed vigour to improve child and maternity welfare. The outbreak of war, far from diverting energy into other areas of social concern, seemed to increase the momentum of work started prior to 1911. In a speech to the 1915 Congress, the president, Mrs Barton, pointed to the example that could be followed by guildswomen:

> While men have been destroying life, women have been building up a system that will diminish suffering and save life. We pay the first cost on all human life. We shall not rest satisfied until every mother can take advantage of all that medical science can offer, which means that every town and village must have its maternity centre. We welcome the wider scope now open to married women of serving on town councils, and hope in the near future that many of our women will have the opportunity of doing useful work on our local health committees. (*Cooperative News* 19 June 15.)

Such work was of very real and direct relevance to impoverished areas which suffered chronically high infant and maternal death rates, in large part because of inadequate provision of medical help and uncontaminated milk. Efforts in West Ham were directed to extending existing meagre facilities, most of which were charitable and voluntary, by enlisting the active support of the Public Health Committee. Understandably, the south of the borough, where areas such as Tidal Basin had death rates nearly seven times higher than wealthy wards in the north such as Park and Upton (see, for example, West Ham Medical Officer of Health 1918) received prior claim. By far the largest provider of maternity welfare in the south was the Plaistow Maternity Hospital. Originally established in 1889 to 'provide for the poor of the neighbourhood ... nursing in their own homes in maternity and other cases' (Plaistow Maternity Hospital 1903), it charged no fee for the attendance of a midwife where the husband's wage was less than 21 shillings. In 1910, 4793 cases were attended (ibid. 1936).

Of less significance as a provider, but in the long term a more powerful agent of change, was the Canning Town Health Society. It was established by the Canning Town Women's Settlement in 1906, with a wide brief to improve local health by giving advice and information, investigating sanitary conditions and promoting improvements. A baby visiting committee was immediately set up and in 1909, with cooperation from the Public Health Committee, an anti-TB exhibition was organised in Canning Town Public Hall attended by over 30,000 people (Canning Town Health Society 1911).

Work was handicapped, however, by low funds. A budget of £7.17.10 in 1910 meant that only twenty-five babies per week could be seen at the clinic; but the work continued, and expanded. Under the forceful guidance of Rebecca Cheetham and Edith Kerrison, both guildswomen, the society sought to strengthen links with the Public Health Committee as part of a longer-term aim to secure local authority and state responsibility for maternity services (for the context see Rowan 1985). A milk depot was opened in 1912, home visits increased and health lectures were given regularly at women's meetings. This work was intensified after the outbreak of war, financed by grants from the Local Government Board and the Board of Education. By 1915 expenditure was £263, by 1916 £420: 'nothing shows more clearly the growth of our work than the way in which this help from the government has doubled, trebled, even quadrupled since the school started four years ago' (South West Ham Health Society 1916-17).

By 1917 the main energy of the society was devoted to infant welfare. Following a 'very vigorous conference' at the initiative of the guild and the society on the need for day nurseries, a campaign was launched. In the last year of the war 2706 infant consultations took place, regular classes on cooking, sewing and infant care were held, and 2.5 tons of dried milk supplied to necessitous mothers (ibid. 1918-19).

Such initiatives intensified the pressure exerted by the guild for the state to take responsibility for public health. The 1918 Maternity and Child Welfare Act may have been designed both to satisfy the lobby and assuage opposition from powerful vested interests to a Ministry of Health, and it may have lacked prescriptive power (Rowan 1985), but it did provide a more formal institutional framework for health provision and an extension of state funding. It required local authorities to establish maternity and child welfare committees, to include at least two women, and specified services for which grants would now be made available including home helps, food for expectant and nursing mothers and children under five, creches and day nurseries. Much of this bore the unmistakable stamp of guild thought and policy.

West Ham Council initially decided that the Maternity and Child Welfare Committee should comprise the Public Health Committee, plus the matron of Plaistow Maternity Hospital. Edith Kerrison, the other woman member, however, successfully moved that two married women also be appointed and later that a member from the South West Ham Health Society be co-opted (West Ham Council *Minutes* 23 November 18). Pressure was immediately brought to bear. The first meeting of the committee received a resolution from a conference held under the auspices of the society and the Canning Town branch of the guild which rejoiced in the wider powers given under the act, and urged the council to 'take steps to exercise any, or all of the powers given, and especially that steps be taken as soon as possible to establish a creche or day nursery in the southern part of the borough' (Maternity and Child Welfare Committee *Minutes* 20 November 18). The committee responded by increasing grants to voluntary agencies, entering into an agreement with Queen Mary's Hospital and the Women's Settlement Hospital to set aside beds for maternity cases, and producing monthly statistics on the work of health visiting staff (ibid. 16 January, 12 June and 11 September 19).

The supply of milk also increased. Under the 1918 Milk (Mothers and Children) Order, the council was empowered to supply milk to expectant and nursing mothers, and children under five at cost price or less. In January 1920 a conference with milk retailers agreed on a voucher scheme through which 76,764 gallons were supplied until it was decided in August, because of the continued difficulty of guaranteeing uncontaminated milk, to substitute dried milk powder. The supply of powdered milk increased from 8 tons in 1920, and 33 in 1921 to 106 in 1924 (Medical Officer of Health 1925).

This pattern of activity in child and maternity welfare lasted throughout the 1920s. The council, in the absence of state schemes, continued to rely heavily on the voluntary sector for essential services. In the third quarter of 1920, council health workers were responsible for only 512 of the 4424 visits to expectant mothers, and 11,329 of the 27,062 visits to children (Maternity and Child Welfare Committee *Minutes* 12 October 20). By 1924 the proportion had fallen. In the last quarter, council workers accounted for 468 of the 5004 visits to mothers, 13,796 of the 44,169 visits to children (ibid. 12 March 25).

In both spheres the influence of the guild remained powerful. New branches were established in Forest Gate in 1919, Upton in 1919, Plaistow in 1920, West Ham in 1921, and Custom House in 1928, making a total of eight in the borough. By 1939 (the only year for which figures are available) the borough had ten branches with a total membership of 788 (WCG *Annual Report* 1939). Three branch officers – Kerrison, Parsons and Bock – all of whom were to become key political figures, were included among the eight women serving on the Maternity and Child Welfare Committee by 1922 (MCWC *Minutes* 11 May 22). Kerrison was elected chair in 1926.

In 1928 the Medical Officer reported that maternity and child welfare had developed remarkably over the last two years. There was now an Assistant Medical Officer with special responsibility for this work, systematic visiting of all expectant mothers, careful supervision of the work of midwives, cooperation between the service and ancillary health services, in particular the school medical service, municipal antenatal clinics, and health advice and information. He concluded:

> There is now a firm grip on the conditions affecting the health of the populace of the borough and it is certain, given time, the innovations put into practice during the past few years will prove to be of enormous benefit, particularly to the health of infants and mothers of West Ham. (Medical Officer of Health 1928.)

The effect of the service on infant and maternity mortality rates was striking (Table 2.1). Data suggest that reductions in infant mortality rates outpaced those at a national level; it was in the early postwar period that levels in West Ham fell below the national average for the first time. Maternity mortality rates, on the other hand, followed closely movements at the national level, although local levels remained consistently lower. Given the extent of economic deprivation, it was an impressive record.

And it was a record that came to be seen and recognised by the local electorate, in particular the newly enfranchised women, not least through

TABLE 2.1 *Infant and maternal mortality rates in West Ham, selected years, 1896–1935*

	Infant mortality rate		Maternal mortality rate	
	West Ham	E & W	West Ham	E & W
1896-1900	182	156	3.39	4.69
1906-1915	127	117	2.16	3.74
1916-1920	94	90	2.27	4.12
1921-1925	72	76	2.35	3.90
1926-1930	66	68	2.50	4.27
1931-1935	62	62	2.68	4.13

Source: West Ham Medical Officer of Health 1935.

the efforts of Labour candidates to exploit it to political advantage. In the 1921 election a leaflet in support of the candidature of Kerrison argued that the Labour Party had been responsible for implementing the 1918 Act, providing home helps for poor mothers and supplying free milk in necessitous cases. It concluded, 'On all questions relating to health, housing and education, the Labour Party can be trusted to attend to the interests of the women and the children'. In 1922, Collins promised on behalf of the Labour Party that 'all that can be done under the Maternity and Child Welfare Acts in the way of helping necessitous, and expectant and nursing mothers, and caring for young children would have our support' (Election leaflet 1922).

Irrespective of the damaging consequences that child welfare reforms may have had on gender relations within working-class families by promoting ideologies of motherhood inscribed within bourgeois conceptions of domesticity (Rowan 1985), they served to strengthen the identity of Labour amongst the female electorate. It was by actively promoting such reforms that the Labour Party in West Ham succeeded in capturing the female vote when it was first exercised. In this process, the Women's Cooperative Guild played a key role. It spread the cooperative gospel amongst women as consumers and purchasers. But also the whole agenda of maternity and child welfare and its subsequent implementation was promoted by the guild. Thus it spread the Labour gospel of women as mothers.

2.6 Opposition from the Municipal Alliance

Labourism successfully established hegemony in West Ham during the immediate postwar period. Drawing on an earlier record of municipal activity and labour representation, it was able to consolidate its position at a time of hope for a new future by an active fusion of Labour Party, trade union and cooperative effort. Sufficient common ground existed for a programme of reform to be formulated and presented to an electorate, so constituted as aggressively independent working class – males as producers, females as consumers and reproducers. But what was the nature of the opposition, in particular from the Municipal Alliance, which had in 1900 brought down the first labour council in West Ham? What alternative was offered, and how can we account for its lack of success and ultimate demise in the interwar period?

Formed in 1899, the Alliance brought together antisocialist Liberal and Tory members, whose interests had until the ascent of the labour group in the 18908 dominated local politics (Marriott 1984). This intervention reconstituted the boundaries of political allegiance. Strong party ties were forged, and a polarisation forced between Labour and Tory/Liberal. Within the antisocialist camp Liberalism occupied a subordinate position, forfeiting a tradition of Radical progressivism that had informed much of the alternative municipal discourse during the 1890s, and leading to its extinction as a force in local politics.

Within the Alliance interests of local petit bourgeoisie and industrial bourgeoisie converged. Although small local employers were the initial moving force and tended to dominate the committees, prestigious offices were held by manufacturers, providing them with a platform in local politics. Arnold Hills of the Thames Ironworks was the first president, followed by R Broodbank of the St Katharine Dock Co. Among the vice presidents were S Boulton, D Howard, W Knight, C Lyle, H Marten and Dr Messel, all of whom headed large local industries. Indirect support was given by others. Hill reported at the first general meeting that Lord Hamilton and Sir William Birt of the GER Co. had promised to help the Alliance in 'every way they could' (*SE* 14 October 1899).

Membership of the Alliance suggests just how successful its appeal was. Local ratepayer organisations, trade associations, the Church of England Lay Council, the West Ham Chamber of Commerce and several craft unions were involved. Thus within the new boundaries old hostilities between anglican and nonconformist, publican and temperance reformer, and even manufacturer and sections of skilled labour were buried by an overriding concern to forge unity against the municipal politics of the labour group.

This unity enabled the Alliance to intervene into the discourse of municipal politics in a skilful and decisive manner. Claiming to be 'Non-Political, Non-Partisan and Non-Sectarian', it asked

the support of every intelligent Burgess for its candidates not because of their political or sectarian views, but because they will work and vote without fear or favour:

FOR	AGAINST
Good roads	Reckless extravagance
Pure water	Blundering and plundering
Sanitary houses	Tyranny and tammany
Trade union rates of pay	A privileged few at the expense of unprivileged many
Fair play	Crude experiments in socialism for the benefit of socialists at the ratepayers' expense
The common good	Wrecking the trade of the borough.

(Election manifesto of the Municipal Alliance 1900.)

Herein are contained significant elements of the dominant nineteenth-century ideology of local government–depoliticisation, economy and utilitarianism – around a limited conception of municipal enterprise that bore few traces of the brand of municipal socialism forced onto the political agenda by the labour group. But centre-stage were the issues of rates and expenditure. Deep concern was expressed at the recklessness of the labour group, and the inevitable effect that such expenditure would have upon assessments and rates. The problematic was a false one. Expenditure was relatively high not because of extravagant socialist schemes, but because the labour group attempted to overcome years of neglect by providing basic needs for a rapidly increasing population. But the issues of rates and economy served to unite antisocialist forces in a persistent attack on every aspect of the labour programme. The labour group, unable to free itself entirely from structural constraints during its period of office, effectively capitulated, losing power in the 1900 election.

The record of the Alliance in power was one of pragmatism, perhaps not very different from that of labour had it retained control. Pledges to check expenditure were not kept; indeed, it continued to rise, as did the district rate, a fact that was conveniently blamed on the unfortunate legacy of labour's investment programme, but was due rather to the desire of the Alliance to extend municipal enterprise and trading, particularly in tramways and electricity. During 1902-12 expenditure increased by 60 per cent. At no time, however, were the economy and rates resurrected in local elections.

As electioneering resumed in 1919, and the Alliance recognised the strengths of Labour's renewed challenge, so much of the old political rhetoric was recycled. Rates again featured centrally. Symes, the Alliance candidate in the High Street Ward campaigned for social reform with strict economy (p37 below). Wybrew in Plaistow spoke in similar terms:

> No elector will wish to deny responsibility in respect of, and no elector will wish to avoid payment for, necessary and enlightened progress in Housing, Education and Recreation and especially with regard to the welfare of the large army of children committed to our care... I do ask that plans are conceived and carried out, after due deliberation, in a practical manner to ensure the best value for the expenditure involved. (Election leaflet 1919.)

And there was even tacit recognition of the existence of the female electorate:

> Ladies, you must be keenly interested in the rental of your home, especially now that you have to pay the increased rate. The children are your constant care, and their education is something to you. Prove this by using your vote.

In terms of specific details of necessary improvements in health and welfare it is difficult to distinguish between the programmes of the Alliance and Labour. But it was through linking reform to the rates issue and a particular conception of the 'people' that political specificity was conferred and revealed in the programmes.

The Alliance was committed to economy in local government, and the rates issue had been an effective ideological weapon in the past. Underpinning this commitment, however, were powerful structural factors. The Alliance was indissolubly linked to local ratepayers' organisations – most notably the Forest Gate Ratepayers' Association (FGRA) – which functioned as an effective lobby for those who felt most threatened by rate increases, namely, the manufacturers and petit bourgeoisie. There was a wide overlap of membership especially among the officers. The associations professed political neutrality and because of this could not become involved directly in local elections; the Alliance, on the other hand, could – indeed this was the principal rationale for its existence – but even then claimed the same neutrality, helping to cloak manifest sectionalism. It was inevitable that both would act in the same interests, and command support against putative extravagance and recklessness.

Now the climate was different. Reconstruction meant for many a potential realisation of hopes for better housing, education and health. Those erecting barriers on the grounds of economy courted political disfavour. Mann, Labour candidate in Forest Gate, presented the alternatives:

> The town council does not make laws, it only administers them. This can be either broad, with the full expression of human feeling common only to the Labour movement, or it may be narrow, niggardly and mean with only the objective of shirking responsibility, and never carrying out in the spirit of those laws work which could be applied to make the conditions of the working people easier, and the lives of their children brighter and better. (Election leaflet 1919.)

Furthermore, charges of extravagance were difficult to sustain. Before regaining power in 1919, Labour's last term of office was in 1911-12. Since then the district rate had risen steadily; so too had rents, responsibility for which was laid firmly at the door of landlords and hence the Alliance: 'Vote Labour and keep out Alliance landlords', concluded E Reed after a brief analysis of increases in rents (Election leaflet 1920). Such responses, however, were isolated. Labour clearly recognised the fragility of the rate issue compared with the desire for progressive reform amongst an enlarged electorate.

The Alliance attempted to mask the narrow sectional basis of 'economy' by popular appeals to the whole electorate; in this it contrasted sharply with Labour, and so the nature of the appeal is worth closer scrutiny. In a leaflet entitled *What is the West Ham Municipal Alliance?*, Lt Colonel Luscombe explained that the Alliance had originally been formed 'to oppose the Socialists and save West Ham':

> Men and women of all schools of thought joined; all parties were welcomed if they were against socialism... In West Ham we have a special brand of socialists. They can be 'Labour' or 'Cooperative' or

conscientious objectors when it suits, but whatever they disguise themselves as, their object is the same – to bring about a 'class war'...
The Alliance again appeals to all unselfish men and women – and to the electors who desire to see West Ham governed in the interests of all classes, for all to receive just and fair consideration – to take their part in bringing this about. This they can do by rallying under the Alliance motto of 'The Common Good'. (Election leaflet 1920.)

The necessity of constructing popular consent among the electorate was an important component of Conservative thought, and had been since extension of the franchise to sections of the urban working classes in 1867. Without demonstrable concern for their welfare and the active promotion of an identity of interests it would have been difficult for a party of landed and industrial power to retain authority (for an historical survey of this see McKenzie and Silver 1968 pp42-73). Guided by an apparent recognition of the obligations of power toward the people, Conservatives could show evidence after 1867 of a consistent record of legislative reform to improve working-class conditions. Increasingly, as Britain expanded its imperial rule, this pragmatic concern for the people was articulated with a distinct sense of the British (English) nation (Schwarz 1986). Within this discourse nation and people converged under the natural leadership of a Conservative Party which appointed itself as guardian, committed to the defence of their integrity against attack from hostile or alien forces. Furthermore, the Conservative Party was, it argued, the only party fit to assume this role. Liberal policy was unpatriotic because it recognised other national interests and threatened dissolution of the empire.

In the immediate postwar period as the franchise was again extended, and as Labour emerged as the principal opposition, so Conservatives retrained their guns. Some of the older imperialist rhetoric remained, but it appeared obsolete in a new world order in which Britain occupied a subordinate position. Now nation and people were linked in a nationalism constructed from a common inheritance rather than from opposition to potentially antagonistic nationalisms (ibid. p169). This inheritance, because it was available to every loyal English man and woman, effectively displaced political specificity. The 'people', the 'common good', 'all men' (sic), the 'community' were mobilised against a putative self interest, in particular that of class, whose divisive influence threatened national traditions and institutions. Thus the Alliance in West Ham could claim to be 'non-political and non-sectarian' and

> to combine the forces working for good government of the borough, and to combat the policy of the extremists who seek to create a privileged section of the community at the expense of the rest. (WHMA 1920.)

Extremists, therefore, were responsible for diverting the working class from allegiance to common interest, to the path of class conflict:

> Already we have had a taste of [socialism] in West Ham. No one but a Socialist stands a chance of promotion or employment under the

Council today. Shopkeepers are afraid to express their political views and free speech is denied to others than Socialists. Class war and self-interest are taking the place of Cooperation and the Common Good. Words are taking on new meanings: 'workers' are those who talk the loudest, and the honest worker who shows the slightest independence is a 'traitor to his class'. (WHMA 1923.)

The political rhetoric of the Alliance constructed the working-class electorate in quite specific ways. Subsumed within the people, it argued, the working class had no needs distinct from those of the population as a whole. At times, its organisations, in particular the unions and cooperative societies, were persuaded by socialists acting out of self interest to take unpropitious courses of action; against such leaders, genuine, common-sensical (English) workers must assert their authority, restore equilibrium and so provide conditions under which production would increase to the benefit of all.

Within Labour rhetoric, on the other hand, working-class identity and exclusivity was asserted against class enemies. The Alliance, it was argued, in spite of popular appeals, represented the interests of landlords and employers who had committed working-class families to a life-long struggle against poverty and distress. Extremists, defined here as intellectuals imbued with (foreign) revolutionary thought, preach violence and terrorism, against which the steadfastness of labour must prevail.

I have described the appeal of the Alliance as popular, that of Labour as populist. This is no semantic nicety; rather, it is arguable that the distinction reveals something of their political specificities. The work of Laclau (1982) is of interest. In a careful study, he distinguished between popular and populist. Both can be seen as popular traditions in that they appeal to 'the people', but while popular interpellations tend to absorb and neutralise potentially antagonistic elements, populism tends to develop them:

> What transforms an ideological discourse into a populist one is *a peculiar form of articulation* of the popular-democratic interpellations in it. *Our thesis is that populism consists in the presentation of popular-democratic interpellations as a synthetic-antagonistic complex with respect to the dominant ideology*... Populism starts at the point where popular democratic elements are presented as an antagonistic option against the ideology of the dominant bloc. (Laclau 1982 pp172-73.)

The popular appeal of the Alliance, attempted as part of a hegemonic strategy to mobilise support by neutralising antagonistic class relations, exploiting discontent with, *inter alia,* the intrusion of 'extreme' political forms, and incorporating working-class demands for social reform. The project failed because the Alliance could not disguise the class basis of its appeal in the eyes of working-class electorate, numerically stronger, with powerful industrial base, and tradition of independent, at times aggressive, action. The poor law struggles up to 1926 sealed its fate (Chapter 4 below).

Instead, this constituency turned to the populism of Labour. The perspective may not have developed antagonistic elements to the extent to

TABLE 2.2 *Votes for Labour, Conservative and Liberal candidates, and members elected in West Ham parliamentary contests, 1919–29.*

| | VOTES | | | MEMBERS | |
	Labour	Tory	Liberal	Labour	Tory
1919	26,591[a]	21,570	7,201	2	2
1922	41,480	30,338	7,396	3	1
1923	46,537	21,716	9,598	4	0
1924	56,278	35,194	-	3	1
1929	78,454	28,543	9,386	4	0

Notes: [a] Includes Jones as unofficial Labour candidate.

TABLE 2.3 *Votes for Labour and Municipal Alliance candidates, and change in Labour seats in West Ham municipal elections, 1919–29.*

	Labour	Alliance	Change
1919[a]	13,339	5,665	+4
1920	11,975	11,029	+1
1921	17,170	18,276	-1
1922[b]	37,078	27,909	+6
1923	18,685	16,184	+1
1924	14,638	13,511	+3
1925	18,014	19,287	-1
1926	23,551	8,337	+1
1927	20,505	13,572	+1
1928	24,929	14,023	+2
1929[c]	10,090	6,926	+3

Notes: [a] Includes W Hughes, an independent allied to Labour.
[b] Wards increased from 12 to 16.
[c] Only 8 wards contested.

which, at a generalised level, it could have been a genuine challenge to extant political power, but the populism did articulate working-class interests and demands assertively and independently. In this, it accorded with the consciousness of sufficient of the electorate to consolidate power.

2.7 Electoral consolidation of Labour

Independent working-class activity in West Ham, most notably through trade unions, cooperation and political representation, coupled with an ineffective Tory/Liberal opposition, laid the foundations for Labour's accession to power in the immediate postwar years. By 1920, it had secured a comfortable majority on the council and had two of Greater London's four Labour MPs. This authority was consolidated through the 1920s to the point that Labour possessed an unassailable majority on the council and MPs in all four constituencies (Tables 2.2 and 2.3).

This process of consolidation, influenced as it was by a variety of local and national factors, was uneven but real enough. In large part, Labour was successful because it responded more effectively to political and structural change. Consider, for example, 1920, which in some respects was the most critical year for Labour. 1920 witnessed a downturn in postwar militancy as the boom lost momentum and the economy plunged into recession. And yet Labour in West Ham lost little ground.

The recession had no discernible consequences for the ability of Labour and its supporters to maintain political work. Activities of the local cooperative movement were facilitated by a strong trading position. Early in the year, scs could report a record quarter for increases in sales, capital and membership, reflecting a picture of growth over the year that did not dispel fears of the adverse influence of political involvement on trade. Opposition remained but it was muted. C Hughes spoke against the parliamentary candidature of Barnes on the grounds that he was a member of the ILP, and 'for him to force the members to support him was downright tyranny' (SE 31 January 20); he could muster little support. By the end of the year, on the eve of amalgamation into the LCS, Barnes could report:

> The work that had been put in in the past year was now showing results and he was absolutely confident that the spirit that had animated the society, the progressive feeling and the strong loyalty would continue throughout London. He felt that they had an opportunity of spreading to a greater extent than ever before. (SE 30 November 20.)

This animated spirit, however, was less evident in Labour's programme as the immediate postwar idealism and optimism began to be replaced by more pragmatic demands. At a meeting organised by the South West Ham branch of the ILP, councillor Wood thought it necessary to remind some of the people that a war had taken place:

> There was a danger of people having short memories, and forgetting even that they had taken part in the war… He was still looking for the end of the war and the land fit for heroes to live in. (SE 5 June 20.)

Temporary upsurges in militancy during the year, in particular around the question of British intervention in Russia and Ireland, provoked principled stands at national and local levels, not least because it deflected anti-Bolshevik propaganda that had been used consistently against Labour. Wood continued:

> The Russians who went to war on their side were now regarded as their enemies, and he contended that the reason why the British government was trying to prevent the Russian Government trading with this country and was using Polish forces to fight the Russian people was because the people of Russia had set up a form of Government which was antagonistic to a capitalist Government like theirs. (SE 5 June 20.)

A local Council of Action was established. It held a series of well attended meetings, bringing together diverse elements within the labour movement on a unified platform. At one such meeting, Davis (ILP) appeared with Pollitt (CP) and Groves (ILP). The message was a militant assertion of class hostility. Davis said:

Ever since he could think at all he had realised that the class which exploited the worker in every country would fight to the last ditch for the sake of keeping the worker where he was and where he had been all his life. They were afraid that if the Russian workers proved by demonstration that they were quite capable of managing their own affairs the workers of other countries would ask why their countries were not being governed in the same way... What they wanted was not to deal with individuals, but with principles. (*SE* 4 September 20.)

But this was a rare moment of unity in the expression of oppositional definitions of the 'national interest'. By this time Lloyd George, in response to generalised militancy against the government's policy on Russia, had conceded that no British troops would be sent, and so defused a potentially dangerous situation (Miliband 1973 pp79-82).

Labour's campaign in the weeks leading to municipal elections bore all the traces of populist pragmatism. In support of Mansfield, A E Killip challenged the Alliance to demonstrate how rates could be reduced without disadvantage to the community. Since it had been in power Labour had improved conditions, particularly through provision of milk to mothers and children (*SE* 16 October 20). Thorne asked the people to vote for Mansfield

not because he was Mansfield, but because he was a man of their own party and had done a great deal of work in connection with municipal, industrial and trade union affairs generally... They claimed the people's votes because they had worked in the people's interest and not their own... Nobody could represent the interests of the workers as well as the Labour party had done. (*SE* 16 October 20.)

Andrew Allison in Hudsons Ward felt it unnecessary to argue the merits of Labour's programme: 'Our principles and policy are well known... We stand for people before property' (Election leaflet 1920).

The Alliance and its supporters busied themselves in rates and exposés of socialist malpractice. In an analysis of council expenditure, E W Wordley told the FGRA that the majority intended to spend as much as they could on labour; as a result, bankruptcy was imminent (SE 27 September 20). Meanwhile, Walter Sanders expressed indignation at Labour's scheme to provide nursery schools, not merely because of the cost but because he thought mothers should look after children at that age. J H Rooff claimed that the socialist regime was committed to revolution, the first step in which was enforcement of a closed shop among council employees (*SE* 16 October 20).

Immediately prior to polling day the Alliance played the extremist card. In a large advertisement in the local press it pointed out

the grave danger to the people as a whole from the extreme section of the Socialists, who are now beginning to openly admit they are out for REVOLUTION and CONFISCATION. In the council chamber quite recently one of the Socialists supported the position taken up by the

Soviet Government in Russia in a way that showed what would happen here if they got the power in their hands. DON'T BE MISLED, whether Socialists run in their true colours, or in an underhand way as 'Labour' or 'Cooperative', they are out for the same end, and your only remedy is to VOTE THEM DOWN. (*SE* 23 October 20.)

In an increased poll the Alliance nearly doubled its vote, while that of Labour fell slightly. Labour gained one seat but lost two in the by-election following appointment of aldermen. Much of the Alliance advance occurred in its traditional heartlands of the north, where it successfully exploited economic and political insecurities of the local bourgeoisie. The Labour vote suffered from increasing local distress caused by the strike which was still in progress. At the subsequent AGM of the Alliance, Charles Ward argued that following the electoral truce of the war years conscientiously observed by the Alliance but not its opponents, the organisation had made up lost ground through steady educative work, and was now able 'to get in closer touch with the people' (*SE* 12 February 21). With increases in rates paid by the tenant, the people were 'awakening to the fact that the Alliance stood for a saner and wiser administration of public affairs'.

In the course of 1921 the programmes of Labour and the Alliance contained nothing that was new. The conditions underlying the integrity and confidence of the working-class electorate, however, deteriorated. From the record levels of 1920, LCS trade fell sharply with the inevitable revival of opposition to political involvement. By July, the committee reported that in spite of an increase in the number of members over the last quarter, there had been a loss of trade and a decline in share capital. Unemployment was to blame. Large numbers of cooperators were unemployed; they had been forced to withdraw savings and buy less (*SE* 30 July 21). Progressive cooperators disagreed. King declared that

> they were suffering throughout the ramifications of their Society because of their political action. Any man [sic] who had opposed political action had simply been insulted at quarterly meetings, and they could not keep on doing that without feeling the effects. Members became tired and withdrew their money and their trade. (*SE* 8 October 21.)

Efforts to abolish the political fund were unsuccessful, but in the event were unnecessary anyway. Net trading surpluses, from which funds were allocated, evaporated; for most of 1921 and 1922 the LCS Political Committee was forced to carry on without a grant. All propaganda was seriously affected, not least the publication of its newspaper *Citizen* which had been launched throughout London early in 1921.

At a national level the Triple Alliance collapsed in April; with it went socialist hope that a united union movement could challenge the government. Members of the newly-formed Communist Party saw an opportunity to expose the complicity of trade union and Labour leaders, but their appeals met with little success (Miliband 1973 p89). In response to the charge in a leaflet by Tom Mann and the Red International of Labour Unions that the NUGW had refused to support the miners on Black Friday, Thorne adroitly deflected criticism by declaring that this was malicious propaganda designed to 'disrupt everyone of the workmen's organisations' (*SE* 20 August 21). It was easily done. Communist influence, although disproportionate to the number of party members, remained small and, because of persistent failures to affiliate to the Labour Party and vehement hostility from labourism, quite outside the main spheres of formal political activity.

Communist influence was strongest in the trade unions and amongst unemployed, and in the period of union militancy around the miners' strike many of the anxieties about extremism were aired. 'Under the shadow of the very great crisis', Lyle argued at the North West Ham Conservative Club, 'nobody knew what the result might have been':

> the object of certain people was very different, was very definite. It was not and never had been a question of wages. Certain people were out for other and more sinister designs. (*SE* 30 April 21.)

Cooper, chair of the club's political committee, while welcoming defeat of the Triple Alliance, pointed to the consequences for the future:

> They were all thankful that the moderate influence in the trade unions had beaten the Communist element. The Socialists had captured a large number of the Councils and Boards of Guardians throughout the country, and there was only one thing left for them to take charge of – the British Empire. (*SE* 30 April 21.)

In a lecture to the FGRA on 'The undercurrent in trades unionism,' Pike combined such anticommunist rhetoric with popular appeals to commonsense:

> Wherever a general strike had threatened the community the community had organised and beaten it... The great mass of the people did not want revolution, or else they would have elected a Labour Government. Trades unionism, functioning in its proper field, was an asset to the whole community, but when it was used by ambitious men for their own ends it was a danger. (*SE* 7 May 21.)

The dominant tone of formal labourism was asserted at the annual conference of the SDP in Stratford. Most of the key Labour councillors attended, including Thorne, Jones, Davis, Godbold, Rumsey, Killip and Husband. Thorne opened with a characteristic attack on extremism. After reference to the unfortunate existence of the BSP, he stated that it had been completely destroyed by amalgamation into the Communist Party 'pledged to follow the Bolshevist dictatorship of Lenin'. Because of this and the high levels of unemployment

> never was Socialist propaganda on sane and sound lines so needed as it was today... The greater grew the size and strength of the Labour Party, and it was growing steadily, the more was Socialist propaganda and organisation required to educate and influence the workers inside and outside the Labour Party. He declared that the

sane and sound advocacy of social democracy by the SDP would outlast all the various actionist 'will o' the wisps' which, while apparently indicating easy roads to the promised land of social and economic emancipation, finally led to anarchical swamps and morasses (*SE* 6 August 21.).

A resolution was passed condemning direct action as a means of bringing about the Social Democratic Commonwealth, while the importance of support for the cooperative movement was recognised in spite of doubts on the advisability of its political involvement.

Such complacency allowed the Alliance to take the initiative temporarily. In a heavier poll, the rates issue and antisocialism seemed decisive. Carroll in Forest Gate argued that 'class legislation' was impossible, 'especially at a time like the present when the nation is stirred to its very vitals by unemployment and general stagnation of trade' (Election leaflet 1921). Labour candidates looked to the record of reform. Kerrison, for example, claimed that 'On all questions relating to health, housing and education, the Labour Party can be trusted to attend to the interests of the women and children'. It was not enough. The Alliance polled a total of 18,276 in winning five seats; Labour polled 17,657 in winning seven. Overall the Alliance gained one (*SE* 5 November 21).

Portentous signs had been seen, however, of an issue that was to dominate the political landscape of West Ham beyond the boundaries of local representation over the next five years. In the face of unprecedented levels of unemployment, the unemployed themselves were pressing demands on the West Ham Board of Guardians for adequate levels of relief – demands that the guardians could not meet without heavy borrowing from the government. The ensuing struggle brought the unemployed into direct conflict with the state, at the culmination of which in 1926 the government superseded the guardians. The act was widely seen as a direct challenge to local representational democracy, and revealed much about the capacity of labourism to respond to perceived threats to its authority. (The episode is examined in Chapter 4.)

Although the struggle took place outside the formal boundaries of local politics and the council was involved only at the margins, it forced unemployment onto the agenda, much to the advantage of Labour. 1921 had witnessed the launch of the Poplar Council's bitter struggle for equalisation of the rates; by September 5000 unemployed men and women were marching to the West Ham guardians threatening trouble if demands for increased scales of relief were not met. Allison described unemployment as 'the problem of the most pressing importance', and declared that the Labour Party had a duty to 'do all that is humanly possible to find work locally for our unemployed fellow citizens' (Election leaflet 1921). Such commitments, in spite of their essential unfeasibility, were to be restated time and again in future elections. The Alliance response was characteristic. Hickford in High Street Ward argued that females employed by the council should make way for unemployed ex-servicemen.

The unemployed continued to press demands through 1922, simultaneously asserting the political significance of unemployment. No party, ratepayer, church or trade union meeting took place without some discussion of the issue. At a musical evening of the Upton Liberal and Radical Association, Nicholson attributed unemployment to the lack of confidence people had in the men who were directing the destiny of the world (*SE* 1 February 22). Later that month at a Liberal Party rally in Stratford Capt. Wedgewood Benn blamed the loss of foreign markets (*SE* 25 February 22) Local ratepayer associations, on the other hand, took a pragmatic view. Cooper, at the inaugural meeting of the Stratford Ratepayers' Association argued that high rates were forcing manufacturers to leave the district, necessarily increasing levels of unemployment (*SE* 25 March 22).

Labour took the offensive. Beginning the campaign, Killip, councillor and guardian, welcomed the new political dimension of unemployment:

> The FGRA were continually talking about the apathy of the working classes. The apathy of the people towards unemployment was one of the things that caused so little notice to be taken of it. They should let the people who were responsible for it see that they were beginning to take an active interest in what was the most important issue of the time. (*SE* 2 September 22.)

Rumsey denied Alliance charges that Labour had failed to make full use of opportunities provided by the government for provision of relief works. On the contrary, West Ham had been in the forefront of relief, but had been obstructed by a government enjoying full support of the Alliance (*SE* 28 September 22).

What proved decisive, however, was part of the hidden agenda of unemployment. Outside the formal political discourses of Alliance and Labour there emerged a genuine popular resentment against Alliance candidates based on a simple identification of them with threats to relief. The charge was not made openly by Labour candidates, but there is little doubt that the belief was fostered that a vote for the Alliance was a vote for cessation of relief. Some Alliance supporters made statements that did little to allay such fears. At a meeting of the FGRA shortly before the election, Ward stated:

> The Socialists were trading on the giving of relief... At the last election he heard someone ask 'Who's Killip?' and the reply was 'The man who gives you relief at Cumberland Road'. The Municipal Alliance does not believe in doles, and if their candidates were returned they would do their best to stop this out-going of public funds and try to see to it that schemes of relief were brought forward under the plans which the Minister of Labour had outlined. (*SE* 7 October 22.)

The 1922 election was an important one since the number of wards had been increased by four to sixteen (Table 2.3). In a relatively heavy poll Labour won eighteen seats, the Alliance six. Prior to the election Labour had twenty-eight seats and the Alliance twenty, now it stood at thirty-six and twenty-four respectively, and after the by-elections subsequent to the election of aldermen, forty and twenty-four. Fears expressed by an Alliance member on the eve of the election that they were 'to go into the wilderness for seven or eight years' were to prove rather optimistic (*SE* 4 November 22).

At the postmortem conducted by the FGRA, Alliance candidates analysed the reasons for their disastrous performance. Cresswell believed that the 'dole business' in the south was responsible; Cooper claimed that on election day 'when children went to get free dinners they were told to tell their parents that if Cooper was returned no more free dinners would be given'; Coath said that electors had been told that if they voted for him 'they would get no more doles'; and Clare had been accused of voting against the guardians' grant of coal to the unemployed (*SE* 11 November 22).

It was a position from which the Alliance never recovered. Unemployment exposed more effectively than Labour's pragmatic programme the sectional basis of the Alliance appeal, and the potentially harsh realities of 'efficiency and economy' in public expenditure. As the struggle over levels of relief intensified, so the Alliance lost further ground. 1926 was a particularly bad year. Defeat of the general strike during which Alliance members served on the Emergency Committee, and supersession of the guardians leading to drastic cuts in relief revived charges that the Alliance and its supporters were 'baby starvers'. Its vote fell by more than half. By the end of the decade it could claim only eight seats out of sixty-four on the council, and was a negligible influence in municipal affairs.

This loss of power was reflected at the parliamentary level (Table 2.2). Less than three weeks after substantial Labour gains in the 1922 municipal election, Groves won Stratford from the Tories, while Thorne and Jones were re-elected on a platform of working-class advocacy. At the election Labour in Greater London quadrupled its members to sixteen. In 1923, Labour won all four seats in West Ham, but lost Upton the following year as Labour members in outer London fell from fifteen to seven. The franchise for the 1929 election nearly doubled the number of women voters; Labour again captured four seats with hugely increased majorities.

In the early postwar years potentially damaging splits within the ranks of the Labour Party in West Ham forced by the war were healed, and the party embarked on a campaign to consolidate power around a unified populist programme of reform. At a time of political instability militant opposition proved ineffective against the commonsensical assertion of working-class identity and a vehement nationalism at the heart of labourist discourse. The political involvement of a powerful tradition of cooperation contributed to Labour's success. Tens of thousands of local cooperators were urged to recognise the identity of their cause and that of Labour.

The Womens' Cooperative Guild played a decisive role in helping to secure for Labour the newly-enfranchised female vote. Guildswomen had pioneered child and maternity welfare, and given working-class women a sense of political obligation. They successfully politicised lived experiences of women in such a way that their concerns came to be seen as the concerns of Labour.

Against Labour, antisocialist interests cohered around the Municipal Alliance. It too articulated social reform, but in spite of popular appeals to the people and to the common good, its narrow sectional base was sharply exposed by discourses around the struggles of the unemployed. The Alliance advocacy of cuts in relief undermined its support so drastically that the ground it lost on the council was never recovered. By the end of the 1920s Labour dominated the formal political terrain.

The Royal Docks in south West Ham, looking east, 1950. Although now firmly in decline, the area displays abundant evidence of the communications infrastructure that promoted congested industrial settlement some thirty years earlier. *Courtesy of the Museum in Docklands Project.*

Left. Will Thorne in his uniform as a Colonel in the Essex Volunteers, 1918. 'A pupil of Eleanor Marx, in the long ago', Sylvia Pankhurst was to write in *The home front*, 'he was one of the noisiest war men'. *Right*. Will Thorne and Jack Jones at the TUC, Southport, 1926. Both used their positions as officers in the National Union of General Workers to secure and consolidate power in local politics. *Courtesy of Newham Local Studies Library.*

A party of the Stratford New Town Women's Cooperative Guild, 1931. The Guild branches remained an important influence on the political involvement of women in the interwar years. *Courtesy of Newham Local Studies Library.*

TOWN COUNCIL ELECTIONS.

Wednesday, November 1st, 1922.   Polling from 8 a.m. to 8 p.m.

BECKTON ROAD WARD.

Mr. F. C. ANDREWS.   *Mrs. B. PARSONS.*

Fellow Citizens,

    Councillor EDITH KERRISON, of the Independent Labour Party, has represented the Tidal Basin Ward for the past five years. Previous to that she was a Member of the West Ham Board of Guardians, representing Custom House and Silvertown and Tidal Basin Wards for nearly twenty years, and her work for the aged and sick is well known to residents in the District. Councillor Kerrison has served on the Public Health, Maternity and Child Welfare and the Education Committees of the Council, her former experience (she was first Matron of the Seaman's Hospital) specially fitting her for service on these important Committees.

    Mrs. D. PARSONS, of the S.D.F., is very well known in the District. She was particularly active during the agitation for securing the right of every woman to exercise the franchise. For the past three years she has been a member of the Maternity and Child Welfare Committee.

    Mr. F. C. ANDREWS is a full time Trade Union Official, has lived in West Ham practically all his life, and has been an active worker in the Trade Union and Labour movement for the past twenty-five years.

    We have every confidence in recommending their candidatures.

Alderman W. THORNE, J.P., M.P.,

Alderman JACK JONES, M.P.,

And all the Members of the Labour Party.

P.T.O.

A Labour Party election leaflet, 1922. Edith Kerrison and Daisy Parsons came to prominence in the impoverished southern wards through their work in child and maternity welfare. *Courtesy of Newham Local Studies Library.*

A deputation from the West Ham Board of Guardians to the Ministry of Health, September 1925, seeks to prevent forced reductions in relief. Comprising left to right, Bert Killip, Mrs Lebden, GA Paul, HE Price, Charles Ward and SW Maude, it represented various shades of Labour and Moderate opinion. *Courtesy of Newham Local Studies Library.*

WEST HAM-LET IN PLAIN CLOTHES.

"Alas, Poor Yorick!"
(The West Ham Board of Guardians have been "playing Hamlet" with
the Borough's resources.

A cartoon from the *Evening News* dated 12 September 1925,
demonstrates hostility to the supposed extravagance of
West Ham Guardians.   Such public attention influenced
events leading to the supersession of the guardians in an
unprecedented attack on local representational democracy.
Courtesy of Associated Newspapers plc.

Councillors Ridgwell and Ward, Municipal Alliance members of the West Ham Board of Guardians, discuss the impending crisis, July 1926. *Courtesy of Newham Local Studies Library.*

Years of physical toil and neglect are shown on the faces of women as they gather to celebrate the Jubilee of George V, Custom House, May 1935. *Courtesy of George Taylor.*

3

TRADE UNIONS, POLITICS AND LABOUR REPRESENTATION

It is no answer to say send labour men to Parliament; with the best of intentions, they are as helpless as the rest of them. (Tom Kirk, secretary NUR West Ham branch, *Railway Review* 23 May 1919.)

3.1 Historical perspectives

I have attempted to demonstrate that the ascent of the Labour Party in West Ham to a position of unchallenged authority was in part due to its ability to articulate the expectations and demands of a working-class electorate in the postwar period. In this the party was aided by a politicised cooperative movement that was instrumental in capturing the newly-enfranchised female vote, and an opposition whose sectional interests were exposed as social conditions deteriorated.

But of all the bodies of the organised working class, the trade unions are generally held to have exerted most influence on the fortunes of the Labour Party. Surveying the growth of the Labour Party from 1918 to 1923 in his major study of trade unionism, Clegg (1985 p353) concludes that 'The increase in the Party's strength ... mainly reflected the growth of the unions'.

Such a perspective is very much part of received wisdom, particularly since McKibbin (1974) interpreted the rise of Labour as the political mobilisation of industrial consciousness in which support automatically reflected union membership. The point seems obvious and uncontentious. Financially and organisationally the two bodies were bound firmly together. The party had, after all, been established by the trade union movement, and continued to rely almost exclusively upon union contributions and affiliation fees. And at the constituency level, local parties were based on trade union branches and trades councils which provided not only administrative structures but also human resources for party work.

Yet the identity of unions and the Labour Party is not one that can be sustained without considerable qualification. Consider, for example, data on respective memberships (Table 3.1). These reveal a direct correspondence between party membership and trade union affiliation, much as we

TABLE 3.1 *Membership of trade unions and the Labour Party (m), density (%), union affiliation to the Labour Party (m), Labour vote (m), and Labour MPs, general elections, 1910-29.*

	Union member- ship	Union affili- ation	Density	Labour member- ship	Labour MPs		Labour vote
					Total	Union	
1910[a]	2.57	1.39	54.3	1.43	42		0.4
1918	6.53	2.96	45.3	3.01	60	49	2.2
1922	5.63	3.28	58.3	3.31	142	85	4.2
1923	5.43	3.12	57.5	3.16	191	98	4.3
1924	5.54	3.16	57.0	3.19	151	86	5.5
1929	4.86	2.04	42.1	2.30	288	114	8.4

Sources: Butler (1972) and Cole (1948b).
Note: [a] December.

would expect given that the vast majority of party members comprised affiliated trade unionists, even after 1918 when individual membership was introduced. The relationship between union membership and party affiliation, however, is less obvious. Affiliation was influenced by the attitudes of unions and their members to political activity, and laws governing the administration of political funds. Perhaps significant is the steady increase in density of affiliation, suggesting that those remaining in unions during the recession were more committed and loyal to the party.

Little of this helps to explain increases in the Labour vote and number of Labour MPs. Even before the 1931 National government played havoc with figures on the state of political parties, there is no relationship between party membership and performance in the parliamentary sphere. Figures on union-sponsored MPs served only to complicate an already complex picture.

For some time studies have attempted to unravel the links between trade unionism and politics. The classic work of G D H Cole and Asa Briggs periodises the relationship by detecting 'pendulum swings' between union activity in industrial and political spheres. As disillusionment sets in with one form of struggle, they argue, or it becomes less effective, so attention is diverted to the other (Cole 1948a, 1948b; Briggs 1959). Here, then, an inverse relationship is posed between industrial and political trade unionism. And the influential analysis of Nairn (1965) sees a Labour Party dominated by trade unions. From it we learn little of the moveable and sometimes volatile nature of the relationship between trade unions and the party, or of the factors that cause such shifts to take place (pp6-7).

More recent work has been concerned to stress the value of specific historical studies. Pimlott and Cook (1982) note the lack of attention to the 'political role of unions in an historical context', and contributors to their collection of essays attempt to fill the gap by examining the development of this role from the eighteenth century to the present. Although union activity had a political dimension from the outset, it was not until the formation of the TUC in 1868 that trade unions were recognised to have a significant presence in local and national politics (Stevenson 1982). This presence was expressed through the two major parties until the perceived necessity for independent representation, in part as a means of safeguarding the unions' industrial position, led to the formation of the Labour Party. Not that such moves had a wide acceptance amongst the membership. Socialists within the unions, many of whom emerged from the struggles of new unionism, exercised considerable authority over an indifferent membership and took much of the responsibility for political advance. Moreover, party fortunes were bolstered by legal attacks on the unions, in particular the Taff Vale decision, which began to undermine the basis of industrial power (Lovell 1982).

The Liberal Party, however, continued to command the loyalty of most of the enfranchised working class until 1910, when the unions embarked on a period of unprecedented growth and militancy. The Liberal government was forced to intervene in industrial disputes, thereby consulting with union leaders and implicitly accepting their importance in management of the economy (Rubinstein 1982). Thus was laid the foundation upon which unions built so effectively during the war, immeasurably enhancing their prestige and power at national and local levels. By 1918, the Labour Party, largely as a result of this enhanced political authority and an enlarged electorate, was on the road to parliamentary power. At the local level, 'Where the Labour Party was strong in 1918 and subsequent elections its strength stemmed from a strong trade union presence... On the whole the Labour Party was strong where trade unionism was strong, and weak where trade unionism was weak' (Wrigley 1982 p86).

Useful though this broad historical survey is, there is, deliberately, no thrust toward theoretical unity. As a result, implicit interpretations of the relationship between industrial and political trade unionism differ, and there is no compatible explanation for sharp changes in the nature of the relationship from one period to another. Theoretically more consistent is the attempt by Martin (1980) to explain patterns of change in the political role of the TUC. Drawing on systems theory, he isolates organisational structure, government policy, social attitudes concerning the legitimacy of TUC activity as a pressure group, and the politically relevant resources of the TUC as key determinants of its political ascent from humble beginnings to triumphant emergence as a vital component in the British political machine.

Neglected in all this work is union involvement in local politics. Given the importance attached to the constituency by several of the authors, it is unfortunate that so little attention is directed to the contribution of union branches and leaders to the development of local Labour parties. Profitable lines of inquiry are opened by one study of local labour leaders in the 1920s (Howard 1983), which argues that Labour failed to build a solid basis for expansion in the immediate postwar period, so frustrating expectations of

continued success and engendering a recognition of fundamental structural weaknesses. Much of this failure rested with an inability to capitalise
on the strength of unions:

> What was naturally assumed has that the party would continue to
> grow (as it had done during the war and the first years of peace)
> owing to the growth of trade union membership and the attraction
> of particular pressure groups within the party's orbit. Trade union
> membership continued to expand, but the Labour Party never fully
> built on the foundations laid during the war. (ibid. p66.)

Detailed local studies should help to reveal the nature of the relationship between trade union and political activity by examining its structural
underpinnings, social and political networks, and political discourses.
Evidence from local studies, including that on East London during the war
and the 1920s (p28), however, reveals no more consensus than that shown
in national studies. Bush (1984) argues that the power acquired by unions
in the course of the war was the single most important factor in the success
of the Labour Party, since they provided organisation, finance and a
channel for high political expectations of an enlarged working-class electorate. In contrast, Gillespie (1981) contends that political advances were
secured not because of trade union support but in spite of it. Union strength
in East London during the war has been overestimated; the industrial
structure of the area remained distinct and relatively unchanged from
prewar decades, and although the traditional weakness of unions has been
challenged by a brief militancy, its subsequent collapse left a political
vacuum that Morrison's London Labour Party filled with alacrity.

But what of West Ham in this period? I have suggested that the
experience of East London politics is not one that can be applied
unproblematically to West Ham. From the outset, trade union involvement in local politics was distinctive. Gasworkers' struggles at Beckton led
directly to the formation of the Gas Workers and General Labourers' Union
(GWGLU) which became the most representative body of nascent new
unionism. The union was committed to the extension of labour representation at local and national levels (Marriott 1984). Unlike older craft unions,
which had tended to rely on industrial security at the workplace, unions of
semiskilled workers were conscious of their strategic weaknesses and
sought demands through the state.

It has been argued that the experience of West Ham questions the
general applicability of the model posing an inverse relationship between
industrial strength of new unions and their leaders' commitment to
independent labour politics (Lovell 1982). It is important, however, to
distinguish between numerical strength of the union and its confidence
and ability to use that strength in pursuing demands. It was precisely
because of the recognition by union leaders of members' limited industrial
power, particularly when defeat at the South Metropolitan Gasworks
exposed their vulnerability to replacement labour, that the union turned to
labour representation.

This shift was articulated well by Will Thorne and John Burns at the GWGLU anniversary celebrations of 1892 and 1893:

> The Gas Workers' Union has spent £20,000 on strikes to maintain an eight-hour day. It would have been better to spend £5,000 in supporting twenty five labour candidates so that they could get by law what they failed to get by organisation (*SE* 2 April 92.)

> The future policy for trade unionists would be to get the control of public institutions and, through them, bring about the amelioration of social conditions. (ibid.)

> The policy of the union from the beginning had been to recognise that trade unionism of itself could not obtain for the workers that which they required, and hence the wise policy had been adopted of invoking municipal action and parliamentary aid. The fruits of that policy were seen in the ten labour members on the [London] County Council, and in the two or three hundred in local municipal bodies up and down the country. (*SE* 8 April 93.)

> During the past twelve months the workers in different parts of the country had been able to maintain their position, but they found at the present moment that the employers were banding together to crush what was called the new and progressive trade unionism... If they had good and sound labour men on all local bodies, then the workers would not be placed in the present deplorable position. (ibid.)

For many union members, gasworkers and others, the series of industrial defeats inflicted in the early 1890s confirmed the legitimacy of struggles for municipal power. This was heightened by the sense of civic identity and responsibility recently engendered by the gain of borough status for West Ham in 1886, as a consequence of which it became one of the principal sites of this new terrain of working-class struggle, returning the first independent labour MP in 1892 and the first labour council in British electoral history six years later.

These successes, however, cannot be attributed exclusively to union involvement. The franchise remained restricted, effectively debarring the main body of semiskilled and unskilled labour. In addition, political involvement was not accepted universally. J Walsh, a leading local figure in the GWGLU, represented a substantial body of opinion:

> A man could be a good Liberal or a good Tory, or Nationalist or Radical, and yet be a very good Trade Unionist... The sooner the unions left politics alone, the better it would be for the organisation. They did not want to convert the House of Commons or the Corporation; they wanted to convert the minds of men at large... You have stated that a man has no business to belong to a new union who is not an active Socialist or I.L.P. man, and who is not prepared for the State takeover of the whole industrial machinery of the country. Now I say that is wrong. I say the working men of this country are not prepared for any such step. (*SE* 25 January 96.)

But secular trends gave impetus to labour representation in the course of the 1890s as unions lost members and industrial authority. It was during this period that trades councils emerged as important political agencies. Having failed to secure local bargaining machineries, and after exclusion from the TUC in 1895, they looked increasingly beyond workplace interests of their constituents to wider social and economic concerns.

The role of the West Ham Trades Council was decisive in capturing municipal power. Founded in 1891 during a time of bitter union struggles, it immediately set its sights on labour representation and assumed responsibility for organising union support. It was in a good position to do so since from the outset it could legitimately claim to be the one body representing the interests of local unions. The inaugural meeting attracted forty delegates from a variety of skilled and general unions including the ASRS, ASE, GRWU and UBWU (SE 12 December 1891). Within four years it commanded the support of the largest local unions, in particular, the GWGLU and DWRGLU; thirty-eight branches in all were affiliated, representing a membership of approximately 8000, making it the seventh largest in the country.

At a demonstration to mark the council's fourth anniversary a resolution urged the need to impress 'upon our representatives on Imperial and local bodies the necessity of speedily carrying out those reforms which have been so long promised' (SE 25 August 1894). Speaking in support, Thorne stated:

> The influence of a Trades Council was undoubtedly great, and one of the most important duties of such a body was to get labor men on to the local administrative bodies. Work of that kind was very necessary in West Ham.

Keir Hardie emphasised the point:

> You draw representatives from a class other than your own. If you drew men from your own ranks, who believed as you believed, who think as you think, and who feel as you feel, you would not require to impress on them the necessity of [labour reforms].

Without sufficient funding, however, the political work that the trades council could undertake was limited. The council's Labour Representation Fund had £3.7.9 in hand at the end of 1894, and during 1895 received only £2.12.6, this thanks to the Stratford and Plaistow branches of the ASCJ (WHTC, *Annual Report* 1895). By 1897 it was in deficit, prompting the council to introduce a levy of 10 shillings per branch 'toward paying election expenses and loss of time when possible to its Labour representatives' (idem 1898). Under these circumstances, political activity was confined to vetting candidates and addressing meetings. All candidates were invited to meet delegates and explain their views. Occasionally, the trades council forwarded prospective candidates to the West Ham Socialist and Labour Council for official endorsement; when they were rejected, as two were prior to the 1894 election, it promptly withdrew its delegates (SE 29 September 94).

Thus the trades council established a role which it held well into the

1920s. Although not formally in a position to select candidates, because the council represented trade union interests it was able to propose candidates, wield veto power against others it did not accept, and give active support to those it did. After victory in the 1898 election, the secretary claimed 'your Council were very largely responsible for this magnificent result, 138 meetings being addressed by its delegates in support of those candidates adopted by them' (WHTC, *Annual Report* 1898). In the subsequent by-election 'representatives addressed 90 meetings, besides assisting in the canvass and attending as deputations the various branches affiliated to the Council'.

The Labour Council, reflecting the mixed base of its support, was a fragile alliance of SDF and ILP members, augmented by Radicals, Christian Socialists and Irish Nationalists. It held authority for only a year; after that the Alliance intervened, eventually winning control in 1900 (p26 above). From then until the outbreak of war Labour intermittently held power. The experience of war laid the foundations for Labour's ascent in the immediate postwar period. This and the role of cooperation was described in the last chapter; here the focus is more exclusively on trade union activity and involvement.

3.2 Trade unions, politics and the war

War strengthened the position of unions in virtually all areas of their activity and influence (for good general accounts see Martin 1980, and Clegg 1985). Recognition of the need for cooperation of the unions in war production, changes in patterns of collective bargaining, involvement of union leaders in the state apparatus to an unprecedented extent, and active exploitation by the rank and file of their strategic position at the point of production all contributed to a massive growth in union membership, financial strength and self confidence. Overall membership increased from 4,145,000 in 1914 to 6,533,000 in 1918, rising to a peak of 8,348,000 in 1920. Most of the wartime growth occurred in 1917 and 1918 which witnessed a 40 per cent increase, compared with only 12 per cent from 1914 to 1916. Within this the number of women trade unionists nearly trebled, helping the four largest general unions to increase their membership threefold (Clegg 1985 pp196-7).

Political involvement of the unions during the war took the form of lobbying government and its agencies, a process that was intensified by the absence of parliamentary elections and the apparent success of the unions in gaining concessions. Individual unions tended to negotiate directly. Leaders were reluctant to empower the TUC to act on their behalf, as a result of which its role was circumscribed, and it became merely one of a number of the more important labour organisations (Martin 1980). The unions also succeeded in strengthening their grip on the Labour Party. The threatened split between prowar union leaders and antiwar ILP members was avoided because there was enough common ground to sustain working relationships. Most union leaders refused to sacrifice working-class interests at the altar of German annihilation, while pacifists feared a German victory. Attempts by right-wing leaders to establish an alternative in the Trade Union Labour Party were overwhelmingly defeated.

Unions participated in discussions around, and benefited from, the new constitution of the party. Now they had virtual authority over the composition of the executive through domination of the conference vote. The introduction of individual membership did nothing to threaten this domin-0ation. *Labour and the new social order* was based largely on wartime experience of labour in government, and the manifesto of the TUC Parliamentary Committee drawn up for the 1918 election was close to party thinking.

The authority of trade unions during the war was also consolidated at a local level. Government pressure on employers to recognise unions and establish joint committees was an important influence, especially in those industries that had not been unionised (Wrigley 1982 p86). But the influence was reciprocal. Relatively full employment, a shortage of certain skilled labour, an increasing presence of women, and a greater density of unionisation strengthened unions at the workplace, and laid the foundation for change nationally.

Such arguments tend to support the view that Labour Party gains in the immediate postwar period were most evident in constituencies where unions had been able to establish their authority (ibid. p87) But the picture was complex and far from uniform, and an understanding of it depends on an elaboration of the relationship between unions and Labour within individual constituencies. Some of this complexity is illustrated by the changes forced on the trades councils over this period. Until the outbreak of war the main responsibility for electoral work remained with trades councils despite their commitment to industrial activity. In the early years of the party, only they could affiliate; after 1905 other electoral bodies were admitted, but only in constituencies where trades councils had not been formed. Attempts by the party to place responsibility for electoral work in the hands of bodies which had no other interests were successfully resisted by trades councils, in some instances because unionists feared the consequences of ILP control. Of the 145 local bodies affiliated to the party in 1913, eighty-five were trades councils (Cole 1948b p50).

Increased labour representation on local committees during the war promoted trades councils. Many could claim that their efforts had done much to expose the harsh and inequitable consequences of profiteering, conscription, food control and rent increases (Clinton 1977 p73). New councils were established, while the authority of existing councils, in spite of a chronic shortage of funds, continued to expand. By 1917, they comprised 153 of the 260 affiliated bodies; but now the Labour Party was determined to create a national network of local electoral bodies, in part as a drive toward parliamentary power enshrined in the new manifesto, in part as a conscious attempt to consolidate union support by curbing the perceived political authority of trades councils. Councils were pressed to become local parties, thereby subordinating their political responsibility.

Whether or not they did so depended on the character of individual councils and their desire for autonomy. Those that chose to remain outside the party, its leaders hoped, would gradually fade into obscurity since their role was irrelevant to the exigencies of modern political struggle. By 1918 only seventy-three trades councils were numbered in the 398 affiliated bodies.

Others saw trades councils as crucial to the development of militant trade unionism. Syndicalism, in particular, with its belief in industrial power and distrust of union and party officials looked to the potential of trades councils in overcoming sectional rivalries and providing the basis for a national federation of labour. Since this belief accorded with much that trades councils did to promote the industrial interests of trade unions, syndicalist influence was pervasive (ibid p88). Later the newly-formed Communist Party attempted to transform trades councils into the nuclei of a network of shop and works committees that could act as local soviets, eventually assuming administrative control from local authorities.

Trades councils, then, were contested areas in the labour movement. If in the struggle for control the Labour Party and TUC eventually secured victory, it was not by annexing the councils, but by gradually stripping them of their role and authority, and dismantling communist influence (p108). Individual councils, however, were able to resist this attrition long after 1918, and continued to exercise a considerable influence on local politics.

Irrespective of the experience of trade unionism in East London during the war, and the extent to which it contributed to the political advance of Labour in the interwar year, unions in West Ham consolidated their position in both the industrial and political spheres of their activity. Structural conditions were propitious. West Ham was not immune to sweated trades and smallscale production, but had never experienced the worst excesses of East London. Heavy industry had a considerable presence, particularly in the south where the massive factories of Henley's cable works, the sugar refineries of Tate & Lyle, the Beckton gasworks, Silver's India Rubber, Gutta Percha & Telegraph Co. among others lined the Thames.

War temporarily eliminated the single largest barrier to trade union growth and effectiveness, namely, endemic casual labour. The flow of able-bodied men to the armies, coupled with increased demand for a whole range of skills, guaranteed work for most who wanted it. Production of munitions was at the heart of this expansion. Within a year after the outbreak of war the demand for skilled labour was urgent. Appeals from the Ministry of Munitions to 159 engineering firms in East London, including Stratford and Canning town, for any spare labour uncovered only eight men (Bush 1984 p108). One solution adopted was to subcontract out appropriate work to other firms with less-skilled workforces, thus passing on the benefits accruing from government contracts.

West Ham and Poplar were the centres of East London engineering, but equally important to West Ham was its chemical industry, which also was adapted to munitions. Beckton, Henley's, Silver's and Brunner Mond were amongst the largest that switched lines of production (ibid. p109). South of the river from West Ham but employing considerable numbers of its residents was Woolwich Arsenal, which at its peak in 1917 had a workforce of 74,467, including 28,000 women.

Trade unions took full advantage of this expansion in employment. Membership of the general unions grew rapidly, especially in controlled firms where arbitration to settle disputes was compulsory. Local branches of the National Union of General Workers (NUGW, previously GWGLU) at Canning Town and West Ham had by 1918 quadrupled their quarterly income, largely as a result of the union's success in arbitration (ibid. p115). Even the Workers' Union, which had none of the same historical roots in the area and only three small branches in 1914, was able to expand. The breakthrough came with recognition at Silver's; by 1918 the Canning Town branch could claim 1000 members.

From the outbreak of war unions recognised that in order to protect members' interests it was necessary to take up political issues through appropriate representation. The West Ham Trades Council initially had control of labour representation on local committees' but faced opposition from union branches which felt that unions should be consulted. The NUR Canning Town branch approached the Local Distress Committee to ensure adequate representation, and Stratford 1 asked the West Ham Citizens Committee to co-opt three representatives from the branch (ibid. p105).

Major campaigns were conducted by unions on issues directly affecting working and living conditions. A meeting in Canning Town organised by the NUGW demanded government control of price inflation and appropriate working-class action in support (ibid. p145). Profiteering, dilution of skilled labour, conscription and war bonuses were also subject to attention. As the end of the war approached minds turned increasingly to postwar reconstruction. The NUR West Ham branch responded to an appeal from *Railway Review* to submit a detailed programme; it included demands for an end to the industrial truce, higher pay and shorter hours, a Citizen army, workers' control of the food supply, and tariff protection for industry (ibid. p144).

Early in 1918 a new banner for the branch was unfurled by Thorne at a meeting of the NUR Eastern District (*SE* 12 January 18). In many ways, the meeting encapsulated the current state of local unions. Thorne, who in November 1917 had fulfilled a long-cherished desire to be mayor, spoke of the 60,000 increase in membership of the NUGW during 1917 to 270,000. Tom Kirk, branch secretary, local councillor and close personal friend of Thorne, stated that in 1907 West Ham had only the Stratford branch. Now there were branches at Forest Gate, West Ham and Canning Town, with a total membership counted in thousands instead of hundreds. Words on the banner combined industrial and political demands:

From wage slavery to industrial freedom.

Away from profiteers and exploiters to the cooperative common-wealth.

The precise mechanics of political involvement are difficult to untangle. Trade union branches had campaigned actively for labour representation and on a variety of political issues in the course of the war, but responsibility for coordination of effort and political direction rested elsewhere. Two bodies in particular were of critical importance: the West Ham Trades Council was the only representative body capable of linking industrial and political struggles, while the BSP (later NSP) South West Ham branch could through its individual members exert considerable influence in both spheres. But in spite of an overlap of membership (G Shreeve, for example, was secretary of the trades council and BSP member) latent hostility existed between the bodies, largely because of attitudes to the war held by the different constituencies (see also pp29-32) .

As war progressed the trades council came increasingly under ILP influence. It began to express dissatisfaction with the conduct of the war and those individual union leaders who had actively voiced patriotic sentiments. The NSP South West Ham branch, on the other hand, was dominated by such leaders. Not that the war was entirely responsible, for relationships between the ILP and SDF (from which the BSP emerged) had been uneasy during the 1890s when labour representation was ascendant, and did not improve. Just prior to the outbreak of war, a resolution at the BSP South West Ham branch to support G Croot (ILP) in a municipal election was defeated on the grounds that the ILP 'started under false pretences and had been false ever since' (BSP South West Ham branch, *Minutes* 2 March 13). War widened the split, even though not to the extent of formal separation as in the case of the BSP North West Ham branch (p30).

Indeed, for the most part local struggles were not compromised by political differences. The BSP South West Ham branch campaigned for a coordination of effort to deal with distress (ibid. 6 August 14), against the government's scale of separation allowance (ibid. 25 September 14), for direct labour on government contracts (ibid. 12 January 15), and so on, none of which was opposed by the trades council. It was not until the 1918 Representation of the People Act forced parliamentary representation onto the agenda that open fissures appeared. The episode of Thorne's rejection by a Trades Council Parliamentary Conference has been described (p31). ILP and BSP members successfully outmanoeuvred Thorne's supporters, thus threatening to oust a sitting MP. Thorne turned to the Labour Party and for a time it seemed that a major split on the council would occur. But the decisive move was taken when he appealed to the main constituency of his support – members of the NUGW. Since the Military Conscription Act has been introduced, he argued,

> there were a number of men who had been engineering all kinds of things for the purposes of trying to get him down. They had said he sneered at the conscientious objector. If they thought that he, as a member of the Socialist and Trades Union movement, was going to

let Macdonald or Snowden jeer at him and not return it they were mistaken. (*SE* 19 January 18.)

Thorne approached the union executive in the knowledge that a recent ballot of branches had revealed 12,403 to 70 in favour of the union sponsoring his candidature. It passed a motion which subsequently appeared in the local press:

This General Council regrets the action of the conference in West Ham in failing to place Mr. W. Thorne M.P. in the list of candidates for the next Parliamentary Election. The Council regrets the decision of the Conference on the ground that it misrepresents the wishes of the West Ham electorate, and that Mr. Thorne has consistently and fearlessly supported the war policy of organised labour in its resolve to support the country in continuing the war… The Council therefore asks Mr. Thorne to submit his conduct to the test of public meetings in his division, and either to meet in an election context any opponent nominated in opposition to him, or to establish in the division a responsible organisation with a view to securing his re-election at any future Parliamentary contest. (NUGW General Council, *Minutes* 17 January 18.)

Thorne recognised that he was on safe ground. The main body of rank-and-file opinion, if forced, would not commit itself to antiwar, ILP politics even if they had the authority of the trades council. At a subsequent public meeting of union members in Canning Town, an overwhelming vote of confidence in Thorne was carried (ibid. 13 March 18).

The union also played a decisive role in the election of Jack Jones at Silvertown. Jones had been proposed as a union candidate in spite of the existence of an official Labour candidate in D J Davis. To resolve the dilemma the party had proposed adopting Jones in Stratford where there was no Labour candidate, but the union argued that this would remove him from an area where 'he had carried on his life-work for Labour' (ibid. 25 October 18). Thorne was adamant. Whether or not the local party adopted Jones and himself, they would both contest seats with full support of the NSP. Approaches to the Central Labour Party settled nothing. At a crucial meeting of the General Council, Hayday responded to expressed fears that the relationships with the party would be jeopardised, by arguing that the dispute was purely local and the party should not interfere. It was resolved that Jones contest Silvertown with the full financial backing of the union (ibid. 20 November 18).

The desire for unity and reconciliation among labour ranks in the closing stages of the war prevented further damaging splits or recriminations. Thorne's candidature was settled and the unofficial candidature of Jones at Silvertown, although troublesome, was not a major barrier to cooperation. The West Ham Trades Council did as much as any organisation to clear the ground. At the annual meeting, Alderman Davis spoke of the Labour Party's new constitution and its resolve to field as many candidates as possible in the forthcoming general election. Not all places were as well organised as West Ham, 'where some of the delegates have been working for 20 years', but even here there was much work to be done (*SE* 6 April 18). It was suggested that in order to help capture the female vote, the Women's Cooperative Guild and Railway Women's Guild be invited to affiliate. In the meantime, links with the cooperative movement were strengthened when the council voted to support the candidature of Alf Barnes at West Ham South. The only sour note was struck in a long letter from the Clerk's Union protesting against the threat posed to trades councils by the new party constitution.

Few present would have recognised the prophetic nature of the letter as they prepared enthusiastically to reconstitute the council into the West Ham Trades Council and Central Labour Party. The name was significant for it embodied a formal separation of industrial and political sections. The former had amongst its objects:

1. The Collective Ownership of all the Means of Production, Distribution and Exchange.

2. The establishment of a more intimate connection between all branches of the operative class, so as to secure united action on all questions affecting or likely to affect their interests.

3. To secure direct Labour Representation by nominating and supporting candidates for all Elective Bodies. (West Ham Trades Council and Central Labour Party, *Rule Book* 1920.)

The political section, however, existed:

1. Generally to promote the political, social and economic emancipation of the people, and more particularly those who depend directly upon their own exertions by hand or by brain for the means of life.

2. The industrial objects shall be carried out by the Trades Council, meeting separately to consider and decide upon industrial questions.

This was a curious division of labour, and a rather untidy compromise between conflicting views on whether industrial and political work should be carried out by separate sections of the same body or by two separate organisations. The rather more definite and ambitious programme of the industrial section, including labour representation, reflected its powerful base in organised labour and the legacy of past practice. By comparison the objects of the political section were vague and inconsequential – a grudging recognition of the autonomous political role secured by the Labour Party as part of its attempt to rationalise constituency organisation.

The industrial section was open only to local branches of bona fide trade unions. Affiliated branches paying 3*d* per member were also affiliated to the Central Labour Party, 1*d* of the fee being used for its purposes. From the outset the section was dominated by the large unions, and remained so. Of the £167 paid in affiliation fees during 1928, £89 came from branches of the NUR, NUGW and TGWU (WHTC, *Annual Report* 1928). The political section, on the other hand, consisted of cooperative societies, socialist societies and local Labour parties as well as union branches.

Even with an overlapping membership, financially and organisation-ally the sections were distinct. Rather more damaging, however, was the formal separation of industrial and political boundaries. Over the next few years the separation would widen as the grip of the Labour Party tightened on political activity. The industrial section was shorn of its responsibility for selecting candidates, replacing that object with a new one:

b. To promote suitable educational, social and sports facilities for adult workers. (idem *Rule Book* 1932.)

The first meeting of the West Ham Central Labour Party took place in September 1918. D J Davis, its secretary and president of the trades council, explained that the new constitution opened the National Labour Party to 'men [sic] who earned their living by their brains' (*SE* 28 September 18). Furthermore, the party had an ideal which might not be achieved next year, but would (he hoped) eventually be realised.

On the industrial front, meanwhile, there was much activity. Demands were voiced for substantial wage increases following a period of rapid price inflation. A meeting at Stratford of the National Union of Corporation Workers denounced dilatory local authorities, and demanded a £1 per week increase on prewar rates. Members claimed that it was long overdue; other sections of workers had fought successfully, and the only reason corporation workers had fallen behind was because they were poorly organised (ibid. 6 April 18). The £1 was granted to West Ham Corporation workers but they struck for more. Blame was placed firmly at the door of the Alliance majority which refused to concede.

A compromise was eventually reached, however, when a total of 25 shillings was offered. During the dispute, Councillor Godbold stated:

The Labour [councillors] had had to fight from beginning to end in order to secure what they had got. Every member of the Labour Party without exception had done his best to bring about better conditions for corporation workers. (*SE* June 18.)

Within a month, and at a time of bitter struggle over political control of the Stratford Cooperative Society (p43), 700 employees of the CWS's Silvertown factory were on strike. Directors of the CWS had refused recognition of the Amalgamated Union of Cooperative and Commercial Employees, but granted privileges to 'craft' unions which had no record of industrial militancy. A demand for a 10 shilling increase was also on the agenda.

The strike was part of a national campaign led by the AUCE to improve conditions for cooperative employees. Formed in 1891, the union had grown slowly in a sector historically reluctant to organise. By 1906 it had 15,000 members, but then war and the politicisation of cooperation led to massive recruitment. In 1920 the union claimed 100,000 members, 90,000 of whom were in cooperation, this out of a workforce of 190,000 (Webb and Webb 1922 p193). Shopworkers, many of whom were female, were perhaps treated no worse in cooperative societies than elsewhere, but the union, with active support from the Women's Cooperative Guild, argued that conditions forced on them conflicted with the ideals of cooperation.

At a strike meeting, Salmon, the branch secretary, argued that if the directors persisted in fighting the union and continued to pay sweated wages, distribution of cooperative goods would be disrupted; the strike was not a challenge to the ideals of cooperation, but an attempt to restore them (*SE* 31 August 18). Sylvia Pankhurst also dismissed the charge that the AUCE acted against cooperative interests. Industrial unionism was the way forward. Directors were impeding progress, but the workers

> being in the right would win. They would do more than that: they would transform the Cooperative movement. They would make it a real Cooperative Movement instead of the sham it was at the present time... They had as big a fight against [the directors] as against the capitalist employer, and they would fight with the same sternness.

Concessions were granted by management, and genuine improvements made which guaranteed conditions better than those in traditional distributive and retail sectors.

In September 1918 a brief unofficial strike occurred among NUR members at Stratford over the payment of an additional war bonus. Kirk, Labour councillor and West Ham branch secretary, expressed his opposition to the action. Whilst recognising that the high cost of living and profiteering roused strong feelings amongst railwaymen, he could not condone 'anything in the nature of an unofficial strike' (*SE* 28 September 18). The offer was the best under the circumstances, and would have been accepted had it not been for the fact that

> branches had been honeycombed with 'Bolshevism', and they had seized this time of grave national peril to trade on legitimate unrest... The present strike was against the union.

At strike meetings attended by 500 railway workers various speakers referred to the impossibility of feeding and clothing their families. Others spoke of a commitment, not to national destruction, but to international peace in their fight for all workers. Without official support, however, and with a large detachment of Scots Guards at Stratford Station, the strike faltered. A resolution to return to work expressed dissatisfaction with the settlement, but recommended acceptance on the grounds that a government committee had been set up to review food prices.

These strikes, presaging as they did the unprecedented wave of industrial militancy in the immediate postwar period, demonstrated several features that were to influence the direction of political involvement. They were movements of rank and file members within general unions. Demands reflected a profound unease with living standards, but also reached to the ideals of workingclass identity and advance through dissolution of capitalism and the promotion of peace. This is emphasised by the fact that the strikes occurred during the war and were located in sizable, non-private concerns. Neither the corporation nor CWS were obvious centres of capitalist enterprise, and the GER Co was firmly under state control. There were, however, perceived limits to acceptable industrial action. That which threatened the authority of extant local labour leaders was roundly con-demned. Kirk's attitude to the unofficial strike of railwaymen was entirely consistent with labourist ideology and rhetoric that came to dominate local politics.

For the most part, discourses of class identity and idealism articulated by rank and file unionists gave impetus to the Labour programme at a local level because it was the only one that could embody them; without this political involvement it would be difficult to account satisfactorily for the significant advances made by the local Labour Party in the municipal and general elections.

But what was the precise nature of this involvement? Can we gain a better understanding of the mechanisms through which politics was expressed and facilitated? Such questions are posed obliquely by Julia Bush when she asks 'How much effect did the advice of union leaders have on the political thinking of their members?', and goes on to say 'The question is important and yet difficult to answer' (Bush 1984 p155).

It is indeed! Bush attempts an answer by examining the influence of union leaders on the membership through union journals and reports. Although few unions were prepared to jeopardise industrial authority by insensitive use of political propaganda, most were committed to political education in one form or another. Political comment varied widely from vague and general remarks on the threat to working-class interests posed by the government and profiteering, to sophisticated discussions of marxist economics and specific appeals to vote Labour in national and local elections. Such comment reached all sections of the membership, either through the journals or by word being passed to local branches, and from branches to the shop floor. Even when a cover price restricted the journal's availability, it is likely that readership exceeded sales.

Political education within branches was also important. Local branches of the NUR, which as a union was more committed than others to education, had regular speakers on political issues, and ran classes in Stratford that attracted many students from a variety of unions (p31, and Bush 1984 p159). For Bush, the causal link was clear. Trade unionism preceded politics in East London. Even if branches were not well attended and individual members used unions to improve their living and working conditions, they were introduced to the idea of labour representation, thereby advancing local Labour parties (ibid. p162).

The persuasiveness of these arguments has to be tempered by a recogni-tion that they lack detailed historical verification, are based on the rather limited experience of East London in the period around 1918, and tend to lean on a rather convenient equation linking the ascent of the Labour Party to trade union strength. We learn little of the potential union membership involved in politics, or of the precise nature of political discourses elabo-rated by unions. Arguments that may apply to the traditional East End do not necessarily apply to West Ham (p29 above). Even more those valid for 1917-19 may not have equal validity for the postwar period as the fortunes of unions fluctuated. In the final analysis, the arguments are fruitful speculations that need further empirical and theoretical scrutiny.

3.3 Political involvement: three trade unions

It might be helpful now to explore in some detail the issues which have just been raised, starting with the nature of the commitment of individual unions to political involvement. In the context of West Ham, the National Union of Railwaymen (NUR), National Union of General Workers (NUGW) and Transport and General Workers Union (TGWU) were by far the most influential politically, not only because their branch memberships exceeded all others but because it was from the ranks of these unions that most of the key Labour figures sprang.

National Union of Railwaymen

At the close of war, during which the NUR nationally had expanded from 132,000 to 402,000, railway workers were strongly unionised in West Ham. The union drew most of its members from the massive GER works at Stratford but also attracted railway workers from the smaller LMS depot at Plaistow and from a variety of local employers such as the corporation and dock companies.

The rapid increase in membership during the war was due partly to recruitment of women on the railways, many of whom joined the union when it opened its doors to them in 1916. In his presidential report Cramp noted the consequences:

> It is gratifying to find that the introduction of female labour upon the railways has not resulted in a proportionate decline in railway trade unionism. On the contrary, women have apparently grasped our principles far more quickly than was the case with men in the past and are among our most enthusiastic members. (NUR *Proceedings and Reports* 18.)

In the immediate postwar boom membership continued to expand rapidly, but with the onset of recession it tumbled, and for the rest of the decade failed to recover lost ground (Table 3.2). Overall, shifts reflected those at a national level, although the fluctuations locally were more marked.

Branches drew on different constituencies. The Stratford and Forest Gate branches consisted largely of skilled railway workers. 32 per cent of Stratford 2 comprised Scale D railway workers in 1919, the most highly skilled shopmen in the locomotive works. This compares with 20 per cent in Forest Gate and Stratford 1, 11 per cent in West Ham, 8 per cent in Plaistow and 7 per cent in Canning Town. These latter branches, then, were dominated by relatively unskilled railway workers such as porters and cleaners. Stratford 3 and 4 were formed in 1920, the former out of transfers from 1 and 2, while the latter was for supervisors, one hundred of whom had transferred from Bethnal Green.

As a union, the NUR had a long record of political involvement which it

TABLE 3.2 *Membership of NUR branches, West Ham, 1918-30*

	1918	1919	1920	1921	1922	1923	1924	1925	1926	1930
West Ham	623	813	955	583	416	463	498	643	575	558
Canning Town	557	726	546	501	467	522	450	506	505	450
Forest Gate	419	576	454	365	280	314	312	345	307	279
Plaistow[a]	569	595	570	371	290	291	277	359	326	503
Stratford 1	1872	2638	1939	1478	1183	1232	1186	1337	1088	966
Stratford 2	2240	2690	2620	1783	1324	1636	1379	1942	1650	1356
Stratford 3	—	—	212	113	161	220	299	463	447	416
Stratford 4	—	—	149	138	137	146	145	147	139	108
Total	6280	8038	7445	5332	4258	4824	4546	5742	5037	4636
National (000)	417	481	459	386	337	363	382	399	388	335

Note: [a] Plaistow 1 and 2 combined.
Sources: NUR *Proceedings and Reports*, relevant years.

frequently recalled with pride in the pages of *Railway Review*. Its pred-
ecessor, the Amalgamated Society of Railway Servants (ASRS), was the first
union to follow the miners in sponsoring its own parliamentary candidates, and at the 1898 TUC was responsible for the resolution calling on
Congress to secure 'the return of an increased number of Labour representatives', a proposal which led directly to the formation of the Labour
Representation Committee in 1900 .

As the 1918 election approached the NUR reaffirmed its commitment to
independent representation and its faith in the ability of the Labour Party
to build a new social order. J H Thomas, general secretary of the union and
one of its MPs, successfully moved at the 1918 Labour Party conference that

> the task of social reconstruction to be organised and undertaken by
> the Government, in conjunction with the local authorities, ought to
> be regarded as involving, not any patchwork jerrymandering of the
> anarchic individualism and profiteering of the competitive capital-
> ism of pre-war time, ... but the gradual building up of a new social
> order. (Labour Party *Annual report* 18.)

An Executive Committee meeting held immediately prior to the election, amidst disquiet that the Labour Party should remain within the
coalition, resolved that it

> should go to the country as an independent body, putting forward
> its policy as set out in its reconstruction programme... Further,
> realising that the future of the Labour movement in this country is of
> vital importance to the interests of the working class in considering
> after the war problems, we are fully convinced that these problems
> can only be effectively dealt with by a strong Labour Party returned
> to Parliament at the election. We further decide to recommend to our
> members in the country to render every support to Labour

candidates in their respective constituencies. (NUR *Proceedings and Reports* 18.)

At a special NUR conference in Westminster Hall, delegates accepted unanimously the Labour Party's *New social order* (*Railway Rev.* 22 November 18). And the union was prepared to back this with hard cash to an extent displayed by no other union. It sponsored Labour candidates in national elections, gave grants to candidates in municipal elections, paid without hesitation increases in affiliation fees to the Labour Party, and responded generously to appeals from the party for extra funding during elections. In 1923, for example, the NUR granted £10,000 to the election fund, prompting a letter from Henderson, the party secretary:

> In the years gone by, right from the very inception of our Party, the organised railwaymen of the country have always seemed to fulfil the role of pioneers – at the Plymouth Congress, in the Taff Vale agitation, the Osborne judgement, in connection with the Daily Herald, and again on this occasion they have been prominent in their good works. (NUR, General Secretary's Report *Proceedings and Reports* 23.)

Generous recognition also came from C J Kelly, a councillor from Poplar and member of the LCC, who commented on the record of the union in LCC elections:

> Taking the country as a whole, the N. U. R. stand out above any other union in so far as finding money and providing candidates is concerned. In fact, in almost every trades council, divisional and local labour party, the N. U. R. is the most prominent of all the affiliated societies… At the last L.C.C. election, 80% of the election fund was found by the N.U.R. (*Railway Rev.* 23 May 24)

All this was made possible through the political levy. The columns of *Railway Review* in the postwar period stressed the importance of contracting in: 'Why do we think nothing of spending a bob to see a game, or spending freely when we are "on the swank", or dropping a tidy bit on a loser, and yet begrudge paying a trifle to our Labour Party funds?', a cartoon asked rhetorically in one issue (ibid. 5 March 20). At the end of 1920 Cramp, the Parliamentary General Secretary, reported to the Annual Meeting that notwithstanding the fine political record of the union, in recent years many members had neglected to pay the levy. But now he was able to say that

> there is a considerable improvement in this respect. According to returns I have received from branch secretaries since the beginning of this year, the great majority of our members are now contributing to the political fund. (NUR *Proceedings and Reports* 20.)

The union also had strong historical links with the cooperative movement, and in this period demonstrated a rare appreciation of the advantages to be derived from working together. It welcomed the entry of cooperation into the political arena, and urged Labour to guard against attempted incursions by the Liberals:

Labour hopes to secure the passive if not active support of the cooperative body, and to ensure this we, as trade unionists, must redouble our efforts to link up the two movements... We have so much in common that the fusing process should be not only mutually beneficial, but mark a big stop [sic] forward in the march of progress. (*Railway Rev.* 1 February 18.)

Local members responded readily to such calls. Railway workers in West Ham were steeped in a tradition of political involvement. Stratford locomotive works had been the nucleus of the nascent cooperative movement, and members had taken an active role in returning the labour council in 1898 (p26 above). None did more than Tom Kirk, a signalman who had joined the ASRS in 1897, and was an active member of Stratford 1 before founding the West Ham branch in 1907. As secretary of the branch he campaigned energetically to expand union membership and promote political involvement, in recognition of which he had been presented with an inscribed gold medallion by J H Thomas. He was elected to West Ham council in 1910, and during the war had taken an active interest in food control and the defeat of 'Prussian aggression'. As a member of the South West Ham branch of the NSP, he had strong personal ties with other important local unionists, and through skilful use of the press helped construct and disseminate the programme of labourism (see, for example, his letter published in both *Railway Review* and *Stratford Express*, p30) . Early in 1918 he demonstrated his loyalty to Thorne against 'pacifist intriguers',with the full support of his branch (p32). He was later proposed as a parliamentary candidate of the union, but failed to be selected (*Railway Rev.* 22 March 18).

Although Kirk was the only local politician of note to emerge from the NUR, his brand of labourism was not necessarily shared by other branches. Thus while West Ham branch reported that a proposal for electoral reform had been turned down by 'an alliance of local reactionary forces, comprising Liberals, the I.L.P., Conservatives and the B.S.P.', Stratford 1 asked Thorne to protest in parliament against the continuing imprisonment and maltreatment of conscientious objectors, and pledged support for A Barnes and W Murrell (both ILP) in the forthcoming SCS elections (ibid. 6 April 18).

Common acceptance of the Labour Party programme, however, meant that as the election approached such differences were subordinated to the object of increasing labour representation. The West Ham branch, in a report bearing the unmistakable stamp of Kirk, stated:

Every ounce of our energy, enthusiasm and native resourcefulness was put in the South West Ham contest... In spite of the intriguing Bolsheviks, spirit-rapping pacifists, temperance cranks, Liberals and Tories, on Saturday Will Thorne and Jack Jones will head the poll. Thus endeth a strenuous year. Our motto for the New Year: 'First things first'. Britain for the British. (ibid. 3 September 19.)

Thus NUR members did contribute to the success of Thorne and Jones in the southern constituencies. The extent of this contribution, however, must not be overstated. The south was overwhelmingly working class, with considerable branches of general unions likewise committed to labour representation. Stratford in the north, wherein were located the two largest branches of the NUR with a joint membership nearly double the rest, did not have a Labour candidate, and returned a Tory. Kirk hinted that sectionalism displayed by the largest element of craft workers in these branches had been a barrier to the advance of Labour:

> For years the Great Eastern workers voted solidly against the Labour Party in West Ham municipal elections on the ground that the dustman, the road sweeper, the carman, and the scavenger were accorded by the corporation a social status and economic standing superior to the ordinary working class ratepayer. It was not a just complaint, but it was not entirely without cause, and colour was lent to it by the statements of certain ill-educated and unthinking Socialists. (ibid. 23 May 19.)

National Union of General Workers

The National Union of General Workers had a particularly close relationship to West Ham. As the Gasworkers and General Labourers' Union it had been established by Will Thorne and others at the Beckton gasworks in 1889, and in the early stages drew much of its support from Canning Town. The defeat of the gasworkers in the early 1890s, leading to their advocacy of labour representation, marked a new phase in the development of labour politics (Clegg 1964, Marriott 1984). The union actually embodied the principle of representation in its constitution, and for several years prior to 1889 proposed it to the TUC. On formation of the Labour Representation Committee, it expressed a commitment

> To secure by united action the election to Parliament of candidates promoted, in the first instance, by an affiliated society or societies, in the constituency, who undertake to form or join a district group in Parliament, with its own Whips and its own policy on Labour questions. (*General Workers' Journal* Sept-Oct 25 p2.)

The union campaigned actively to increase the number of Labour MPS and councillors. By the end of 1907, the GWGLU had four MPS – W Thorne, J Clynes, P Curran and J Parker – more than any other union apart from the miners, and it was well represented on municipal authorities.

In this period, however, there was never an uncritical acceptance of party policy. Thorne and Clynes had retained their allegiance to the BSP and ILP respectively, causing friction between the union and the Labour Party in selecting candidates. Opposition from the party to the disaffiliated SDF, for example, had placed Thorne in a difficult position as a candidate in the 1906 election and he continued to voice nagging criticism of party policy (Clegg 1964 p77). In West Ham there was even talk of withdrawing from the Labour group on the council (BSP, South West Ham branch *Minutes* 13 September 12).

War changed all this. Clynes rejected the pacifism of the ILP and witnessed a meteoric rise in his parliamentary career, eventually being appointed Food Controller in 1917. Thorne allied himself with the Hyndmanite faction that split from the main body of the BSP, becoming a rabid patriot (p31). His support for war aims, in particular conscription, and his hostility to conscientious objectors distanced him from local socialist activists, leading to his rejection as a Labour candidate in 1918 (p31). But his position within the union, at a time when membership was expanding dramatically, remained secure.

At the end of the war membership stood at 302,390 – nearly double that of 1916, and a near ten fold increase since 1910. It continued to rise, probably reaching a peak in 1920, fell to a low in 1923, and then began to recover slowly (Table 3.3). As with the NUR, rapid wartime expansion depended in part upon the ability of the union to attract female labour, particularly in munitions where craft unions had little success. This paved the way for amalgamation with the National Federation of Women Workers in 1919, by which time the expansion of female trade unionism had rendered obsolete a separate union for women (Clegg 1964 p100). Initially, women members had a separate district with Margaret Bondfield as National Officer, but in 1923 a system of women's branches was introduced (*Gas Workers' Journal* March-April 23).

Local branches reflected these broad movements, although even with seasonal shifts (winter figures were consistently lower than those in summer), they were less marked thanks in large part to amalgamations with the National Amalgamated Union of Labour (NAUL) and Municipal Employees Association (MEA) in February 1924. The location and size of branches owed much to the history of the union in the area, chiefly around the gasworks. Thus the Canning Town and West Ham branches drew much of their membership from Beckton and West Ham gasworks, while Bromley East depended largely upon the Gas Light & Coke Company's plant in Bow. These three branches were more than 50 per cent larger than any other branch of the union in London. The West Ham branch alone had more members than Southampton, Reading or Norwich.

The troubled relationship between the union and the Labour Party continued into the immediate postwar period. Largely under the influence of Thorne and Clynes, who were in favour of Labour remaining within the coalition, the union approached the party. Thorne wrote on 26 November 1918:

> I am desired by our General Committee to ask your Executive to consider the question of calling a special conference of the Party at the earliest opportunity after the result of the General Election is known. We think that after the election it may be expedient to reconsider the question of the Party authorising its representatives in Parliament to take office in the Coalition Government. (Labour Party correspondence LP/UN/18.)

He received a curt reply from Macdonald who subsequently wrote in *Forward*, 14 December 1918:

TABLE 3.3 Membership of NUGW branches in West Ham and adjacent boroughs, selected years 1918–26

	1918c	1921		1922		1923		1924	1925		1926	
		June	Sept	Mar	Dec	June	Dec	Dec	June	Dec	June	Dec
WEST HAM												
Canning Town 1	2662	3562	3044	2266	1743	1819	1587	1844	2050	1862	2163	1822
Canning Town 2	—	—	—	63	185	196	204	261	280	270	270	271
Custom House	—	—	130	—	—	—	—	—	—	272	389	321
Silvertown	287	183	152	144	256	202	166	412	581	662	962	748
Silvertown sugar[a]	—	—	—	—	—	—	—	1593	1286	924	965	652
Plaistow	—	—	66	173	172	181	374	173	191	188	194	181
West Ham	3021	4400	3990	3045	2481	2439	2434	2672	2870	2874	3096	2718
West Ham caretakers	43	93	73	75	76	76	73	70	68	71	70	64
West Ham poor law	—	160	163	164	167	175	149	515[d]	528	433	631	251[b]
Total	6013	8398	7618	5930	5080	5088	4987	7540	7854	7556	8740	7028
NEIGHBOURS												
Bromley East	2631	4006	3560	2852	2558	2586	2172	2448	2758	2672	2845	2402
East Ham	803	1910	1711	1183	703	613	537	611	623	720	849	822
Total	3434	5916	5271	4035	3261	3199	2709	3059	3381	3392	3694	3224
NATIONAL (000)	302	490	455	301	235	214	201	324	322	314	325	290

Source: NUGW Quarterly Reports relevant years. Membership calculated from branch income submitted to District Office.
Notes: [a] Branch established at Tate & Lyle in April 1924.
[b] Fall due to supersession of board of guardians.
[c] Reports for 1919 and 1920 are missing.
[d] Increase due to amalgamation with MEA in February 1924.

I know that an attempt will be made as soon as the election is over, to get Labour to countenance and join the coalition. Mr. Thorne and his Gas Labourers' Union are even now trying to have a national conference called to consider a renewal of the bargain. The Labour Party will not tolerate any such policy.

Much to Thorne's chagrin, Lupton, his Tory opponent in the 1918 election, made political capital from this by distributing extracts from the article. But Thorne remained within the party, as did Clynes who was soon to be elected leader of the Parliamentary Party and later became Home Secretary.

Similar unease existed about political funding. Following the 1918 Conference decision to double affiliation fees, Thorne expressed disquiet at the serious consequences for the union's finances, while Hord, an executive member, argued that the

> trade union movement was paying large sums to the Labour Party, and being in the majority should rule it; but it seemed that other constituencies of the Party were doing as they liked with the money, hence the agitation for a purely trade union political party. (NUGW General Council *Minutes* 16 May 18.)

The NUGW had little of the campaigning zeal for labour representation exhibited by the NUR. Most energy at this time was devoted to strengthening the union. George Stokes, who at the time worked as part of the small staff at union head office, recalled that:

> except for propaganda meetings on Beckton Road corner, the union wasn't greatly politically inclined apart from its two MPs... The union was more or less a self-contained body only interested in increasing the influence of the NUGW... The union was almost apolitical..., their main concern was increasing the size of the union, getting more members, looking after its members' interests. (G Stokes, tape.)

Thorne, despite his seniority as a Labour MP, remained a minor figure in the Labour Party nationally when compared with Clynes, Thomas and Bevin, and in complete contrast to his stature locally. At heart, one suspects, he was a union boss, although as an MP, union general secretary and alderman it was difficult to see how he could devote sufficient time to any of these roles to do it properly. A rare insight into his role is again provided by G Stokes:

> Thorne merely founded the Gasworkers union. He was purely an organiser, he could merely bring members into the union, he could do nothing on the technical side of finance or anything like that. His attendance at Tavistock Square [head office]: he used to get a workman's train to King's Cross, arriving at the office about 8 o'clock. He'd stay for 2-3 hours, then go off to the House. He'd stay there all day until late at night unless he had other business, or was attending a meeting somewhere, and he'd come back to Upton Park Station, take a tram round to the Duke of Edinburgh for just a couple of drinks, then proceed home to Lawrence Road. He had no

capability as regard administration. Butcher the Assistant General Secretary ran head office solely. He lived on the job, had a flat at the top. (ibid.)

Thorne remained a figurehead within the union, but was not without influence. Late in 1918, he stated its agenda:

> The indications are that the war is now drawing to a close, and we shall soon have to face the period of reconstruction. This will be a testing time for all trade union organisations. Our policy must be that all concessions and advances gained during the war period must be maintained wherever it is possible to do so. The sacrifices that working classes have made during the past four years have entitled them to a greater stake in the country and a higher standard of life than prevailed before the war. Whether the people will maintain this level depends on how they maintain their organisations. We are looking to the loyalty of our members to tide us over the difficult times which certainly lie before us. (NUGW General Council *Minutes* 28 September 18.)

This affirmation of the industrial strength and potential of the working class embodied in the trade unions makes no explicit reference to political advance. But then Thorne was speaking as general secretary of a large union in a position of unprecedented authority.

While the union remained financially secure, however, there was no strong opposition to the political levy and sponsoring of Labour candidates. A vote on the principle of the levy taken immediately after the 1913 Trade Union Act revised the conditions for establishing political funds, revealed a low 29 per cent poll but an 87 per cent vote in favour of the levy (Clegg 1985 p223). This suggests that amidst widespread indifference an active minority held sway. In the 1918 election, the union sponsored eight candidates, granting a total of £3425 in expenses (NUGW General Council *Minutes* 28 December 18). Five were elected; an excellent return on the investment. Corresponding amounts were not forthcoming in municipal elections. In 1922, for example, while the General Council committed £5553 to parliamentary candidates, only £1000 was allocated to districts on a pro rata membership basis (ibid. 23 February 23).

The success of the union in West Ham elections seemed impressive. Following the 1923 elections, the union could claim twelve of the forty-seven Labour councillors. But the extent to which this success can be attributed to direct involvement of the union is not easy to determine. The priority given to consolidation of industrial gains during this period relegated explicit political activity. The union accepted the Labour programme and provided election funds for its parliamentary candidates, but there was little active promotion of the political ideals of Labour, little encouragement of the membership to support work for Labour candidates, and little funding. The only evidence of direct political intervention came when the union interceded on behalf of Thorne and Jones to salvage their parliamentary candidatures. In south West Ham this political role

TABLE 3.4 *Membership of TGWU branches located in West Ham, aggregated into trade groups, 1922–28*

| | 1922 | | 1924 | | 1926 | | 1928 | |
	Branches	Members	Branches	Members	Branches	Members	Branches	Members
Docks	14	5672	15	3572	14	3601	13	4173
Clerical	2	646	2	693	2	470	1	401
Commercial	3	530	3	853	3	649	3	539
Road transport	2	301	3	453	2	423	2	289
Bus and tram	0	0	3	1562	3	1474	3	1582
Coop and dairy	1	229	2	425	2	320	2	437
Total	23	7378	28	7445	26	6937	24	7421

Source: TGWU, *Annual reports.*
Notes: [a] No individual branch returns after 1929.

was in part assumed, not by the Labour Party which was discredited by the war and incursion of middle-class intellectuals, but by the NSP. Small as it was, it became the political voice of local NUGW members, hence mediating between the union and municipal involvement (pp98-9).

Transport and General Workers Union

As a centre of communication, West Ham was to prove an important site of TGWU activity. Membership during the 1920s is shown in Table 3.4.

Before amalgamation with the Workers' Union in 1929, the TGWU was dominated by dock and road transport workers; in West Ham, this was certainly the case. The massive docks complex south of the borough provided the union with approximately half its membership. Here were recruited not only dockers, but workers in industries sited dockside such as the three giant flour mills and the East London Oil Company. Many of the clerical workers were also employed by the Port of London Authority. The docks trade group was followed by that of bus and tram workers, branches of whose union, the United Vehicle Workers, did not exist in West Ham at the time of amalgamation. Bus and tram workers were to prove a solid and loyal group within the TGWU, although their militancy was often to trouble Bevin.

Aggregate membership of the union in West Ham was fairly steady during the 1920s, but the figures disguise some important shifts. The docks branches were badly affected after the early peak of 1922 by recession and the secession in 1923 of a substantial number of stevedores, dockers and lightermen to form the Stevedores Union (NASLWDU – the 'blue union'), but then gradually recovered. In large part recruitment of bus and tram workers compensated for these losses.

Numerically, financially and politically, of the eleven trade unions that amalgamated to form the Transport and General Workers Union in January 1922, the most powerful was the Dock, Wharf, Riverside and General Labourers' Union (Dockers' Union). Formed during the 1889 dock struggles, like other general unions it suffered major setbacks in the 1890s as trade declined and employers counterattacked, but survived as proof that dock labour could sustain viable forms of organisation. Membership increased steadily during the war from 38,000 in 1914 to 85,000 in 1918. It was rather smaller than the NUR and NUGW but had considerable confidence, embodied in its general secretary, Ben Tillett, and national organiser, Ernest Bevin.

From the outset, the Dockers' Union displayed complex and ambivalent attitudes toward political involvement. Dock labour had been notoriously resilient to organisation, and held little allegiance to politics, whatever its shade, in part because the franchise amongst its numbers was extremely low. Although the 1889 strike was led by professed socialists, and figures such as Tillett and Mann continued to hold key positions, this was not because of their socialism but in spite of it (Clegg, Flanders and Thompson 1964 p90). Above all, they were accepted because of their commitment to the dockers' cause and their ability to articulate demands. Largely under the influence of Tillett, as the union's industrial fortunes declined it began in 1893 to press TUC conferences for independent labour representation. In West Ham, organised dockers were wooed by labour candidates, and so contributed to the victory of 1898, but few candidates for municipal honours emerged from their ranks.

As the 1918 general election approached, the union resolved to increase its representation in parliament. In addition to Tillett, who was the sole MP, five candidates were sponsored, and the weight of the union was put behind them:

> It is essential for Labour to be prepared, and to complete its organisation at the earliest possible date... So far as our own organisation is concerned, everything that can possibly be done is being done, and in the course of a few weeks the electoral organisations will be completely prepared for the election, and we are in no way fearing the results. (*Dockers' Record* October 18.)

Tillett had taken a strong patriotic stance during the war; congratulating union members on their conduct, he referred to the absence of damaging strike action and the way in which the union position had been maintained (ibid. November 18). Now he adhered to the 'comprehensive programme' of the Labour Party:

> I shall do my best in the resettlement of the fighters and war workers in peaceful industry, on the most equitable basis. I shall support the Government in the vigorous prosecution of peace... With the Labour Party I shall do my best in demanding such adjustments in industry and trade as shall secure to industrial democracy a high standard of living, full and equitable economic benefit for their labour. (ibid.)

Through the union journal, appeals went out to all union members:

> to do all they can to secure the return of the union's candidates at the head of the poll. All candidates have accepted the constitution and comprehensive programme of the Labour Party. In addition to this,

we appeal to our members, both men and women, in all the constituencies where Labour Party candidates are being run, to do everything within their power to ensure the return of such candidates, and make it possible for Labour to be more strongly represented in the new Parliament than it was in the last. (ibid.)

The union, like the NUR and NUGW, had benefited from a considerable increase in women members during the war, most of whom had been recruited from munitions, cotton and light engineering factories. And it recognised their potential. The *Dockers' Record* had a women's page edited by Mary Carlin, the woman organiser, and devoted to reports of female advances in the industrial and political fields rather than hints on cooking and sewing. Women-only meetings were held at which questions on maternity and child welfare, housing, public health and education were discussed. Particular attention was given to the role of women in an enlarged electorate:

We have had quite enough of being governed, now we are determined to take a hand of governing. We know all of our women who have the vote will use it for the Labour candidate, and those who have not yet reached the age of thirty can see to it that their mothers are enlightened on this subject. (ibid. November 18.)

Tillett and Wignall were elected to parliament for North Salford and Forest of Dean respectively. Bevin was defeated at Bristol Central, and W Devenay defeated at Mile End, East London, where he had been adopted as a candidate after failing nomination in one of the hotly-contested constituencies in West Ham. The union contributed £2512 to the election (ibid. October 19).

Soon after the election, moves toward amalgamation, and defence of hours and wages, most notably at the Shaw Inquiry, commanded much union time and energy. A proposed amalgamation with the NUGW failed because the necessary 50 per cent poll was not reached by the Dockers' Union. Bevin, who had shown little enthusiasm for the proposal, immediately set in motion alternative proposals that were to come to fruition with the formation of the TGWU.

It was in Bevin that the political ambiguities of the TGWU – inherited in large part from the Dockers' Union – were most manifest. Experience and instinct determined his priorities:

So long as he was thinking or talking about trade unions and industrial affairs, Bevin's grasp was sure. When he ventured into politics (where he had no experience on which to draw) he was far less effective. (Bullock 1960 p72.)

The war years confirmed this. Although in favour of active prosecution of the war effort, Bevin refused to ally himself with sentiments expressed by patriotic union leaders of an older generation, and demanded that there be no compromise on the industrial front. Quite apart from that, with the commitment he had to work on various government committees, the Dockers' Union and the Transport Workers Federation, there was no time for politics (ibid. p78). His defeat in the 1918 election merely strengthened identification with the industrial sphere and led to a period of self-imposed exile from politics.

Bevin placed faith, then, in the potential of industrial action to effect change. Not that this was ever thought to be a form of direct action as the first step in revolutionary struggle, but rather as a means of exerting pressure on government. Nor did it mean that political intervention was abandoned – merely subordinated. This faith led him to campaign in 1919 for the replacement of the Parliamentary Committee of the TUC by a General Council, arguing that 'Congress should develop the industrial side of the movement as against the "deputising" or "political" conception' (ibid. p111).

It also informed his determination to forge the TGWU, in spite of the collapse of the Triple Alliance and attendant decline of the Transport Workers Federation while negotiations with constituent unions were proceeding. The structure of the union was formulated by Bevin, and once he had assumed control as General Secretary, successfully ousting Tillett in the process, he imposed political authority by asserting the integrity of organised working-class power, particularly against potential class enemies:

> We are satisfied the General Council (of the T.U.C.) is on the right lines... We are awaiting the development of the Council with keen interest, and we sincerely hope that it will not be influenced by middle-class place seekers whose interference has already lost the movement the statutory eight-hour day and legal minimum wage at a time when the now much abused Triple Alliance had given a lead which would have won it. This type of mind knowing nothing of the real working class struggle, and lacking farsightedness and experience, sits with superior smiles, enjoying economic security, telling others how easy it all is and how it 'ought to be done'. We prefer the fighter with a good soul to the cynic with mere brain. (*The Record* September 21.)

This suspicion of the middle class, however, did not prevent work with a Labour Party that could be forced to represent genuine working-class interests:

> For centuries these classes [employers, aristocrats, etc], by trading upon the ignorance and political prejudices of the working class electors, have held the monopoly of power to shape the laws which control and regulate the economic condition of the working classes... If the [labour] movement goes on developing during the next dozen years as it has during the past twelve, this economic advantage of the employers will be nullified by the organised advantage of the workers, and therein lies our hope... Every trade unionist must realise that when the election comes he must appreciate that his Labour politics are useless to him without the backing of strong trade unionism. The two go hand in hand, and this close cooperation will ensure victory. (ibid. August 22.)

It was a perspective to which Bevin adhered with customary tenacity. Even when criticised for pursuing industrial action during the time of the first Labour Government, an editorial in *The Record* responded:

> Governments may come and Governments may go, but the workers' fight must go on all the time and in every possible way. A strong industrial army must be the best support a Labour Government can have. (ibid. April 24.)

On amalgamation the TGWU agreed to honour commitments undertaken by individual unions in financing parliamentary candidates. Among the nine candidates accepted were four sitting MPS; £3750 was to be allocated to their expenses. Applications from a variety of non-union candidates and organisations were also considered, and smaller grants made, including £50 to the ILP (TGWU General Executive *Minutes* 1 November 22). A general manifesto was issued by the executive urging the whole of the membership to vote for Labour candidates. Bevin advised all officers to render 'all possible support to the candidates, consistent, of course, with the maintaining of their industrial work during the contest' (TGWU General Secretary's Report, 30 October 1922). But at branch level little political direction was felt, or probably desired. Frank Robinson recalls meetings of the West Ham dockers:

> Meetings used to last 4-5 hours. Some political issues that came up in the press or in the news, if we thought that they had any effect on what was going on in the docks then they would be put on the agenda. But it was not general throughout the TGWU. Nothing ever came through the branches to say go and support [a Labour MP]. Nothing like that. You never had a political awareness who even the MP was. The attitude was I suppose that if you wanted to get into that, go and join your local Labour Party branch. We was never encouraged to go forward politically. (Robinson, tape.)

The nature of political involvement displayed by the NUR, NUGW and TGWU in the immediate postwar period denies an easy and convenient equation between trade unionism and politics. All three unions adopted unhesitatingly the Labour Party programme and were anxious to finance candidates in parliamentary elections. But here common ground ends. The NUR had close ties with party leaders, particularly through Thomas and Cramp, and on the whole supported them by expressing confidence in their action, and backing the party financially. The NUGW, on the other hand, remained suspicious of the leadership because of its ILP and middle-class associations; Clynes and Thorne launched right-wing critiques in spite of the former's prominence within the party. Some of this suspicion was shared by Bevin, but this had less to do with discredited war records and class affiliations than with subordination of the political to the industrial.

In broad terms, the direction of a union's political activity at the local level was determined by national policy, although a preoccupation with parliamentary representation meant that relatively less attention and funding were devoted to municipal politics. Most active in West Ham was the NUR. Branches of considerable size, some of which had a large presence of skilled labour, campaigned actively, but were located in the north of the borough where Labour's electoral base was relatively weak. Other branches, dominated by less skilled members, provided a platform for a brand of labourism best exemplified by Kirk. The NUGW and Dockers' Union (later TGWU) derived their strength from the south. But here political intervention was ill-defined.

This tendency towards separation of trade union and political spheres was not averted by labourist discourses. Programmes launched by Labour candidates interpellated the electorate as industrial workers, as mothers, as citizens, as consumers and as tenants, but rarely as trade unionists. Demands for trade union reform, such as abolition of restrictions on union activity or improvements in collective bargaining, formed no part of the Labour platform.

Into the political space left vacant by the unions in this period stepped not the Labour Party, which at the time did not have an independent local organisation, nor the West Ham Trades Council, whose militant industrial section was losing political ground, but the South West Ham branch of the NSP. Compared with local union branches the NSP was minute – the largest attendance at a branch meeting over the years 1912-22 was thirty-six, the average about twenty-four – and yet the extent to which its members came to dominate municipal politics was remarkable. Apart from figures such as Kerrison, Groves, Barnes, D J Davis and Gardner, all of whom retained ILP affiliations, the large majority of prominent local politicians were NSP members. The list is an impressive one: Jones, Thorne, Stokes, Moule, Killip, Godbold, Parsons, Husband, Scoulding, Rumsey, Mansfield, Kirk, Allison, Croot and Shreeve came to exercise effective control over the political machinery of West Ham at national and local levels. This authority, however, was based firmly within the unions. Most of these councillors were members of the NUGW (Kirk, NUR branch secretary, and Scoulding, who was London area secretary of TGWU, being notable exceptions), and when necessary could seek sanctuary therein.

Control was facilitated by the dual loyalties of those like Thorne and Jones who did not wish to devote a lot of time to routine, local political work (p91). At a meeting to discuss this it was recorded that

> Comrade Thorne said that whilst our 6 M.P.s were all members of the N.S.P. they nevertheless were also active members of the trade union movement and as their time was very much engaged in their trade union work they could not be expected to give every week end to the Party. (NSP South West Ham branch *Minutes* 23 March 19.)

The branch organised public rallies, provided speakers at Barking Road every Sunday morning, distributed leaflets, but also proposed candidates and held members accountable for their actions. Kirk, for example, was asked for an explanation of his article in the *Democrat* 'which was not favourable to our policy' (ibid. 18 February 21).

Ultimate political and financial authority in the immediate postwar period, therefore, rested on considerable union power, particularly in the south of the borough. But at a time when the NUGW was confident in its industrial strength, that authority was articulated and directed by a close-knit caucus of NSP members. Thus were laid the foundations of oligarchical power.

3.4 Labour representation in the immediate postwar period

1919 was a troubled year. In the aftermath of Labour victories in the southern constituencies of West Ham, the party sought to weld fissures created by the war. NSP and ILP members demonstrated unity in preparation for municipal struggles (p31 above). Rallies addressed the common problems of reconstruction. But pockets of resistance to labourist hegemony remained, the most important of which had an industrial base. At a meeting of the West Ham Trades Council, Godbold urged delegates to

> give the Labour group a chance. The group had now got a bare majority, and they found the tramway in an acute financial muddle. The responsibility taken by the Labour Party was so grave that they wanted a little time to consider it. He was very glad to say that the Labour group in the Town Council were united. (*SE* 24 May 19.)

In reply, Holden, a council worker, suggested that they boycott the trams; 'whether the Labour group was in power or not made no difference'.

Such divisions were most blatantly exposed, however, by the question of military intervention in Russia. At a June meeting of the trades council, Pankhurst of the Operative Brickworkers' Society moved that the council view 'with suspicion and alarm the growing hostility of the governing and capitalist classes in this country... to the new-born democracies of Germany and Russia', and called for 'the withdrawal from Russia of all British naval and military forces' (ibid. 7 June 19). Shreeve (NSP and NUGW) responded that until the Triple Alliance could be persuaded to act the best hope lay in educating the Labour Party that this was 'too serious a matter to be trifled with any longer'. This proclamation of faith in political action brought sharp rejoinders from delegates. One declared that 'The Labour Party is going to do what we tell them', while Goodham

> thought it useless to send the resolutions to the Labour party, because there were among them too many Rt. Honourables who associated themselves with politicians of other colours, and they did not do as the workers expected them to do. (ibid. 7 June 19.)

Dawson also criticised the party, and said that the TUC was 'nothing more than a trade union official's holiday'. The motion was carried unanimously and the chair ended the meeting with a call to organise strikes.

The question of Russia, therefore, raised in very real terms the legitimacy of state intervention and the nature of the relationship between industrial and political action. The use of strikes as an explicitly political weapon directly challenged labourist views on the boundaries of legitimate politics and on the subordinate role of industrial action, almost rendering obsolete the need for independent labour representation. Trade union leaders who were inscribed within labourism, even if they accepted the importance of industrial action, could not take this step. The TUC Parliamentary Committee refused to call a special conference on whether industrial action should be used to enforce withdrawal of troops from Russia. But the Labour Party conference voted two to one in favour of direct action. The NUM, NUR, ILP and delegates from trades councils and local Labour parties were in the majority, the Dockers' Union and NUGW in the minority. In an apolitical assertion of trade union independence, Tillett and Clynes objected to the principle of a political party dictating industrial strategy, and argued that the matter be dealt with by recourse to conventional political methods. Thorne and Jones along with other delegates cast the large block vote of the union against direct action.

A meeting organised jointly by the East London Federation of the ILP and the West Ham Trades Council demanded 'complete and immediate cessation of the intervention against Socialist Republics' (*SE* 26 July 19). Gardner blamed the British government, members of which obtained their seats by fraud, and declared that the 'Labour movement in West Ham was getting on it feet again'. But these were lonely voices. More powerful ones were being mobilised by NSP members. The West Ham branch of the NUR, under the guidance of Kirk, resolved 'That this branch expresses itself against the principle of using the strike weapon as a means of settling political questions' (*Railway Rev.* 22 August 19). An amendment 'That before the N.U.R. is committed to strike action on political questions the members should be consulted by ballot' was also carried. Thorne stated from his Sunday morning platform that he was

> not in favour of direct action for political purposes; to use the strike weapon for political purposes would mean bloodshed and violence, but if all the wage earners in all parts of the country had the same commonsense as those in Plaistow and Silvertown, they would not now be in the position they were. They should use their political votes to bring about industrial emancipation, and he believed that it could be done without resort to any methods of direct action. (*SE* 16 August 19.)

An editorial in the local press agreed. It was quite legitimate to use the vote for industrial purposes, but the reverse leads 'perilously near to anarchy' (ibid.), not least because it allows a comparatively small number of extremists in trade union meetings to force the membership as a whole into precipitate action. Ballots should be taken.

Thorne was to provide the clearest statement on political action at the NSP Annual Conference later that month:

> To every form of anarchy, whether it be called by its real name, or disguised as Bolshevism or direct action, they as Socialists were resolutely opposed. Men and women who could or would not submit themselves to the task of organisation and discipline necessary to secure the return of a legislative and administrative majority

of working-class delegates or representatives to Parliament and to local bodies were not likely to have the material force and courage necessary to achieve social change by any other method. (*SE* 23 August 19.)

Here is the total delimitation of working-class politics to Labour representation. It is only through parliamentary and municipal action that working-class advances are likely to be secured. Within this process, trade unions had a role, but it was sectional and subordinate to organisations such as the NSP. Outside this process, trade unions had no political role. Trade unions and politics must march together, but separately.

NSP members were active in the run-up to the municipal elections of November. The Plaistow and Silvertown Divisions Registration Committee was established, a parliamentary agent and organiser, B Killip, appointed, and numerous meetings addressed, particularly in support of Scoulding and Rumsey. The trades council, meanwhile, sought to strengthen links with the Stratford Cooperative Society. A meeting between the council and the Political Representation Committee of the SCS expressed hope of future cooperation in political work, and decided that joint conferences should take place before elections (*SE* 26 April 19).

Electioneering was rudely interrupted by the national railway strike. Precipitated by government attempts to standardise wage rates which, if implemented, would lead to widescale reductions, the strike was total among local railway workers. In spite of charges in the local press that it was an anarchist conspiracy, the West Ham Trades Council, Plaistow Labour Party and the church expressed support. The trades council agreed to form a committee to negotiate with the SCS on the best means of ensuring adequate food in the stores for strikers' families (*SE* 4 October 19). A strike fund was set up by the Canning Town branch of the NUR, to which contributions were made by local unionists.

A compromise settlement was reached after nine days. Kirk, who had been active during the strike, later reviewed the lessons to be learned:

> I believe it will be found to have put an end to much of the industrial unrest, particularly among the lesser unions... I am not in favour of political direct action. I believe in constitutional government as opposed to the Soviet form. I am anxious to capture the political machinery for social democracy. It has been my object, no less than that of Mr. Thomas, with whom I have been in constant association, to avoid this strike, but it was forced upon us, and we had no alternative. (*SE* 11 October 19.)

The union detected signs that the success of the strike would boost Labour votes in the impending municipal elections:

> The singular indifference shown in the past by many trade unionists to the success of local candidates is not quite so evident on this occasion, and we do not think we shall have the spectacle of only half a dozen men of a big branch of the N.U.R. going to support one of their own members at the poll... Our duty is to satisfy ourselves by

showing the same solidarity at the poll as in the strike. (*Railway Rev.* 31 October 19.)

Immediately prior to the election, a meeting held by West Ham Central Labour Party showed a united face to the electorate. ILP and NSP candidates under the Labour banner spoke of the potential the election had for real change. Thorne declared that

The trade union vote was not nearly so strong in 1913 as it was today, and in future it would be even stronger because the Socialist, Labour and co-operative movements were rapidly combining. (*SE* 29 October 19.)

The four seats gained by Labour were in the north of the borough where the railway workers' vote was likely to have been strongest. Devenay was elected mayor – the first docker to head a Labour council. Alderman Davis expressed hope that the people of West Ham would not expect too much of the party; it had inherited considerable social problems that were not going to be solved in twenty-four hours.

Much of the political arena after the elections was occupied by struggles around control of the SCS. West Ham Trades Council pledged support for Barnes as president, and McGiff and Clements as members of the management committee (*SE* 24 January 20). Railway workers also had good reason to be interested. During the strike cooperative societies had supplied food to railway workers and placed their financial resources at the disposal of the NUR (p45) This, W J Abraham declared in his presidential address to the 1920 Annual General Meeting, had saved the strike (NUR *Proceedings and Reports* 1920). The Forest Gate branch, which reported better attendances than ever, resolved that members vote for the same three Labour candidates as the trades council (*Railway Rev.* 25 January 20).

The NUR seemed anxious to build on its success in the industrial and political fields. An appeal from Herbert Morrison for continued support claimed that NUR members affiliated to the London Labour Party had increased from 2872 in 1914 to 10,068 in 1919 (ibid. 27 February 20), and a campaign was launched through the *Railway Review*. Page advertisements announced:

Labour's awakening. The call of the N.U.R. to every member to join in the BIG CAMPAIGN for the right to live during sickness and old age, better houses, pensions for mothers, state medical service, farm colonies for consumptives, etc. What part are YOU taking in the great fight? Do not dream about better times, but work for them. (ibid. 6 February 20.)

Thus the NUR continued to display a greater commitment to political action than most other large unions. Its conception of such action, however, was little different. Thomas argued at the 1920 TUC:

There are some in our ranks who have no faith in political action and who point to the alleged failure of the Labour Party as justification of their views. Political action has not failed; it has never been fully tried. Labour has not yet returned to Parliament the number of members its voting strength warranted. (ibid. 19 March 20.)

The Stratford Labour Party adopted Councillor T Groves, a coachmaker at the GER locomotive works, as parliamentary candidate for the division. All four constituencies would now have Labour candidates in the next election. At a meeting of the South West Ham Labour Party Thorne expressed a belief that there would be a revolution over the next ten years in wages and hours 'if the workers used their trade unions and political powers jointly' (SE 31 January 20).

However, the immediate postwar boom was faltering and unions were beginning to lose hold of the economic privileges secured in recent years. A resolution forwarded to the West Ham Trades Council demanding that the TUC call a special conference to 'consider the acute problem of unemployment' was carried, despite feelings expressed by one delegate that the TUC was useless, and that appealing to it was like approaching a relieving officer. During the debate the chair described conditions in the docks as shocking (SE 29 May 20); indeed, casualism had returned. An official of the Dockers' Union claimed that work in the docks had been maintained until recently, when some ships had been diverted to other ports, but demand had increased dramatically. Better conditions granted by the Shaw Inquiry had attracted large numbers of labourers, the majority of whom were regularly turned away (SE 28 August 20).

Sections of the trades council apart, few employed workers were to express interest in the plight of those without work. Trade unions voiced anxiety about the use of casual labour and the financial burden of unemployment benefit, while leaders seemed content to recycle beliefs in national solutions and organising meetings with ex-servicemen's associations. Occasionally, militant assertions of resistance to deteriorating conditions were heard. The newly-formed Stratford 4 branch of the NUR resolved to

> urge the T.U.C. to fix a date to present a demand to the Government to reduce prices of commodities by 100 per cent, and on the Government failing to do so Congress to call a general strike. (Railway Rev. 23 April 20.)

The Canning Town branch of the NUGW complained to the trades council that some corporation employees were working double shifts, and demanded cessation of overtime (SE 26 June 20). Later the West Ham Corporation Employee Federal Council organised meetings when bitter criticism was levelled at the Labour Council for refusing to accept a closed shop and equal pay. The secretary, A Jones, recounted that

> the Labour Party had agreed that there should be equal pay for equal work irrespective of sex. They had asked the Council to agree to this, but the Special Wages Committee reported to the Council that they were unable to accept the principle; but women should receive one-fifth less. It was degrading to the Labour Party that this sort of thing should be going on, and it was up to the Federal Council to see that it was altered. (SE 16 October 20.)

Councillors Wooder and Scoulding (both NSP) were described by the

chair, G Clark, as 'two of the dirtiest tykes he had ever been before'.
Scoulding replied later that the attack was 'one of the most despicable
things that a white man could do to a white man' (*SE* 29 January 21).

The Local Council of Action held an occasional meeting to sustain
protest against intervention in Russia, and support was expressed for
miners during the national strike. At an ILP meeting Devenay argued that
> the miners were forced into the strike. When the war was over…, a
> very large number of people in this country expected that they were
> going to have a new land. It was because of that false impression that
> there had been so many struggles and disputes ever since. (*SE* 23
> October 20.)

Leggatt, district organiser of the National Union of Vehicle Workers,
saw the strike as a new chapter in the history of labour; but at a time of
retrenchment and confusion such assertions were symbolic and isolated.
At the municipal elections, although Labour gained a seat, its poll declined
relatively and absolutely.

3.5 Militant challenges to official labourism

Summing up 1921, Thorne wrote in his union journal:
> Not during the existence of the Union, which commenced 33 years
> ago, has the condition of the wage earners been more pitiful and
> painful than now. The distress in some parts of the country is
> deplorable, and many are crying out at the appalling injustice of
> things. (*Gas Workers' Journal* Jan/Feb 22.)

The NUGW had fared badly in the recession. Membership in December
1923 was a mere 41 per cent of that in June 1921 (Table 3.3), although a
figure of 59 per cent for West Ham suggests that local traditions of loyalty
helped sustain the branches. The damaging effects of this on union finances
were in part mitigated by increased subscriptions; in 1921, for example, the
union claimed a record income of £605,000. Far more serious was the drain
on funds caused by payment of unemployment benefit. In 1921 alone
£550,000 was paid out; at times such expenditure exceeded income. So
serious was the problem that the political fund was suspended (NUGW
General Council *Minutes* May 21), and the general council recommended
that members pay an extra levy of 3 shillings per week. Thorne expressed
surprise to find that as many as 50,000 members voted against the increase
(*Gas Workers' Journal* May/June 21).

Other unions seemed more resilient. Over the same period local branches
of the NUR lost only 20 per cent of their members – a figure close to that
nationally (Table 3.2), while the TGWU actually gained over the first two
years of its existence. These figures compared favourably with the much
higher losses sustained by shopworkers' and labourers' unions, a feature
that Clegg (1985 pp346-7) attributes to the economic performance of the
industries, traditions of loyalty among the membership, and changes in
collective bargaining.

Many unions moved toward amalgamation, paralleling that within cooperation. In the period of frenzied activity promoted by the 1917 Trade Union Act and the influence of syndicalist ideas, the NUR had failed to reach agreement with the craft-based ASLEF, and the NUGW, in spite of discussions with numerous smaller unions, remained essentially unchanged. It was not until 1924 that the desire for 'one big amalgamated Workers' Union' (*Gas Workers' Journal* Jan/Feb 21) was in small part realised by incorporation of the MEA and NAUL. Failed negotiations with the Dockers' Union had taken much time and energy, and now the Dockers, with Bevin at the helm, were steering toward the TGWU.

A series of meetings was organised by the Amalgamation Committee to explain the scheme to members of constituent unions. One at Canning Town Public Hall, filled to overflowing, heard Devenay describe the scheme as the

> finest that had ever been put forward in the interests of the workmen... It gave every workman the opportunity of working out his own salvation without the interference of any other section of workers... Employers were amalgamating in such a way that it was absolutely necessary for the workers to come together and make common cause against their common enemies. (*SE* 15 January 21.)

A resolution endorsing amalgamation was passed unanimously. These sentiments were echoed by Thorne at the thirty-second anniversary celebrations of the NUGW. He hoped

> that they would all stick to the Union, and that instead of there being so many damned foolish unions they would have one huge organisation, and so compete with organised capital and not have the silly jealousy and friction they had today. (*SE* 7 April 22.)

Moves to amalgamate were the most visible attempts of these unions in a period of retreat to reverse declining fortunes. They were specifically industrial measures that built upon and served to perpetuate the schism between the industrial and political spheres, in spite of the militant rhetoric. The collapse of the Triple Alliance in April 1921 merely increased the momentum.

Against this backcloth communists and extreme left-wing members began to exercise an influence in the unions quite disproportionate to their numbers. Repeated denial of entry into the Labour Party and faith in the organised working class, particularly after manifestations of support for the Russian revolution and hostility to British intervention, encouraged communists to devote most effort in this period to work within the trade union movement. Through resources and strategies provided by the Red International of Labour Unions (RILU) – effectively the trade union arm of the Commintern – militant unionists from the Shop Stewards' and Workers' Committee Movement worked within the mainstream to promote revolutionary change (Martin 1969). In the belief that organised workers would soon recognise the irrelevance of reformism and accept the need for such change, this work was regarded as an expedient. With the downturn of industrial militancy after 1920, it became a longer-term strategy.

Although this political current was never able to gain momentum or a significant body of support among trade union branches in West Ham, it was to provide nagging and persistent opposition to labourism, and gave direction to struggles of the unemployed (Chapter 4). Expressions of dissent voiced by the Federation of Corporation Employees, NUR branches and elements within the NUGW were communist inspired, but it was within the industrial section of the trades council that communist influence was strongest. Given the propensity of trades councils to attract union militants, and their perceived potential as agents of radical political change, this was hardly surprising.

A motion from NUGW Plaistow branch to the trades council was used as a vehicle to renew attacks on Labour councillors. The motion registered an emphatic protest against continued interference with free speech, and the wholesale arrest and imprisonment of trade unionists, socialists and communists (*SE* 25 June 21). Whitlock moved an amendment that so long as comrades were in prison, Labour councillors be instructed to boycott royal functions – an explicit reference to the recent attendance of councillors at the royal opening of a war memorial, for which Jones had been censured by the branch.

The matter was not allowed to die. Following a visit from the Duke of York at which Davis, the chair of the trades council had presided in his capacity as mayor, a motion of no confidence in him was forwarded by NUGW Canning Town branch. Monk, in moving, said that

> a kind of disease had come about afflicting some of their so-called Labour leaders… If asking the people to give three cheers for the Duke of York was not violating the principles of Socialism, he did not know what was… It might be the duty of the Mayor of the Borough to do such a thing, but it was not the duty of chairman of such an advanced body as the Trades Council. (*SE* 1 October 21.)

Lake launched into a general attack on the local Labour leadership. He had

> sworn allegiance to the King several years ago. He was 'codded' by the Thornes and other rabble of the Borough, those twisters who had let down the unemployed repeatedly and left them a thousand times worse off. [Davis] was one of the clique and as soon as they realised that there wasn't one with true Socialist principles, and that the Labour Party was a 'wash out' and humbug in the Borough, the sooner would they would be better off.

Davis defended his position vigorously, arguing that he had been asked by the unemployed of Plaistow to attend the function which had raised £700. The vote of no confidence was defeated 44-20, but at the next meeting Davis submitted his resignation, ostensibly on the grounds that his work as mayor left little time for trades council meetings (*SE* 29 October 21). Soon after, the trades council affiliated to the Red International of Labour Unions (*SE* 26 November 21), a decision that prompted the NSP South West Ham branch to write to the Labour Party requesting guidance on their position

(NSP South West Ham branch *Minutes* 23 December 21).

The role of labour leaders in the industrial sphere was also open to attack. The perceived betrayal of the miners by other members of the Triple Alliance on Black Friday provoked particularly hostile reactions. Following a communication from Thomas calling off the proposed strike, NUR Canning Town branch reported:

> Members were solid in support of the miners. The telegram caused a kind of shell shock, stuttering and stammering and loss of speech prevailing. The official explanation awaited with keen interest. (*Railway Rev.* 15 April 21.)

This was the prelude to concerted efforts within the NUR to unseat Thomas. The subsequent handling of a libel case against the *Communist* for publishing a cartoon on his 'betrayal' of the miners, and his appointment as a Privy Councillor provided opportunities for further assaults. Stratford 3 and West Ham branches demanded his resignation from political office, and failing that from union office (ibid. 16 June 22), but Thomas' position within the union was secure. A similar resolution at the 1922 Annual Conference was defeated 76-3 (ibid. 14 July 22).

Thorne was not immune. A RILU pamphlet criticising the NUGW for failing to support the miners was denounced by him at a Sunday meeting (p63). The object of the propaganda, he proceeded to say

> was to try and disrupt every one of the workmen's organisations. They (the General Workers) had found, and the Dockers had found, that there were little bunches of fellows in the branches who were trying to make trade unions almost impossible, with a view to carrying out their ideas and principles. (*SE* 20 August 21.)

With such small numbers, and against the dead weight of labourist hostility to all forms of communist activity and thought, the effectiveness of militant strategies in the political sphere was severely circumscribed. The constituency of the unemployed was to provide a more fertile terrain (Chapter 4). Local communist strength was yet further weakened by a determined union campaign to undermine its structural basis in trades councils. At the 19th Biennial Congress of the NUGW a resolution from Plaistow branch recommended affiliation to the RILU on the grounds that 'if they had to compete with the capitalist class they had to down it' (NUGW General Council *Minutes* 24 November 22). Jones, in reply, asked:

> What was the Red International? Its home was at Moscow, and its promoters were the very people who had prostituted Socialism to such a condition of affairs that today it stunk in the nostrils of serious minded workers in the Labour movement.

In contrast to the RILU, Clynes suggested,

> their union was part of the National Labour movement..., attached to the Labour Party, the T.U.C., and so on, and operating through democratic practice on authority vested in majorities, and again through elected institutions.

The motion was defeated 89-5. As we shall see, when the union turned increasing attention to local representation, so the endorsement of candidates came under more critical scrutiny. A special executive meeting in June 1922 affirmed that financial support would be given only to candidates who were endorsed by the General Council and accepted the constitution of the Labour Party (NUGW General Council *Minutes* 7 June 22). A subsequent request from the Communist Party that the union repudiate the decision of the Labour Party executive to refuse endorsement of communists as Labour candidates was supported; there was no opposition in principle to communist candidates who agreed to accept and conform to the Labour Party constitution and programme. Union affiliation to the Communist Party was refused (ibid. 2 October 24).

More significant was the decision to withdraw from trades councils to which the Minority Movement (successor to the RILU) was affiliated. Replies to questionnaires issued to district committees had indicated 'unanimous opposition' to the affiliation of the Minority Movement to trades councils. This gave the executive necessary justification to recommend that

> where the Minority Movement is officially recognised as part of the Trades Council our Branches should by required to discontinue their affiliation with that Trades Council. Also that Districts should give no financial or moral support to recognised Communists during the municipal elections. (ibid. 20 November 25.)

Affiliation was subsequently withdrawn from West Ham Trades Council. The secretary of the political section immediately requested reaffiliation, 'as that section was entirely separate from the industrial section, and was not in any way connected with the Communist or Minority Movement, as was the industrial section' (NUGW Executive Committee *Minutes* 28 October 26). It was granted, but the threat remained. The executive was soon able to claim that 'In all Districts steps had been taken effectively to combat the pernicious influence and propaganda of the Communist and Minority Movement' (ibid. 18 November 26). A resolution at the 1926 Congress to reverse the decision on trade council affiliation was defeated 85-8 (NUGW General Council *Minutes* 19 November 26).

The TGWU followed a similar trajectory. Early in 1924 it was decided that political funds should be used to sponsor only those candidates endorsed by the Labour Party (TGWU General Executive *Minutes* 17 May 24). An application for a grant from the NUWM 'for the purpose of enabling the Movement to continue the duties entrusted to it by the unemployed workers' was refused (ibid.14 March 24), when less than a year previously £25 had been authorised. No doubt communist attacks on the leadership during the 1923 dock strike and their attempt to form a breakaway union encouraged a change of heart. Bevin was later to record:

> We are harassed by movements like the Minority Movement which are continually publishing and broadcasting false statements regarding the Union, and setting our members by the ears. (TGWU *General Secretary's report*, First Quarter 1926.)

And although the union 'viewed with alarm the prosecution of communists as an attack on free speech', it simultaneously endorsed the action of the Area No 7 secretary in withdrawing affiliation from the Glasgow Trades Council because of its links with the Minority Movement (ibid. 20 November 25), so establishing a principle.

Thomas was no better respected by the communists than Thorne or Bevin, but the NUR showed little of the vituperation expressed by the NUGW. It accepted the 1925 Labour Party conference recommendation 'to refrain from nominating or electing known members of non-affiliated political parties, including Communists' as delegates to Party meetings, but did not hound them in branches. Indeed, there is little evidence of strong anticommunist feeling in local branches. Stratford 2 donated 5 shillings to the RILU; Forest Gate protested against the arrest of communists, and instructed delegates on Leyton Trades Council to vote against their expulsion from the Labour Party (*Railway Rev.* 2 December 21, 30 October 25)

The marginalisation of communist influence within West Ham Trades Council effectively blunted the political edge of its work. By the end of the decade the once powerful industrial body was reduced to submitting suggestions on traffic control and the prevention of smallpox, arranging a conference on the reorganisation of education, and collecting money for hunger marchers. Jim Enever, a delegate to the trade council as early as 1925 recalls that the most frequent resolution discussed concerned the urinals at West Ham football ground. Inadequate provision had forced spectators to use an alley under one of the stands, thereby flooding the adjacent Priory Road. More urinals were demanded (Enever, tape). Municipal employment had taken up much time as the trades council attempted to establish joint conciliation machinery, but here 'nothing of a tangible character had evolved' (West Ham Trades Council *Annual Report* 1929).

Thus the communist challenge to labourist hegemony in West Ham was frustrated by a general antipathy to its ideals and an effective dismantling of its base in the trades council. Individual communists were able to operate with limited success in the industrial sphere, but attempts to destabilise the local Labour leadership, often by recourse to personal invective and disruption of meetings, were an unqualified failure.

3.6 The shift to labour representation

The sudden plunge into economic depression led to a period of union retreat and retrenchment. This in turn engendered political confusion and inertia. The significant advances in West Ham from mid-1921 were made by the unemployed in their struggle against the the board of guardians (Chapter 4), and by the London Cooperative Society, consolidating its authority as a political machine of considerable power (Chapter 2). Trade unions were forced to re-examine political strategies. A report by the Parliamentary Committee of the TUC on joint action with the Labour Party proposed to the 1921 Congress that a National Joint Council be established comprising members of the TUC General Council and executive of the party. It argued:

> The need for coordination of policy and effort within the Labour movement as a whole is recognised. In view of the enormous growth of the Labour movement and the importance of presenting a united front upon the great problems which lie before it, the need for coordination becomes more urgent every day. The effectiveness of the Labour movement has in the past been dissipated by the over-lapping of functions, by duplication of effort, and by confusion arising from conflicting policies. (TUC *Annual Report* 1921.)

The party itself directed attention to the constituencies in an attempt to place local organisation on a more sound and rational footing. This included finance which, owing to widely different trade union rules governing political affiliation, lacked uniformity. With the help of the TUC Parliamentary Committee, pressure was exerted to secure the affiliation to the party of all TUC unions, and on individual unions to encourage their local branches to affiliate to constituency parties and assume attendant obligations (National Agent's Report, Labour Party *Annual Report* 1921). In all districts a woman organiser was appointed, and in most constituencies women's sections with their own officers were established.

This all suggested a groundswell of opinion that the political involve-ment of trade unions should be intensified. Thomas, whose union could demonstrate a continuous record of political intervention, noted with some satisfaction the 569 NUR members on borough and urban councils and 152 on boards of guardians:

> The above figures reflect how widely the sense of citizenship has spread amongst our members. We have every right to be proud as a union of our contributions to Local Government. If the whole movement were only to keep pace with the N.U.R. Labour would soon be on the high road to power in local affairs. (*Railway Rev.* 8 July 21.)

But if other unions had in the past subordinated political activity, there were signs that the balance was being redressed. The NUGW London Or-ganizer, C E Knight fatalistically accepted wage reductions, although he had hoped to see stiffer resistance to them among the membership. As a canvasser during LCC elections he was impressed by the 'new outlook evinced by the younger men and women voters':

> There is no need to despair, as the future is full of possibilities and there is abundant evidence on every hand of a growing intelligence and desire for the new social order; and the work of our branches is to mould the mentality of our members in working for that elevated standard of life when the exploitation of the many by the few will be impossible and the fuller life will be assured to every member of the body politic. (*Gas Workers' Journal* May/June 22.)

It was at this time that Tory pressure mounted to reform legislation governing the political levy. Bills sponsored by backbenchers went so far as to propose a total ban on trade union political intervention (Coates and

Topham 1986 p122). Clynes, clearly anxious about the threat, used the opportunity to assert in unambiguous terms the critical importance of politics:

> While workmen have been defeated in the workshops they have been scoring victories at the ballot box... Unemployment and conditions in the workshop have been turned into political questions... Those who have nothing but their labour possess political power great enough to win economic victories when they have made up their minds to do it. (*Gas Workers' Journal* July/August 22.)

Here are all the components of the new political discourse being constructed by trade union leaders in this period. Industrial retreat may have been forced by employers and the government, but there was no setback to the advance of labour representation. Unemployment and matters affecting work intensified this process. No longer were they questions to be resolved through industrial action, since the unions had relinquished much of their authority in this sphere, but through exercising political power. For although the industrial working class may possess labour power, it possesses greater power in the vote. Once workers recognise this, it was agreed, they can begin to improve their working and living conditions. The point was also emphasised by G Oates, an NUGW officer:

> No trade union nowadays can abstain altogether from political action in protecting its members' interests without taking a vigorous part in promoting, enforcing, or resisting legislation affecting education, sanitation, poor-law, factory, mines, railway, shipping, shop hours, trucks, industrial Arbitration and Conciliation and Trade Board Acts. (ibid. Sept/Oct 22.)

Even if Bevin in the newly-formed TGWU was not as devoted to political work as were the leadership of the NUR and NUGW, the union did sponsor candidates and substantial bodies of opinion within constituent unions were now strongly in favour (p97). Among the principles accepted at the unification conference as 'the furtherance of political objects of all kinds', although an amendment 'having their sole object the abolition of the capitalist system' was defeated (*The Record* October 21). An editorial in the union journal insisted that 'organised labour claims the right to expression in the field of politics just as every other organised section of the community claims that right' (ibid.July 22). Prior to the 1922 municipal elections, the case for exercising the vote was put forcibly:

> We know that there are many who do not pay much attention to municipal affairs, but in our view local politics are quite as important as national politics. It is often said that given good local government there is much that can be achieved towards our ideals, even without an alteration of the present law. It is the duty of every member resident in a municipal borough to cast his [sic] vote on November 1st for the Labour candidate. Apart from the general principle underlying this advice we have to remember that many thousands

of our members are employees of port authorities – tramwaymen, dockers, and numerous other sections of municipal workers. (ibid. October 22.)

Prior to the December General Election, an appeal was made to members 'to renew every possible assistance to the Labour candidate... There is so much that the humblest worker can do to help' (ibid. November 22). At no time, however, was this interest in politics allowed to assume primacy; in the eyes of Bevin strong trade unionism remained the bedrock of Labour politics, for without it 'politics are useless' (ibid. August 22).

There is evidence in West Ham during this period of industrial calm (between the three-month ship joiners' strike that ended in March 1921 and the wave of industrial struggles early in 1923 there was no major conflict) of an intensified concern with political action, felt by virtually all the labour movement. At a NUGW meeting in support of the candidature of Barnes in East Ham South, Thorne and Barnes expressed the hope that the gloom and large-scale exodus from unions would soon be reversed. While Jones declared he

> was not at all despondent over the present economic position, but the more determined, because he realised there was one place where 'Jack was as good as his master', and that was at the ballot box. (*SE* 1 April 22.)

Frank Hodges, secretary of the Miners' Federation, was invited to address a public meeting of the Stratford Labour Party. He detected a new mood among trade unionists that would eventually bring the government down:

> If the six million trade unionists were all politically conscious there could be no possibility of doubt that the first Government after this one was turned out would be a Labour Government. This political consciousness, in spite of the industrial depression, was growing stronger and stronger every day. Don't mistake the feeling in the country, everywhere you can see indications of the new spirit growing out of the desire to show their condemnation of the present Government. (ibid. 22 April 22.)

Meanwhile NUR branches continued to give active support to favoured candidates. Crawford and Batley, both shopmen at the GER works, were returned to the general committee of the LCS, for which they thanked Stratford 2; and the branch instructed its delegates to the political section of West Ham Trades Council to vote for Topham and Davis (*Railway Rev.* 5 May 22). As the municipal and general elections approached Thomas appealed to branches that 'no stone be left unturned in order to ensure that every N.U.R. member shall exercise his vote in favour of the Labour candidate' (ibid. 3 November 22). Stratford 2 held a special branch meeting to introduce Carter and Groves, candidates for East Leyton and Stratford respectively, to members and their wives. Mrs Carter asked the large number of women present to vote for the candidates (ibid. 24 November 22).

Within a month the general election took place. Thorne and Jones were returned with substantial majorities in the south, and Groves beat Lyle at Stratford. Even allowing for an increase in the number of seats at the 1922 municipal election, Labour expanded its vote considerably. All round, much higher polls were recorded. Kirk greeted the results with acclaim:

> in no part of the country did reaction receive a more crushing blow than in West Ham, the classic home of the docker and democracy. West Ham surpassed all previous efforts, and again justified its world-wide reputation as a pioneer and leader of political Labour... The earnest and voluntary work undertaken by railwaymen, dockers, teachers and every section of the organised workers, shows the great possibilities there yet are, when our ranks are closed for political action and our watchword is unity. (*Railway Rev.* 15 December 22.)

Election receipts of the Labour candidates confirm the advantages of union sponsorship. Jones received a total of £435, £426 of which came from the NUGW, £7 from the London Labour Party, and £2 from the NUR Canning Town branch. Gardner, who lost at Upton, received £200 including £100 from the Workers' Supply Association, £58 from the ILP, £17 from the Labour Party, £5 from the NUR Plaistow branch, and £2 from the NUR Canning Town branch. By way of comparison the Tory candidate at Upton, H Margesson, received £609 from head office (*SE* 16 December 22).

3.7 Industrial struggle and the Labour vote

By the close of 1922, the Labour Party had established a secure base within the electorate. It was one that the party was not to lose, and the Labour vote continued its broad upward trajectory. Toward mid-1923 signs appeared that the period of trade union passivity was coming to an end. Old grievances began to surface once again. In April, workers at Silvertown CWS struck for recognition of the National Union of Distributive and Allied Workers, into which the NUCE had merged. At a meeting supported by Groves, Salmon, the branch secretary, announced that the executive would not allow the strikers to stand alone. If the strike was not settled through conciliation machinery set up between the TUC and the cooperative movement, it would be extended nationally (*SE* 26 May 23).

In the light of events that were soon to follow the intervention of J Foster, chair of the West Ham Trades Council, in the Labour Party Conference debate on local organisation was of peculiar salience to an understanding of the current political mood:

> He was very glad to hear that the Executive had come to the conclusion that the local Labour Parties might be some use to them. They had been taking the wrong line when they depended entirely on the trade unions for support... But when they came to some of the constituencies where the Labour Party had a great majority, such as Will Thorne's constituency of Plaistow or Jack Jones' constituency of Silvertown – they were all dockers who belonged to the Labour Party there – it was possible to get them to do a good deal more than they

had done. The British Labour Party had not yet touched the imagination of the working class. They voted for the Labour candidate because they believed they ought to follow their ticket, but that was all. They had to get beyond that stage. (Labour Party *Annual Report* 1923.)

The conversion to politics, then, was incomplete. The Labour Party had successfully instilled a sense of duty to vote Labour during elections, but the allegiance was a fragile one (see Chapter 5). The theory was soon to be tested amongst trade unionists. The unofficial dock strike of July, which began in Hull, immediately spread to other ports including London. Ostensibly a response to attempts by employers to force down wages and undermine the recommendations of the Shaw Inquiry, it was fuelled by a simmering discontent with the TGWU leadership (Bullock 1960 pp273-4). In the eyes of dissident factions, some of which were communist inspired, Bevin and Gosling had sold out the membership by refusing to call a strike. The Victoria and Albert Docks were at a standstill. Meetings held by TGWU officials urged a return to work, but strikers were firm. Foster addressed open air meetings in support of the strike:

> Mr. Bevin and Mr. Gosling were not the Union; the Union was the men who pushed the trucks and did the work in the docks. They should appeal to the whole of the workers to enter the struggle and help them. (*SE* 21 July 23.)

But that was something other unionists seemed reluctant to do. Thorne and Jones refused to support dissident action. When asked about strikers' attitudes to them, Foster added:

> We absolutely ignore them, but they will feel a draught at the next election. The men would not have been men at all if they had not struck against the reductions. (ibid.)

The strike was defeated. More damaging to the TGWU, however, was the determined effort of the small Stevedores' Protection League, which with craft pretensions had stood aloof from the amalgamation, to attract TGWU members into the national Amalgamated Stevedores, Lightermen, Watermen and Workers Union.

Sectional interests also stirred the Associated Society of Locomotive Engineers and Firemen (ASLEF) into organising a meeting at Stratford to defend differentials. Bromley, General Secretary of the Union, pointed to the serious danger of skilled and responsible men being forced into 'fodder labour'. He then commented on the general lessons of recent industrial struggles:

> He did not mind how the working class were organised if they were class conscious… Since the enthusiasm of a few years ago for making big unions those who had studied their movement and looked into it deeply could see that it was the big general union that often shirked the fight. (*SE* 15 September 23.)

The 1923 municipal elections in West Ham saw a fall in the Labour vote, although at the general election Labour candidates were returned in all four constituencies with a marked increase in the vote. This was part of the national trend that resulted in the first Labour government, an event that was not welcomed by Kirk. In a letter sent to the local press he stated:

Nationally, the Labour Party is to take responsibility without power. A month ago we were a revolutionary army marching to victory. Now, without consultation with the rank and file, leaders have committed us to being caretakers of a capitalist machine. (*SE* 29 December 23.)

Such sentiments expose elements within the labourist discourse which, although contradictory, could readily be incorporated. Revolutionary rhetoric on the nature of a capitalist state sprang from a heightened sense of class combativity, but this could coexist with a hostility to communist practice and the Labour leadership – largely because they were infected with middle-class intellectuals sympathetic to foreign political theory – and to strike action. Advocacy of labour representation did not necessarily mean an acceptance of existing political institutions; working-class candidates elected in sufficient numbers could establish statutorily-constituted bodies better able to represent the interests of their constituents. Thus although Kirk could describe himself as a communist, opposed to the 'instinctive labourist', this was because he favoured communal control not proletarian dictatorship (*Railway Rev* 23 May 19).

Labour representation as a principle was accepted by increasing numbers of trade unionists and activists in West Ham, not because of the Labour Party but in spite of it. Thus the period of renewed militancy after 1922 caused only a temporary setback to the municipal Labour vote; the long term upward climb was unmistakable. If anything, union activity intensified during the Labour government's spell in office. In January, the discontent amongst ASLEF members over recommendations of the National Wages Board provoked a strike. It was described as a grave blunder by the NUR, which had been a signatory to the Board agreements. A resolution calling for action at an open meeting of NUR West Ham branch failed to find a seconder (*SE* 26 January 24). At a well attended meeting in Stratford Town Hall organised by the Communist Party on the eve of the Labour government, R Bishop criticised the NUR for a 'most contemptible piece of treachery', concluding that the battle would not be won until they had 615 Members of Parliament, and had organised themselves outside, so that they could march forward with two weapons, one in each hand – the political weapon to protect what they had gained by the industrial weapon (*SE* 26 January 24).

Collapse of the strike after a week was followed almost immediately by a dock strike in support of a pay increase and a guaranteed week. In March a ten day stoppage occurred among train and bus workers. Both strikes had official backing from the TGWU but engendered much resentment against the leadership, particularly when the terms for a return to work were settled (*SE* 2 February 24; 5 April 24). An unofficial strike of 3500 sugar workers at Tate & Lyle broke out in April over the refusal of some workers to join the NUGW, and in May NUGW members at the Hart Accumulator

Company in Stratford struck for holiday payment (*SE* 19 April 24; 3 May 24). July witnessed a strike by the National Federation of Building Trade Operatives, who demanded a forty-four hour week and pay increases (*SE* 26 July 24).

Soon after the defeat of the Labour government, Bevin, who received criticism from Labour leaders for undermining support by pursuing industrial demands, recorded in his report to the union executive:

> The Union is now beginning to reap the fruits of the amalgamation in their fullest sense. The membership is very sound, and taking a survey of the votes cast at the General Election in the big transport areas one cannot help feeling that our membership is becoming as politically conscious as they are industrially loyal... We must now work and strive for an unadulterated Labour government which will be responsive in the fullest sense to the needs of the struggling masses... The fact that reaction is in the saddle for the moment will, I am sure, drive home to our people the obvious lesson that industrial organization must always be the real foundation of our movement.
> (TGWU, General Executive *Minutes 15* November 24.)

After this period of frenetic industrial activity, calm ensued. From July 1924 to May 1926, when the general strike descended, not a single major strike was recorded in West Ham. Rather it was increasing strife between the unemployed and the board of guardians that took centre stage as the crisis moved toward its climax. In the meantime, Labour again began to improve its performance in municipal elections.

Something of the prevailing mood is caught by a brief episode at Tate & Lyle's refinery. An arbitration award, part of which demanded increased output and abolition of the bonus system, was declined by 400 sugar workers. The company sacked them. A march demanding reinstatement was organised with the help of the South West Ham branch of the NUWM, but on reaching the factory it was met by a large body of police. Speakers attempted to engage the interest of workers leaving the factory, but few stopped; appeals to show sympathy with dismissed workers went unheard (*SE* 18 April 25), and at a NUGW meeting Hollins said he detected signs that employers were preparing for a 'combined attack on the workmen', the only answer to which was to build the unions (*SE* 18 July 25).

Early in 1926 the union held meetings on the 'inseparable link' between trade unionism and politics. 'Long ago', Gardner said, 'they in West Ham saw the necessity of trade unionism and politics being linked together, and the rest of the country followed. It was more necessary as time went on' (*SE* 16 January 26). Examining the record of the Tory government, Hollins concluded that 'sooner or later people in the country would realise that their only hope of economic salvation was to return working class representatives to the House of Commons' (*SE* 6 February 26).

The general strike erupted unexpectedly in West Ham, but commanded widespread support among trade unionists. The docks, public transport and services, including the municipal supply of electrical power were stopped, although convoys with military escorts managed to unload and transport food supplies from the docks. In the aftermath Thorne declared that far from being a general strike it was only partial:

> A general strike would never succeed in this country – and it had never succeeded anywhere else – until they had the political machinery behind them. They had a majority of Tory members but they could not make him believe that if there had been a Labour Government in power they would have had this dispute. (*SE* 19 June 26).

He was constantly heckled by a communist contingent but was not to be moved. Elsewhere he said:

> So far as he was concerned personally he took up an attitude on the matter as far back as 1884, and he had not shifted his position at all. He was convinced they would have to get back to the old programme of many years ago. (*SE* 29 May 26).

It was a fitting epitaph from the single most dominant figure in West Ham politics and trade unionism.

The West Ham Board of Guardians was soon to be dismantled by the government, an act that effectively undermined Alliance support. By now Labour held unchallengeable authority at municipal and parliamentary levels. A decline in the absolute level of Labour voting from this period was hastened by a recognition of this authority, and the fact that an increasing number of impregnable Labour seats were not contested.

The experience of local politics in West Ham during the 1920s does then suggest that trade unions influenced the boundaries of the political arena and, within that arena, the course of labour representation. But the nature of this influence is not one that can readily be described by overarching theoretical scenarios. Not only did the unions have different perspectives on the nature of political involvement, but the perspectives themselves were subject to change over time.

In purely quantitative terms, trade union members in West Ham could dominate voting. The municipal franchise in 1922, for example, was 114,684. Of this, 64,987 voted, 37,078 for Labour candidates. Estimates of trade union membership in the area, on the other hand, are largely speculative, but that of 30,000 cited by Thorne may not have been very wide of the mark, considering that the combined membership of NUR, NUGW and TGWU branches was was about 18,000. This was comparable to the number of cooperators and vastly exceeded membership of the local Labour parties (p165). But this numerical domination did not lead inevitably or unproblematically to a wholesale commitment to the Labour Party. Labourism drove a wedge between industrial and political activity; in this, trade unions displayed an instrumental complicity which in important respects determined the course of future action. Trade unions could legitimately intervene in both spheres, but the political sphere – delimited to municipal and parliamentary representation – was increasingly recognised to be the province of the Labour Party. Thus industrial struggles in

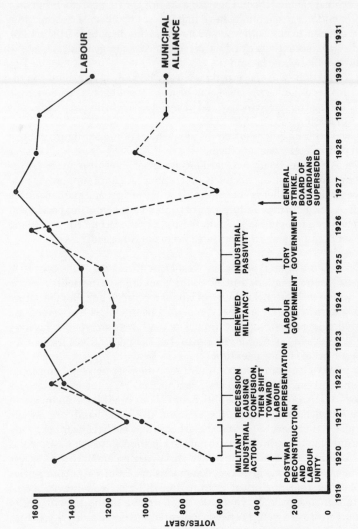

FIGURE 3.1 *West Ham Municipal elections, 1919–1930, votes per seat*

themselves could not be used to promote political change. Change was to be effected through labour representatives who could introduce appropriate industrial legislation or, at the municipal level, improve social and economic conditions for the working class. Outside labour representation, trade unions had no political role.

Not all trade unions were incorporated totally by labourist discourses defining legitimate boundaries of political action. The leaderships of the NUR, NUGW and TGWU were all prepared, with reluctance, to support strike action if necessary to safeguard members' interests, although this was rarely allowed to take the form of direct action in pursuit of political objectives. Differences did exist, however, in the degree to which they were prepared to give active support to the principles of labour representation.

The complex interplay of these forces in a changing industrial and political climate determined the influence exerted by trade unions on the Labour Party. In the immediate postwar period, the Labour vote in West Ham derived its strength from established traditions of Labour representation and expectations of a new social order (Figure 3.1). The impulse toward unity among labour ranks overcame potentially damaging splits. Most tangible progress occurred in southern wards where a favourable electoral base compensated for a less than total commitment among members of the NUGW and the Dockers' Union to the Labour Party. Indeed, direct political intervention by these unions was minimal in this period; it was confined largely to providing support for their candidates when challenged by more radical traditions within the labour movement. In northern constituencies, the unambiguous political commitment of NUR members was not sufficient to overcome a relatively unfavourable electoral base.

As industrial militancy increased and trade unions began to realise their enhanced strategic strength within production, the commitment to Labour representation declined, and the Labour vote fell. This was reversed when the economy plunged into recession, and the industrial fortunes of the unions declined. Following a period of confusion, trade unions and Labour Party members began to re-examine the nature of political intervention. Changes in labourist discourses encouraged unionists increasingly to seek advance through the channels of Labour representation.

There was a temporary setback during the period of renewed industrial militancy in 1923, but the upward climb in the level of Labour voting continued. This movement is reflected in the parliamentary vote (Figure 3.2). Here, although short-term fluctuations are masked, the same steady growth in Labour votes appears. The divergence in the Labour vote at municipal and parliamentary level after 1926 was due to the collapse of the Alliance vote and the increasing number of uncontested Labour seats.

The evidence does suggest that in this period a relationship existed between industrial and political activity of trade unions, so that as one declined the other increased. The precise causal connection is difficult to define. The emphasis here has perhaps been on the political responding to

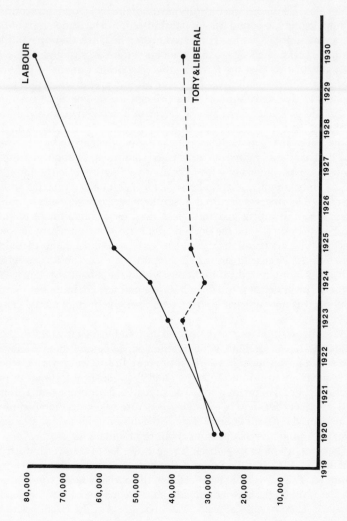

FIGURE 3.2 *West Ham general elections, 1919–1929, votes cast for Labour and Tory & Liberal*

changes in the industrial sphere, but the relationship was reciprocal. Labourist discourses on labour representation articulated by the Labour Party proved increasingly attractive to trade unionists, simultaneously loosening belief in the inviolability of industrial power and the legitimacy of mobilising that power in pursuit of political objectives. This discourse, as we have seen in this Chapter, attracted other constituencies; without this the upward movement of the Labour vote, inflected as it was by trade union intervention, would not have been so pronounced or, indeed, so certain.

4

THE CHALLENGE OF POOR LAW STRUGGLES

He had nothing to regret, and was glad that the opportunity
had been given to him to do some little good while on earth.
(Report of a speech by Sir Alfred Woodgate in response to a
presentation by the Forest Gate Ratepayers' Association in
appreciation of his services as chairman of the government-
appointed Board of Guardians for West Ham, *Stratford Express*
May 1930.)

Amongst the growing, but as yet relatively small body of literature on
interwar Britain, there is a persistent and justifiable interest in unemployment. The advent of widespread, chronic unemployment was one of the
principal structural features of the British economy, and the attendant
distress constituted a massive challenge to social policy. It is perhaps not
surprising, therefore, that much of this interest has been directed to an
understanding of the economics of unemployment, especially since deficiencies in the Keynesian models have been detected in the light of postwar
experience (see Glynn and Booth 1983 for a good review), and, with equally
significant current relevance, to the social effects of unemployment and
policy measures adopted to deal with them (Gilbert 1976, Whiteside 1987,
Mitchell 1985).

By comparison, the politics of unemployment has received scant attention. One contemporary account of unemployed struggles has become a
classic (Hannington 1977), although it understandably stresses the role of
the NUWM; and, more recently, Croucher (1987) has covered similar ground
with the advantage of access to a wider range of documentary material.
Kingsford (1982) has usefully examined hunger marches, and there have
been local studies which, within a wider concern to investigate the
experience of unemployment, have touched on political aspects (Nicholas
1986). But overall our understanding of the political dynamics of
unemployed struggles in the interwar period is superficial.

It would appear that just as the structural basis of unemployment had
a regional bias and shifted over time, so too did the context and nature of
unemployed struggles. Generalisations are always imprecise, here

particularly so; the case for local studies is a valid one. And if attention has been focused on the more obvious manifestations of these struggles – hunger marches, demonstrations against boards of guardians – it has been at the expense of a recognition of the prevailing abstinence in many locations over long periods.

West Ham witnessed unemployed struggles in the 1920s that had a profound impact on the operation of the poor law. In response to repeated failures to deal effectively with the problem, the government intervened and superseded the West Ham Board of Guardians, so accelerating the abolition of the whole poor law machinery. Locally, the unemployed constituted the most determined opposition to the dominant labourist tradition of political action. The nature of this challenge and its subsequent demise is the subject of this chapter.

Although it has been necessary to consider the national context at particular moments, we cannot here embark upon detailed examination of the politics of state action in the dispute. In superseding the guardians, the government threatened not only fundamental principles of the poor law, but also the whole basis of local representational democracy. The historical and political specificity of this action in a national context requires a separate study.

4.1 Unemployment in West Ham

The industrial decline of West Ham in the interwar period (p17-19 above) had a dramatic impact on unemployment. The most complete, reliable and dynamic guide to the extent of local unemployment is data on insured persons registered at employment exchanges. A continuous series based on aggregate numbers of books lodged at each of the exchanges from 1921 to 1938 survive; details are reproduced in Table 4.1. These data were subsequently used by the Ministry of Labour to publish the monthly Local Unemployment Index from 1927 to 1938, in which registered unemployed at individual exchanges are expressed as a percentage of the insured population. Such information for Stratford and Canning Town combined, together with that for London and Great Britain is also included.

The data show that although movements in levels of unemployment within West Ham followed closely those in the metropolis as a whole, overall levels were consistently higher than those of both London and Great Britain. To place the figures in perspective comparisons can be made among different geographical areas and individual exchanges. In January 1927, for example, West Ham had a rate of 19.0 per cent, which was higher than London (6.5%) and Poplar (13.2%) – the worst affected metropolitan borough – and East Ham (8.1%), but lower than Glamorgan (23.7%) and Durham (27.6%) – both areas of the country devastated by the collapse of staple industries. Unemployment registered by the Merthyr Tydfil exchange in Glamorgan was 66.6 per cent. Thus West Ham experienced levels of unemployment among insured workers that were markedly higher than those for the metropolitan area (indeed for the whole

TABLE 4.1 *Unemployed registered at the Canning Town, Stratford and London labour at exchanges, and unemployed as a percentage of the insured population for West Ham, London and Great Britain, 1921–38.*

	Canning[a] Town	Stratford[a]	London[a]	West Ham	London	GB
1921	11,138	8,051	239,660			16.6
1922	11,208	8,001	233,604			14.1
1923	11,460	7,565	195,689			11.6
1924	9,517	6,435	157,131			10.2
1925	9,538	5,405	140,230			11.0
1926	8,951	5,668	142,086			12.3
1927	7,102	4,727	126,457	16.8	5.0	9.6
1928	7,441	3,926	120,296	16.1	4.9	10.7
1929	7,821	3,758	123,194	15.8	5.6	10.3
1930	9,485	5,770	178,761	20.3	8.1	15.8
1931	11,471	8,232	281,058	27.5	12.2	21.1
1932	11,872	9,066	321,839	26.4	13.5	21.9
1933	10,641	8,274	290,464	23.8[b]	11.8	19.8
1934	9,360	6,546	227,538	20.0	9.2	16.6
1935	8,547	5,907	214,783	18.2	8.5	15.3
1936	7,104	4,898	191,741	15.1	7.2	12.9
1937	5,913	4,012	177,173	12.5	6.3	10.6
1938	6,928	5,040	259,071	15.1	8.9	12.6

Source: Marriott (1989).

Notes: [a] Average of Jan., Apr., July and Oct. totals.

[b] Here classification of data in the *Local Unemployment Index* changes from percentage of insured population to percentage of resident population. To ensure comparability, levels for 1933-8 have been calculated as percentage of insured population on the assumption that the numbers of insured workers did not change significantly. This is a valid assumption; July figures for 1933-7 (West Ham Medical Officer of Health, *Annual Report* (1937) Table II) show a variation of less than 5 per cent.

south-east region, whose levels were very close to those of London, see Beveridge 1944 Table 5).

The qualitative nature of unemployment in the interwar period was distinguished by the existence of a hard core of unemployed workers associated with certain depressed industries. The depth and persistence of this depression – a lineal descendant of cyclical movements in demand since 1785 (ibid. Appendix A) – had a profound effect on the employment patterns of some hundreds of thousands of workers. These no longer faced, at worst, intermittent periods of unemployment due to fluctuations in demand, but chronic unemployment with little prospect of work. Three investigations into the circumstances of claimants for unemployment benefit conducted by the Ministry of Labour (Ministry of Labour 1924, 1926, 1928) revealed that a considerable majority would in 'normal' times have been in steady employment (see also Davison 1929). But long-term unemployment was relatively uncommon in the 1920s, averaging nationally about 5 per cent (Glynn and Booth 1983). As the depression persisted, the proportion increased, reaching 25 per cent in the mid-1930s. Ages most affected were the young who failed to gain entry into a skilled trade, and the old who, having lost employment, could not compete for opportunities when they arose.

Quantitatively more significant than this body of chronically unemployed were those subject to fluctuations in demand characteristic of the prewar economy. Intermittent unemployment due to seasonality or casual demand was at consistently higher levels in the interwar period. The amplitude of fluctuation in demand for labour in seasonal industries varied positively with the general level of employment. Thus in the interwar depression fluctuations intensified, although as the depression deepened the relative importance of seasonal unemployment diminished (Saunders 1936). Several structural tendencies augmented their amplitude. Rising standards of living and falling costs of production encouraged the growth of industries that were subject to the vicissitudes of fashion. Mass production also affected the demand for semiskilled labour to operate specialised machinery, making it more difficult for workers to move from one job to another; and general improvement in the organisation of production and distribution rendered it less necessary to stockpile on a large scale.

Most industries continued to be affected by seasonality. Largest fluctuations tended to occur in those dominated by small firms tied to traditional techniques of production, for example, the building and clothing trades, or in those where consumer demand was closely linked to climate, for example coal (ibid. Appendix III). Employment patterns of approximately 75 per cent of insured workers and many uninsured workers were vulnerable to regular seasonal fluctuations.

Of greater magnitude and enhanced state concern was the problem of casual labour. Liberal philanthropic efforts amidst disquiet induced by social unrest in the prewar period had focused attention on casual labour, eventually provoking the state to take measures that, implicitly, were designed to restrict the practice. The hope that labour exchanges would encourage casual labourers to adopt different work habits by instilling a sense of regularity had foundered on the rocks of employer and employee apathy. Compulsory registration, which may have been effective in promoting decasualisation, was abandoned in the early stages of planning. The unemployment insurance scheme deliberately excluded industries with large proportions of casual labour in order to preserve actuarial stability. The state renewed efforts in the immediate postwar period, when there seemed a real opportunity to eliminate casual labour by preventing its re-emergence (Whiteside 1979). But intervention in the labour market was met with hostility by employers, who in the main benefited from a reserve of labour. As a consequence, not only were measures to promote decasualisation advocated with little determination, but also 'decasualising' clauses in the 1911 National Insurance Act were abolished.

Initially, the safeguards built into the enlarged actuarial base of the 1920

Insurance Act prevented casual labour exploiting the system. As the rigid proportionality of benefits to contributions began to be undermined by the introduction of a series of emergency measures (principally the out-of-work donation and then extended benefit) so the practice of casual labour once again seemed attractive to employers and to certain sections of the workforce.

By the 1930s the scale of casual labour probably exceeded that of the prewar period. State intervention, far from providing order to the labour market, actually consolidated the entropy. Casual labour persisted because employers who practised the system, and workers who had been complicit, resisted attempts at reform. At a political level, employers were hostile to decasualisation because they believed that any restriction of the labour supply (including strike breakers) would lead to an increase in wages and a strengthening of the unions. At a practical level, employers wished to retain the flexibility in hiring labour that the casual system provided. This was crucial to an industry like the docks where the demand for labour fluctuated violently; but even in industries not so affected, employers were able to exploit the system to their advantage, particularly during times of high unemployment:

> Skilled workers would go around and find themselves temporary jobs whereas unskilled couldn't. A skilled worker could do an unskilled worker's job. If an employer gets a skilled worker he knows he's got skills already to hand. He would always pay his wages as a labourer, so if he's a brickie he would say 'There's a little bit of work over there'. 'Certainly gov', and they'd go over and do it for a labourer's money. That happened quite a lot. (Robinson, tape.)

Unemployment, therefore, was more likely to affect semiskilled and unskilled labour in the interwar period, the incidence increasing markedly in lower status occupations. The evidence for a stratified labour market is strong (Glynn and Booth 1983). Within this broad scenario gender was significant. All the structural changes to patterns of unemployment had a disproportionately adverse effect on women. Female unemployment is considerably understated by the statistics because of under-registration; throughout the interwar period it remained widespread and persistent.

The evidence for a stratified system of relief for the unemployed is even stronger. In response to mounting unemployment the government made concessions to an increasingly restive body of unemployed. Most important among these was a series of unemployed insurance schemes which gradually extended the number of insured workers and the range of benefits available from labour exchanges (Gilbert 1976). For those who were not covered, had exhausted their benefit entitlement or were disallowed, there was the ancient and feared institution of the poor law.

Given that the large majority of skilled and semiskilled workers were insured under the 1921 National Insurance Act, and that most of these in the 1920s were able to find new work after comparatively short periods of unemployment, it was disproportionately the unskilled who were forced

TABLE 4.2 *Persons and dependants receiving poor law relief on account of unemployment, expressed per 10,000 of the population and as a percentage of all relief, in West Ham and Poplar unions, London and England, 1 January 1922–1927.*

	1922		1923		1924		1925		1926	
	per 10^4	%	per 10^4	%	per 10^4	%	per 10^4	%	per 10^4	%
West Ham	471	63.2	696	68.4	716	67.8	612	61.4	621	62.7
Poplar	970	62.7	1164	61.7	1065	56.1	837	48.1	837	44.7
London	266	49.5	299	51.1	227	43.0	159	34.4	204	37.7
England	191	49.9	189	46.9	141	39.7	83	27.5	125	33.8

Source: *Persons in receipt of Poor Law relief (England and Wales)*, PPXVII (1922), PPXIX (1923), PPXIX (1924), PPXXIII (1925), PPXXIII (1926), PPXIX (1927).

onto the poor law. Data on the extent of such relief are as unreliable as those on unemployment. Poor law unions submitted detailed records on relief, but it was not until relief on account of unemployment began to be perceived as a problem that it was identified separately, and even then only in the published annual returns of persons (and dependants) in receipt of relief on the first day of each year.

Data for the West Ham Union together, by way of comparison with those for Poplar, London and England, are given in Table 4.2. This reveals that the level of unemployment relief in West Ham, expressed as a percentage of the population and of total relief, was dramatically higher in West Ham than in London or nationally. Indeed, until the effects of the 1925 miners' strike were felt, the extent of unemployed relief in West Ham was exceeded only by Poplar, largely as a result of the equalisation of rates secured by the guardians' struggle in 1922. Equally dramatic was the shift in the nature of relief forced by unemployment. Prior to the onset of mass unemployment, outdoor relief comprised 58 per cent of all relief. Women and children formed 76 per cent of the total. In 1922, outdoor relief comprised 89 per cent.

I have argued, largely from evidence on the structural nature of unemployment and the poor law and insurance systems, that it was disproportionately the unskilled that were forced to resort to unemployment relief. This picture tends to be supported if not confirmed by returns made possible from the West Ham Union by the appointed commissioners three months after they took office (Table 4.3). A conservative estimate suggests that at least 75 per cent of those receiving unemployment relief were unskilled – a figure that would have been yet higher in the preceding period since one of the first acts of the commissioners was to cut unemployment relief by a third, mostly by expelling longer-term, unskilled unemployed from the books.

And yet it was around the Board of Guardians and not the labour exchanges that the most persistent unemployed struggles were waged in the 1920s. In this context, the experience of West Ham was highly significant, for it was here in 1926 that the state intervened to take control of a

TABLE 4.3 *Occupational classification of unemployed persons in receipt of relief from West Ham Board of guardians during week ending 4 September 1926.*

MALE		FEMALE	
Railwaymen	91	Domestics	158
Road transport workers	319	Charwomen	189
Dock labourers	1470	Clerks and typists	18
Food trade workers	61	Needlewomen and machinists	72
Warehousemen/storekeepers	192	Shop assistants	29
Shop assistants	115	Factory workers	295
Clerks	216	Printing and stationery	25
Building labourers	526	Others	422
Skilled builders	138		
Plumbers and pipe fitters	66		
Foundry and metal workers	213		
Motor mechanics	52		
Electrical workers	59		
Carpenters	132		
Costermongers and hawkers	103		
Other skilled	1328		
Other unskilled	4272		
TOTAL	9353		1208

Source: West Ham Union, *Report of the Board of Guardians on their administration for the period 26 July 1926 to 30 October 1926*, Cmnd 2786, PPXV (1926).

board of guardians that was considered defiant in persisting to administer liberal scales of relief. In what follows, I shall examine the nature of this struggle around poor law relief in the hope of illuminating the dynamics of unemployed politics before the onset of chronic, mass unemployment in the 1930s and the dismantling of the old poor law apparatus in 1929.

4.2 Postwar recession

Toward the end of 1920 signs appeared that the brief postwar boom was faltering. A decline, initially felt in the cotton and footwear industries, spread rapidly to all the principal industries. The miners' strike in October 1920 accelerated a process which continued unabated through 1921. 'The key note of last year's report was development and unprecedented demand', wrote the Chief Inspector of Factories in the annual report for 1921 (PP XII), 'the key note of this is, unfortunately, black depression... By the end of 1920 there was scarcely an industry in the country that was not working short time, and many works were entirely closed down'.

Industry in West Ham was badly affected. Dock work collapsed, and large numbers of workers were made idle in the glass, india rubber and confectionery industries. Shipwrights and boilermakers, already beginning to feel the effects of a rapid decline in shipbuilding and repairing following the end of the war, were laid off by a prolonged strike of ships' joiners. Only chemicals and allied trades seemed immune. Registrations at employment exchanges increased dramatically. Numbers were much higher than any experienced before the war, not only because unemployment reached unprecedented levels but also because sections of the working population previously excluded from unemployment insurance schemes now came into contact with exchanges by virtue of the latter's responsibility for the administration of the 1918 out of work donation and benefits paid out under the 1920 Unemployment Insurance Act.

The scale and suddenness of the increase in unemployment aggravated distress and confusion among the unemployed, and left local authorities responsible for dealing with the problem in disarray. Early responses from the unemployed themselves were tentative and without direction. Local branches of the National Federation of Discharged and Demobilised Soldiers and Sailors organised street collections with the active support of the Labour Party. The West Ham Central Unemployed Committee asked the mayor to make an appeal for financial assistance (WHC *Minutes* 14 December 20).

However, these were never considered by local labour organisations to be more than short-term ameliorations of distress. A more permanent remedy had to be sought in the intervention of central government. A deputation from West Ham Trades Council and Central Labour Party to a conference on unemployment convened by the Board of Guardians late in 1920 argued that many young men were walking the streets and sleeping out of doors. Broken in health and spirit they were being driven to desperate straits. They were not seeking charity, but productive work in schemes organised by the council and financed by the government (*SE* 18 December 20). The local press, while voicing anxieties about the situation, asserted the potential of such schemes:

> The unemployed situation, particularly in West Ham, is developing apace, and the Government have begun to realise that something more than words, something beyond reiteration of past accomplishments, is demanded by the exigencies of the position. It is still true that nothing has been done, but preparations for real activity are in hand, and local authorities may look for assistance in approved schemes devised for local relief of unemployment. (*SE* 25 December 20.)

In the absence of financial support, and in spite of obvious fears of unrest, there seemed little that local authorities could do. Paul, leader of the Moderates on the West Ham Board of Guardians, expressed the essential dilemma of ratepayers:

> As a landlord myself I do not think it is the duty of the Guardians to provide the money. Hungry men, however, are dangerous and I don't know what will happen if these men are allowed to go hungry… Their upkeep should be a national charge and not forced upon the borough. The only thing was to organize, as the workers had done, and force the hands of the Government. (ibid.)

The mayor expressed the hope that

> the unemployed would not take any steps until they found that the Council had failed to do everything that could be done. If the Council

failed to do anything then he would not be responsible for what happened. He hoped the unemployed would work with the Council for he believed it would be better in the long run. (ibid.)

Demands for a national solution to unemployment were neither new nor radical. In the prewar period the official labour leadership, in particular Thorne, had repeatedly defended their refusal to support the local unemployed struggles on the grounds that it was a national problem and hence demanded solution at that level. Now the demand was taken up by Moderate and Labour alike.

Early in 1920, before the onset of mass unemployment and the turn to poor relief, a deputation from the Moderate-controlled West Ham guardians to the Minister of Health pointed to the inadequacy of ordinary grants of out-relief in the face of rapidly increasing food costs. For local needs to be met, 'it was most inequitable that the increased charges should be borne locally, and they urged that the time had now arrived to make expenditure on out-relief a national charge' (WHBG *Minutes* 29 January 20). The minister held out out little prospect of financial aid; to concede the argument would mean dismantling discourses around relief that had dominated since the establishment of the poor law system in sixteenth-century England (p132).

West Ham Council fared no better. As a local authority it had neither statutory obligation nor the appropriate machinery to relieve distress. In the prewar period, however, it had provided a limited number of employment relief schemes in times of severe depression, and these formed the basis of renewed activity. The strategy was encouraged by a cabinet committee scheme to finance in part a national programme of road construction and maintenance, including an arterial road at Dagenham upon which West Ham unemployed would work.

Further pressure was brought to bear on the government in December 1920 by a deputation from a conference attended by thirty~three boroughs suffering high levels of unemployment. Concern was expressed about the menace of the unemployed, and demands voiced for a 75 per cent grant toward local relief schemes. The government, preoccupied with the demolition of the actuarial base of the national insurance scheme by the onset of mass unemployment, remained deaf to the appeals, and nothing more was heard of the programme of relief work. Instead, a £3m fund was established, applications to which could be made by councils willing to advance two-thirds of the wages plus the cost of materials for any relief scheme. West Ham Council, with overdrafts totalling £135,000, a high rate of interest to pay on borrowed money, and facing an unemployed movement without organisation or direction, initiated little relief work. In the winter of 1920-21, for example, 749 men were offered work clearing snow and preparing the memorial sports ground. Of these, 419 reported and worked for an average of ten days (*SE* 29 January 20).

Relief schemes of the interwar period, like those prewar, proved totally inadequate in dealing with the problem of unemployment. And they were recognised to be so. Groves, member of the ILP and future MP for North West Ham, stated at a meeting on unemployment that such schemes would not solve the question, but that it was the duty of the council to maintain pressure on the government (*SE* 6 November 20). A deputation to the council from the West Ham Unemployed Committee shortly afterwards requested that hostels be provided, schools be cleaned by the unemployed, and that road making commence as soon as possible.

Toward the end of 1920 the guardians also were impelled to adopt the first hesitating steps to relieve the unemployed. In doing so they made use of the 1911 Relief Regulation Order which, while denying guardians the right to grant wholesale outdoor relief, authorised them in special circumstances to grant relief to the unemployed, provided their action was subsequently reported to the Ministry of Health. A letter from the ministry gave tacit approval for such action, but at the same time asserted that the guardians needed to exercise appropriate control:

> It is recognised that the Guardians have been led to adopt a policy by natural sympathy with the needs of those suffering from unemployment at present prevailing. It is felt, however, that the Guardians must be reminded of some of the consequences of this policy... If no conditions are attached there is the risk that relief will be abused and the expenditure of the Guardians would rapidly exceed the rate of expenditure upon which their estimates for the half year have been based... It is therefore incumbent upon the Guardians to examine each individual case, especially in view of the continuation of unemployment donations for ex-servicemen until March, of the abolition of the qualifying period for new entrants under the Unemployed Act, and of other special measures taken by the Government for the relief of unemployment, otherwise there would be serious overlapping. (WHBG *Minutes* 13 January 21.)

As a measure to deal with the problem of distress, it was characteristically ill-conceived and dilatory. Doubtless thought to be a means of easing pressure on the national exchequer by shifting the onus of unemployment relief to local taxation, few could have predicted the influence it would wield on future patterns of relief and the course of unemployed struggles.

4.3 Discourses around relief

Pressure was also being brought to bear on the guardians by the unemployed themselves. Following police suppression of a large unemployed demonstration near Whitehall on 18 October 1920, the London District Council of the Unemployed (LDCU) was formed under the leadership of Wal Hannington (Hannington 1977 pl8). Small though it was, it imparted a degree of organisation and political direction to the unemployed. Through a united front policy the LDCU established contact with George Lansbury (Croucher 1987 p31), who at the time was engaged in the Poplar rate revolt in support of equalisation of the rates (Branson 1979). During the campaign Lansbury had come to recognise the potential of the poor law system as a means of relieving distress from unemployment, and through the *Daily Herald* promoted the slogan 'Go to the Guardians'. This was taken up by the LDCU, and with 'Work or full maintenance' was to become its principal platform throughout the 1920s. Given the significance that these demands came to hold, it is worth examining their political specificity in some detail, in particular the extent to which they opposed dominant discourses on relief and unemployment.

'Go to the Guardians' was a deliberate challenge to the institution of the poor law. Through this institution relief was administered by local authorities operating within definite procedures and inscribed within powerful ideologies governing relationships among the state, the guardians and the poor. Previous challenges had been witnessed. In the years of depression following the end of the Napoleonic wars, for example, levels of relief climbed sharply as a result of the inability of a defective poor law machinery to deal with a renewed militancy in the poor. Such defects, however, had been overcome by the implementation of the 1834 Poor Law (Amendment) Act. The effectivity of this Act derived from its ability to assert new definitions and delimitations in networks of differences. After 1834 the poor law enforced boundaries around different kinds of indigence, so differentiating classes of poor subjects as objects of relief, repression or treatment. The principal separation effected was between able-bodied unemployed and the non able-bodied, namely, the young, old and chronically sick (Williams 1981 p36).

The differentiation, however, was not as complete and definite as these categories imply. The report of the Royal Commission upon which the subsequent act was based had as an underlying principle the distinction between poor and indigent (see the meticulous discussion in Himmelfarb 1984). Paradoxically, not the poor but the indigent (the aged and sick) were entitled to poor relief, and in this respect there was no significant discontinuity from the foundations in Elizabethan laws. The poor themselves were differentiated between able-bodied paupers and the independent labourers in a state of poverty.

This separation in part resolved ambiguities in the definition of the poor that had resulted, it was believed, in widespread abuse of the poor law. Under the new system paupers would be entitled to relief, but only to maintain a condition that was 'less eligible' than the lowest class of labourer. The essential principle of less eligibility would rescue the poor from pauperisation, and thus prevent the superior moral condition of the independent labourer from degradation by indolence, dishonesty and dependence; this in spite of the common experience of the poor labourer living on less money than the pauper. Degradation rather than material condition defined the pauper (ibid. p163). More than that, a reduction in pauperisation would help alleviate a cycle of socio-economic pathologies. The consequences of agricultural unemployment, low productivity, population increases, low wages and high food prices could be resolved by minimising outrelief.

The restructuring of boundaries effected by the 1834 Poor Law had a profound impact. The poor law may have been applied unevenly, but statistical evidence suggests that whereas before 1834 it was committed to the relief of able-bodied labour, most notably the unemployed, by the end of the century such relief had virtually ceased (Williams 1981 p41). This process, however, was not merely due to the implementation of new definitions and procedures. Social and political relations were also transformed. With the rationalisation of relief came a reassertion of strict authoritarian values. Those receiving relief were reconstituted as subordinate and obligated subjectivities. The receipt of relief was a shameful act for which the paupers themselves were, through idleness or lack of thrift, largely responsible. The ritual of handing out relief to the assembled poor had strong religious associations through which mercy and paternalism served to reinforce authority relationships far more effectively than could overt power. Under such circumstances, only out of desperation would a labourer turn to the poor law; the stigma attached to the whole notion of relief, especially indoor relief, was a powerful deterrent.

The poor survived significant shifts in discourses on unemployment and poverty that occurred toward the end of the century. The reformulations that resulted from increased concern expressed by social reformers and investigators about the social and political dangers of the residuum merely reinforced differentiations among the poor. There may have been a new recognition of the nature of unemployment, but this led to a preoccupation with preventative measures rather than reform of the poor law through exorcising the underlying principle of individual pathology. Rather, distinctions between poor and pauper were rearticulated; now the separations that had to be secured were 'respectable' versus 'residuum', 'deserving' versus 'undeserving'.

The 1911 Relief Regulation Order appears to be a simple rationalisation of earlier orders governing aspects of the administration of relief. It proposed no changes in the broad principles, and had no effect on the numbers receiving relief before the outbreak of the war. But in other respects it was significantly novel (ibid. pp130-35). All unions were now required to offer outrelief with a labour test to the unemployed, although a guardians' labour yard could be closed and outrelief stopped at any time. More important, guardians had to maintain a strict surveillance on all paupers receiving relief. Data on each claimant, including occupation and earnings, were kept. These would enable guardians to provide more appropriate treatment. Cases would be reviewed regularly, thus preventing outrelief being renewed automatically to longer-term paupers as it had been in the past.

Thus up to the outbreak of the first world war the poor law remained intact. The principles of 1834 had survived considerable shifts in the structure of employment and discourses around poverty; indeed, the most recent proposals had signalled a new strategy with which the repressive apparatus could be controlled more reliably. Changes that were witnessed in the levels and types of relief in the years immediately preceding the outbreak of war were the result of measures introduced in the Liberal phases of welfare reform. Old age pensions, unemployment insurance and national health insurance, all of which affected levels of relief administered by the poor law, were part of an apparatus erected outside its formal boundaries by a Liberal government increasingly concerned by the threat of a Labour alternative (Gilbert 1976 p448).

The slogan 'Go to the Guardians' raised by Lansbury and taken up by the LDCU, later the National Unemployed Workers Movement (NUWM), in the immediate postwar period was in important respects a radical challenge to underlying principles of the poor law.

First, it asserted the right of the unemployed to poor relief. Certain boards of guardians, including West Ham, had begun to acknowledge this right, and administered relief to destitute unemployed on a routine basis. In this they had the support of the Minister of Health, provided that relief was restricted and individual recipients monitored. But the NUWM demanded wholesale granting of relief to the unemployed, and this broke one of the basic tenets of the poor law.

Secondly, it abolished the distinction between poor and pauper, deserving and undeserving. Those without work, for whatever reason, had a right to approach the guardians for relief. Unemployment was not due to personal inadequacy but to the failure of the economy to provide sufficient work. In the absence of suitable work, it was implied, all were entitled to adequate relief.

Thirdly, it removed the stigma attached to the poor law. Just as there was no shame in being unemployed, so there was no shame in receiving relief. Thus the position of subordinate and obligated subjects was inverted as the unemployed asserted their right to adequate relief and the duty of the guardians to provide it.

Fourthly, it directed attention to the most visible and accessible agency of the poor law, namely, the guardians. The guardians had a degree of autonomy in administering relief. Scales of relief, the merits of individual cases and the procedures of relieving officers were decided by the guardians. Under pressure from an active unemployed body, as it was to prove, the balance of power could be shifted.

In other respects the demand was less than radical. Relief offered no solution to the problem of unemployment. Such arguments were frequently voiced by Moderates who, consistent with poor law principles, believed that generous levels of relief provided no new jobs; worse, they removed the incentive to find those that were available. Part of the argument was a telling one that appealed also to sections of the labour movement. The official labourist leadership at local and national levels, even when represented on the Necessitous Areas Committee, repeatedly asserted that since unemployment was a national problem, the solution should be sought at the national level; hence the protracted series of deputations to prime ministers and ministers of health, none of which seemed to advance the interests of the unemployed.

More radical opinion was also sensitive to the problem. When Sylvia Pankhurst formed the Unemployed Workers Organisation as an alternative to the LDCU, she did so out of a belief that demands such as 'Go to the Guardians' were regressive, and favoured instead the abolition of the system of wage labour (Croucher 1987 p50). Hannington himself recognised the weaknesses. Following successful raids on factories that had forced reductions in pay and overtime, he wrote 'George Lansbury's advice is March to the Guardians. My advice is March to the Factories' (*Out of Work*, 4 April 21, cited in Croucher p53) For the remainder of the year such raids were an important part of the LDCU's activities; many were successful in winning concessions from employers to cease overtime and increase pay (Hannington 1977 pp45-49).

The demand for 'Work or Full Maintenance' originated with the LDCU. In some respects it covered the whole spectrum of NUWM struggle in the interwar period. Unlike 'Go to the Guardians', the demand for work went beyond the sphere of the poor law to challenge the ability of the capitalist system to provide work at adequate levels. It was around such demands that hunger marches, mass demonstrations, factory raids and deputations to the government were mobilised; and it was these struggles in the early period to 1923 that fuelled fears of insurrection, provoking a series of panic reforms in the relief and insurance systems, rather than struggles against the poor law. 'Full Maintenance' (at trade union rates of wages) was also directed at the state, confronting its record in the provision of unemployed relief through insurance and benefit systems as the actuarial crisis mounted

However, in one important respect these slogans exhibited a fundamental weakness that derived from their failure to appreciate the significance of distinct constituencies among the unemployed. Such demands had little practical or political relevance for insured workers, who were largely insulated from chronic unemployment and hence entitled to unemployed benefits on scales that increased steadily during the 1920s. Only when thrown onto poor relief by strike action or by exclusion from benefit for, say, failing to meet the requirements of the genuinely-seeking-work clause, was there a potential for united resistance. Without this, the political fate of those on unemployed relief was viewed with indifference, even hostility, by other sections of the working class, an indifference that the slogans did nothing to dispel.

4.4 Communist influence

Discourses around unemployment relief in the interwar period, then, differed in their perception of the nature of the problem and the appropriate strategy to deal with it. The historical lineages of these discourses, their political specificity and their ability to engage different constituencies are crucial to an understanding of the course of unemployed struggles in this period.

Throughout 1921, as unemployment climbed, the influence of the LDCU increased steadily. Hannington had been dismayed at the tactics of ex-servicemen's associations, and set out to formulate a new programme. In the first issue of *Out of Work* the newspaper of the LDCU, a manifesto appeared:

> In the past the unemployed tolerated petty doles and charity, but now our Council is determined that the Government must take very different provisions. The aims of the Council are:
> (a) Full maintenance for the unemployed at trade union rates of wages
> (b) As a means of finding employment for the unemployed in the trades with which they are associated, the Council wants the re-establishment of trade with Russia, and the recognition of the Soviet Government. (*Out of Work* 19 March 21.)

The programme developed through 1921, as did struggles against boards of guardians. By September, Hannington was claiming a new consciousness among the unemployed:

> Last year they concentrated their whole efforts on collecting money with a view to endeavouring to alleviate the distress prevalent amongst their members (which of course was only tinkering with the evil), and were unconsciously allowing the local and central government authorities, who should have been shouldering the burden of providing relief, to go unassailed and free, while they themselves were shaking the boxes under the nose of somebody possibly who could ill afford to give. But this year it is good to record an entirely different psychology dominating the organizations and directing them into channels of class conscious agitation. (ibid. 17 September 21.)

It is unlikely, however, that the LDCU could legitimately claim responsibility for this shift. The organisation was still a small, loose-knit federation of local unemployed committees, whose main programmatic thrust lay outside the sphere of the poor law. The programme adopted by the national conference held toward the end of November 1921 emphasised the point. Among the demands were provision of work, preservation of civic rights, representation of the unemployed organisation on all employment exchange committees, relief granted to unemployed persons to be a charge on the national exchequer not on the local rates, and abolition of all overtime (Hannington 1971 p44). LDCU members did participate in struggles against the guardians as, for example, at Wandsworth in July 1921, but they did not provide the initiative or leadership. More representative of their activities at the time were the series of mass demonstrations on the streets of London, the factory raids, and the deputations to the TUC and the government.

Little of this programme, and of the platforms more generally adopted by unemployed organisations, was informed by an understanding of the nature of unemployment itself. Apart from premises underlying vague references to the aftermath of the war and the deepening trade recession, which in part could be alleviated by re-establishing trade with Russia during the period of reconstruction, there was no systematic analysis in the early interwar years. This may seem surprising given the advanced state of economic theory in Britain at the time. Keynes, Pigou, Hawtry and Beveridge were in the forefront of debates about the efficacy of manipulating interest rates, and the desirability of reflationary policies and a return to the Gold Standard as measures to stimulate the economy and reduce unemployment (Garraty 1978 pp154-64).

On the other hand, no consensus had emerged in state thinking, and for unemployed workers facing what for many years was a qualitatively and quantitatively new phenomenon, such debates were remote. The structural basis of unemployment had changed. There had been a shift from the underemployment of prewar periods to chronic unemployment affecting sections of the labour force previously immune from the problems of casualism; but underlying much of the strategy of unemployed struggles was the same fatalistic acceptance of their state of unemployment. This merely consolidated the overwhelming concern with local struggles to relieve distress, particularly in the 1920s.

The most significant struggle against the poor law was that at Poplar, where at a meeting on 22 March 1921 the council refused precepts of the London County Council and other metropolitan authorities (for a full account of the struggle see Branson 1979 and Gillespie 1989). Since the election of 1919, the council had been dominated by labour, political leadership of which derived from the ILP. The decision was a culmination of a series of events. In the context of rapidly deteriorating conditions in Poplar, the council had prepared a £31,000 unemployed relief scheme, towards which the government had agreed a grant. Conditions were later attached to the grant that the council found unacceptable.

Subsequent debates in the council were bounded by discourses around perceived realisable municipal strategies. To the suggestion that unemployment could be prevented only by the 'abolition of interest and profit and the ending of the whole capitalist system', Lansbury had urged practical steps to alleviate the problem rather than pious resolutions (Branson p25). The refusal of precepts in furtherance of a demand for equalisation of the rates in the metropolis was a form of action that would force the issue, and at the same time provide positive relief through a reduction in local rates from 6s 10d to 4s 4d. Uncertainty over the precise legal status of the action and the steps that could be taken to deal with it through the machinery of the poor law led to protracted court hearings. Eventually, thirty councillors were sent to jail for contempt of court in the first week of September 1921.

The council hoped that similar action would be taken by other Labour councils in poor boroughs, but there was no widespread resistance. Leadership of the London Labour Party viewed such a course with suspicion, even hostility. Herbert Morrison, the secretary, was vociferous in condemning the Poplar action. Committed to winning control of the LCC by establishing a reputation of responsible and efficient administration in municipal affairs, he saw unconstitutional action as a threat, and was determined to resolve the dispute before it could do real damage.

Much of the leadership of the Central Labour Party and the TUC shared these feelings; support, some of it financial, for the action taken by Poplar was forthcoming after the imprisonment, but it amounted to little more than token gestures. Effective support was confined largely to local people, the *Daily Herald* and the LDCU, in the eyes of whom Poplar provided to the rest of the working class an example of how the principles of the poor law could be challenged effectively. Only Bethnal Green and Stepney councils decided to support Poplar and refuse precepts; both bordered Poplar and were no doubt infected by the spirit of local revolt.

Faced with mounting political embarrassment and an obdurate body of detainees, the Minister of Health and the LCC secured the release of the councillors on the pretext that they should be allowed to participate in a conference to discuss the financial situation. They had been in prison for six weeks. By the time the conference met, Mond had hastily prepared a draft bill to revise and extend the Metropolitan Common Poor Fund and the Rate Equalisation Fund, neither of which had operated effectively since the war. Such proposals only in part met the demands of Labour councillors who placed greater importance on making unemployment relief a national charge and pooling the cost of outdoor relief. And equalisation of rates was politically unacceptable to wealthy boroughs.

A compromise was eventually reached within the terms of which equalisation of rates was sacrificed in favour of pooling of outdoor relief through the Common Poor Fund. The settlement provided Poplar with an additional £350,000 per year – more than it would have received under equalisation of the rates, and far more than it needed to repay precepts. It was widely seen to be a victory for direct action.

Poplar continued to flout the principles and operation of the poor law by exceeding the Mond scales of relief. This brought them into conflict with the Ministry of Health, but it did not again precipitate direct confrontation; in the final analysis the Common Poor Fund was effective enough in preventing chronic financial crises. Within the restricted terrain of the poor law the action of Poplar Council, without the support of other authorities, failed to challenge the underlying political and financial stability.

4.5 Pressures on the West Ham guardians

In certain important respects West Ham resembled Poplar. The postwar depression intensified the problems and attendant distress of casualism, and increased dramatically levels of unemployment. Large areas contin- ued to be plagued by endemic poverty, and the borough suffered from the consequences of low aggregate rateable values. In 1919 a Labour council had been elected which could trace its lineage to a pioneering tradition of municipal activity in the late 1890s. Labour did not hold a majority, however, on the West Ham Board of Guardians, largely because the Union included other boroughs such as East Ham, Leyton and Wanstead. More important, the Union, being outside the metropolitan administrative boundary, was excluded from the Common Poor Fund, and hence exposed fully to the ravages of high levels of relief.

Reverberations from the Poplar struggle reached West Ham, but the equalisation of rates in the metropolis was not of direct interest. A letter in the local press called for a similar scheme nationally, but it was subsequently dismissed as too naive (*SE* 15 August 21). At the same time a meeting of the West Ham Trades Council discussed the advisability of supporting Poplar. In response to a suggestion that the West Ham Council should take a stand rather than go down separately at a later stage, Councillor Groves argued that such a course would be impractical since it would only increase their obligations and halt relief from the guardians. The matter was referred to trade union branches for discussion (*SE* 27 August 21).

Concerted action on unemployment lay elsewhere. As the guardians returned from their summer recess they were met by an orderly crowd of over 5000 unemployed. Knowledge of the availability of unemployed relief from the guardians, combined with a new political awareness of strategies for securing and extending relief, appealed to a steadily increasing constituency. The demand was for increased scales of relief – a demand that was resisted by the Moderates on the grounds that local ratepayers could ill afford the burden already imposed on them. Councillor Killip, principal representative of the Labour group, wanted the government to take responsibility:

> They would be prepared to move a more adequate scale provided the burden did not fall on the ratepayers within the Union. These people were not the unemployed of the old days. It was a new kind of problem they had to face. During the progress of the years the men had become better educated, and had a better grasp of matters. They asked 'Can the guardians provide us with work?' They were told... that they could not provide work, and they then said 'In that case we want maintenance'. (*SE* 10 September 21.)

An increase in the scale of relief was agreed, however, provided that it was sanctioned by the Minister of Health. When informed the unemployed dispersed quietly, much to the relief of the local press:

> The men and women who marched to West Ham workhouse were extremely quiet and orderly, but such has not been the case elsewhere. Riotous and foolish scenes have occurred in places, and it was merely a matter of precaution that the police were in attendance on this occasion. (ibid, Editorial.)

There were to be numerous re-enactments of such scenes in the ensuing months. Decisions taken by the guardians, and the ultimate course of events, were governed by an awareness of the delicate balance that existed among competing interests. The guardians themselves were split between

Moderate and Labour. In the early interwar period Moderate members of the Municipal Alliance had control but found it impossible to pursue ratepayer interests with determination and consistency. Their desire to reduce rates, or at least minimise increases, was tempered by a recognition of the particular economic difficulties of the area, the genuine distress forced on the unemployed, and the attendant rise of militant forms of action. As the state, through measures such as relaxation of the 1911 Relief Regulation Order and reductions in unemployment insurance benefit, imposed greater responsibility on the guardians to relieve distress, so the Moderates came to appreciate the inherent difficulty of their position and the ambiguities in their stand on the poor law. For the most part their concern was to prevent the unemployed forcing unacceptably high scales of relief or abusing relief already conceded; but the very act of granting widespread relief to unemployed was an abandonment of the differentiation between poor and pauper. Excluded now were the loafers and cheats. Given this, the invocation of the principle of less eligibility in order to maintain relief below the district rate of wages for unskilled labour seemed the most they could achieve, and on this the Moderates voted consistently as a body. The only real solution, however, was for the government to assume responsibility for unemployed relief – a measure that would effectively demolish the poor law at a national level but reposition the guardians within the structure erected by nineteenth-century principles. A resolution from the Leyton and Leytonstone Ratepayers Association to the September meeting of the guardians represented Moderate feeling:

> this Association is satisfied that the West Ham Board of Guardians is dealing with the problem of unemployment relief in a generous and sympathetic spirit, and that the existing scale of relief is the maximum that can be given, having regard to the pressing financial burden of the districts within the Union without directly encouraging unemployment. The Association urges the Board to resist the attempt to increase the scale, and to refuse to submit to an organized species of intimidation, engineered for political ends... At the same time, the Association is of the opinion that the problem of unemployment, being a national matter, should be dealt with by the Government on national lines, and be removed from the atmosphere of local prejudice and partisan passion. (WHBG *Minutes* 9 September 21.)

The Labour presence on the guardians was more sympathetic to the plight of the unemployed, and less concerned to reduce rates; but labourism was never able to distance itself from the dilemma faced by the Moderates and the same ambiguities toward the poor law. Killip argued in response to the above motion:

> The Leytonstone Ratepayers Association said that [the question of maintenance] was being used for political ends... He did not believe anyone looked at it from the point of view of political kudos. The principle of maintenance without work had been in existence in this

country as long as the capitalist system had existed. There was a class of people who never worked and never intended to work, but so far as the unemployed were concerned the allowances were inadequate... He knew dozens of cases where the maximum allowance was not paid. [The Moderates'] attitude was: 'If we give you the full scale it will make you too lazy to work'. One wondered why the men who were told this did not raise the roofs of the buildings... He wanted the government to take the responsibility. He had heard people say that the unemployed were getting more money than people who were working outside. In reply to that, all he had to say was 'God help the people outside if they are getting less'. (*SE* 10 September 21.)

Manifest here were an acknowledgement of the right of the unemployed to full allowance and a challenge to the principle of less eligibility, but both were inscribed within the existing structure of the poor law, the new boundaries of which excluded those who refused to work. As with the Moderates, the only solution to the problem was thought to be in the hands of government.

Arrayed against the guardians was a body of unemployed with an increasing presence and political direction that came to expose the inherent weaknesses in their position. At the October meeting of the guardians Paul, effective leader of the Moderates, proposed that the scale of relief be rescinded and replaced by a money grant to cover rent, the rest being relief in kind. It was a drastic measure, forced by the crippled finances of the Union, that voiced anxiety more about the future ability of tenants to pay rent than the plight of the unemployed:

What was the working man to do? His rent was going up with every increase in the rate... It was a gross injustice to every ratepayer in the Union to be called upon to pay these enormous sums of money... He was not against the unemployed – God forbid – but he did feel that it was up to the Board to take such drastic steps as would force the Government to realise their duty to that Board, which had probably saved an incipient revolution. (*SE* 22 October 21.)

The motion was deferred to await the reopening of parliament, but it did demonstrate the extent to which some of the Moderates were willing to reform the machinery of the poor law to press their demands. By November Paul was willing to abandon it altogether and re-establish the principles of the nineteenth century. The Union now faced bankruptcy, he claimed, and since the Ministry of Health refused financial assistance toward the cost of unemployment relief, he proposed that the Board should cease to administer relief (*SE* 5 November 21). Again the motion was defeated, ostensibly on the grounds that such a measure would inflict even worse hardship on the unemployed.

The fear of unrest expressed by Paul was shared by the guardians as a body and by the official labour leadership in West Ham. At a public meeting of the Labour Party, Killip claimed that the party had done more

than any other to bring attention to the problems of the unemployed. On
the board they had never refused a deputation from the unemployed and
had protested against the action of the police, but when

> the leader or a member turned round and in effect told them that
> unless they did what they demanded they would be treated with
> physical violence, he was not going to stand it. Violence either to
> person or property would avail them nothing. (*SE* 26 November 21.)

At a meeting of the West Ham Trades Council, while delegates were
voting to affiliate to the Red International of Labour Unions (p106), concern
was expressed that because the unemployed were being denied free
speech (in this instance by the council's decision to let them use the Town
Hall provided they discuss only questions on local unemployment), the
unemployed were being driven to pursue 'the most dangerous course that
could be pursued' (ibid.). These fears soon seemed to be realised when a
march of over 2000 converged on the workhouse where the guardians were
meeting. The demonstration had been planned; a band and banners
appeared from various districts, and prior notice of deputations had been
submitted. In spite of protests from some Moderates, the deputations were
heard. West Ham Trades Council submitted a claim for increased scales of
relief and a coal allowance. Of the 20,000 organised workers in the area, the
deputation argued, 6000 were unemployed. These were suffering from
cold and hunger, and losing self respect. It concluded that there were
periods in history 'when the unconstitutional method becomes the right
one' (*SE* 11 February 22).

The threat of such action was reinforced by a deputation from the LDCU.
Expressing frustration at the indifference shown by the guardians to the
unemployed, a member continued:

> We are going to be more audacious than we have been in the past.
> This is the last time we are coming to you in a constitutional
> manner… The longer the [guardians] continued to delay, the more
> they would drive these men to desperation. You will be sorry if,
> through your inactivity in the near future, these men take to looting
> shops and helping themselves… We are out for work or main-
> tenance, and the work must be at trade union rates… If all the
> unemployed had been of the same political mind as himself he
> would have taken the same action as was taken at Poplar and locked
> the doors; but as the deputation had no mandate from the men to
> take that drastic step it was not done. (ibid.)

The local press, anxious to avert open conflict, suggested that the
unemployed direct their attention elsewhere. In an implicit reaffirmation
that unemployment was a national problem, an editorial stated:

> Encouraged by the 'success' of their Poplar brethren, the unem-
> ployed of West Ham Union area who style themselves the militant
> section, looked forward to emulating the Poplar example… It is
> difficult to understand what they hoped to gain by such tactics. For
> their own good entirely the men must proceed constitutionally and

they would be well advised to drop the leaders who are inclined to incite them to violence… The men should understand that when they abuse the guardians they are quarrelling with their best friends. Their grievance is with the government, and if, as was intimated by one of the deputation, they decide to adopt unconstitutional methods, let them see that their efforts are directed against those to whom the responsibility belongs and by whom it is ignored. (ibid.)

A motion on an increased scale of relief was narrowly defeated by the Moderate majority. At the next meeting a deputation from the LDCU was refused on the grounds that insufficient notice had been given, but the unemployed assembled outside, numbering about 500, were informed that a coal allowance had been agreed. During the march back to Stratford a fight broke out with police, who charged with truncheons. The ringleaders were arrested and charged with obstruction. All were declared to be members of the LDCU (*Out of Work* 27 February 22).

4.6 Historical specificity of the politics of unemployment

The moment was in some respects a watershed, and it is worth pausing to reflect on its historical specificity and significance in the context of national developments. Although the available evidence on the potential of revolutionary rupture in the immediate postwar period is inconclusive, recent interpretations suggest that most of the social measures on unemployment introduced by the state were essentially designed to prevent widespread civil unrest (Gilbert 1976, Cronin 1982, Deacon 1977, Schwarz and Durham 1985). They were hurried and ill-conceived, in part because statistical series upon which they were based were unreliable. The onset of mass unemployment demolished their actuarial foundations.

Toward the end of 1921 the inherent deficiencies of the 1916 National Insurance (Part II Munitions Workers) Act, the 1918 Out of Work Donation Scheme, and the 1920 Unemployment Insurance Act precipitated a financial crisis in response to which the government saw only two realistic options – further revision of unemployed insurance, and a shift toward the relief of unemployment through the poor law. Numerous revisions followed which defined and redefined those unemployed who could claim particular benefits over certain periods of time. At no time, however, did these measures prove adequate in relieving the distress that continued. In areas such as West Ham, where large numbers of workers were excluded from the 1920 Act, a disproportionate burden fell on the poor law. The increase in relief after the crisis of 1921, particularly with the cessation of the Out of Work donation, was remarkable (Table 4.4). The increase was due, therefore, to structural changes in relief forced by mass unemployment and the tacit recognition by the government of the need to shift some of the responsibility from the national exchequer to local taxation. It was accelerated by the strategies of the unemployed themselves during 1921 as they directed action against the guardians.

In certain respects, however, unemployment entered the political stage

TABLE 4.4 *Numbers in receipt of outdoor relief, and cost of outdoor relief, West Ham Union, 1918–26*

	1918	1919	1920	1921	1922
Number	4,470	3,844	4,086	7,789	28,545
Cost (£)	41,448	49,420	70,147	261,823	663,779

	1923	1924	1925	1926[a]
Number	42,834	45,246	42,909	40,148
Cost (£)	822,163	831,606	803,244	—

Source: West Ham Union *Statement of Accounts*, relevant years.
Note: [a] Data collected on a separate basis after supersession.

too late to act as an effective platform for social transformation. By the end of 1921, the acute political crisis of the immediate postwar period had abated. During the crisis, unemployment did not feature prominently in political discourses. A Home Office survey in 1919, undertaken as part of the constant surveillance of working-class political activity, identified eight causes of revolutionary feeling. Unemployment came sixth after high prices, bad housing, hatred of the rich, education and leadership (Cronin 1982 p120). The subsequent rapid increase in the scale and extent of unemployment coincided with a decline in revolutionary activity. Collapse of the shop stewards movement and socialist influence in the armed forces, and defeats of the Liverpool police strike and Forty Hour strike in Glasgow engendered a political climate which, at the time of the foundation of the Communist Party in the summer of 1920, was 'bleak for socialists' (Schwarz and Durham 1985 p139). This was followed by the collapse of the Triple Alliance in April 1921, leading to defeat of the miners, and the enforced isolation of the Communist Party from the Labour Party and the ILP as the former turned increasingly to constitutional forms of political activity.

The early success of the LDCU depended on its ability to articulate grievances and provide political direction to growing numbers of unemployed. In this it drew strength from postwar militancy, throughout 1921, in the series of struggles against the guardians; but this success could not be maintained, particularly since different constituencies existed among the unemployed themselves. After a peak of activity in late 1921 into early 1922, the LDCU entered a protracted decline which lasted through 1923 and 1924. Committees were lost, *Out of Work* ceased publication and the NUWM became little more than a skeletal structure. Apart from the broader decline in working-class militancy, there were a number of contributory factors.

First, the NUWM remained a relatively small organisation which represented a fraction of the unemployed. Lacking the appropriate machinery, it remained a loose affiliation of committees until 1924 when the Communist Party decided to strengthen and coordinate the efforts of members within the unemployed movement (Croucher 1987 p38). It was not until

August 1921 that a branch of the Communist Party was formed in West Ham (*SE* 27 August 21).

Secondly, such militant leadership remained outside the main body of labour thought and activity. Occasionally, as in Poplar, the NUWM was able to pursue a united front policy with other socialist currents, but official labour leaders continued to express open hostility. At the 35th Annual Conference of the SDF held in Stratford during August 1921, Will Thorne stated:

> Whatever claim the BSP might have made to carry on the traditions of the SDP it had since been completely destroyed by its having become the Communist Party of this country pledged to follow the Bolshevik dictatorship of Lenin. During the past twelve months the 'impossibilists' of the country had been very active. From time to time they had made ferocious attacks upon members of the SP. (*SE* 6 August 21.)

Later in an article describing the role of the guardians, Killip wrote of the NUWM:

> Their chief stock in trade seems to consist of such epithets as 'political twisters', 'betrayers of the unemployed', 'Traitors to the working class', etc... One does not object to the unemployed being 'organised' but is that the sole purpose of the heads of this body? Why are they not honest about it? (*Justice* 17 July 24.)

Thirdly, during 1920-21 there was a fall of approximately 30 per cent in the cost of living, after which prices stabilised (see the series in Mitchell and Deane 1962, and *SE* 4 July 25). This meant a real increase in relief while scales remained constant, thus easing some of the distress and the most immediate pressure on the guardians for increases in maintenance. More important, it undercut the political discourses that had been effective in mobilising action among sections of the unemployed. Pressure was also relieved by an absolute decline in the numbers of insured unemployed after the mid-1921 peak. There were marked regional variations to this trend; in West Ham there was a steady decline until the end of the decade and the onset of another trade depression (Table 4.1).

Scenes witnessed at the West Ham guardians early in 1922 were not repeated. For the remainder of the year, and throughout 1924 and 1925, the unemployed did not demonstrate the same confidence in challenging the guardians. Anxieties about the influence of communists began to recede. At the annual general meeting of the Municipal Alliance, Ward, its secretary and a guardian, expressed confidence that the 'greater majority of the [working class] were not communists or Bolsheviks at heart, but led by extremists in their midst' (*SE* 25 March 22). Harry Pollitt's prediction in an address to the West Ham Trades Council on the red international that the present apathy of the working class was 'more apparent than real', and that in 'a very short time there would be such a hell of a rumpus' (*SE* 20 May 22), was not to be fulfilled for some years.

This decline in militancy coincided with a new initiative by the guardians to resolve the problem of unemployed relief. Immediately after the February unrest they organised a deputation to MPs within the Union in the belief that the only constitutional means open to West Ham was to draw the attention of the government to the danger of financial breakdown in local administration (WHBG *Minutes* 16 March 22). By now the guardians had incurred a debt of £330,000, and the poor rate had risen to 4s 6d compared with 9d, prewar. Killip pointed to the essential dilemma:

> They had the extreme element on one side in the form of the unemployed, and on the other hand were the business people of the borough who complained that in the event of an increased rate it would not be their unwillingness but their inability to pay. (*SE* 1 April 22.)

Jack Jones, MP for Silvertown, in a statement that neatly summarised official labourist thinking on the question, put the matter more bluntly:

> They were not giving extravagant relief because all their schemes had to be approved by the Minister of Health, and nothing he sanctioned would ever be extravagant. They were not asking the Government to give them anything; they were asking them only to insure against revolution. Suppose they could not give men, women and children sufficient food to keep them, the State would have to spend more on gunpowder than they were now spending to keep these people... This was not a party question.(ibid.)

A decision was taken to convene a conference of representatives from what came to be known as necessitous areas, namely, constituencies which suffered hardship through high expenditure on the relief of unemployment. The conference, attended by 129 MPs in June 1922, resolved to send a deputation to Lloyd George. The case for necessitous areas would be drawn up by Thomas Smith, Clerk to the West Ham Guardians, and put by Thorne. They argued that the poor law machinery was not designed to cope with problems attendant upon widespread, chronic unemployment. Without direct government assistance, those unions that bore unfairly a disproportionately large share of the burden had been reduced or would shortly be reduced to a state of bankruptcy. Loans from the Ministry of Health at high rates of interest were no solution. Unless the government came with substantial grants to the immediate aid of the 200 poor law authorities suffering undue hardship, the consequences would be serious and far reaching.

Lloyd George remained impassive. The government had already distributed £80m in unemployment benefits. In the current economic climate the extra £45m demanded could not be raised. Problems experienced by the guardians were only temporary. There were signs that unemployment was decreasing. The most important task, he argued, was to maintain the trend by stimulating trade.

The initiative taken by the guardians was important for it effectively redefined the boundaries and nature of struggles around the poor law. Hitherto the guardians had been positioned as the principal site by the operation of the poor law itself, and by discourses of struggle adopted by the unemployed. In approaching the state the guardians extended the terrain and at the same time deflected the impact of political rhetoric such as 'Go to the Guardians'. The re-articulation was one that could be made with ease in 1922. The fortunes of the NUWM were declining, and practically all political interests were united against the government in the belief that unemployment was a national problem and should be dealt with at that level. Through this redefinition of the terrain of struggle, the guardians also determined the course of its subsequent resolution.

4.7 Guardians and the state

This new terrain was one formed by displacement and erosion over the previous century. The relationship between guardians and government was complex. To an extent government was never completely divorced from the local administration of poor relief; but the links were tenuous. The Local Government Board had possessed a jealously guarded political autonomy from the government that enabled it to pursue a course unhampered by political interference. The course it chose was largely non-interventionist. Although the Board possessed statutory authority to intervene in the affairs of boards of guardians, in a climate antithetical to centralised bureaucratic control it maintained a respectable distance. As the state reluctantly assumed some responsibility for relieving social distress, so it began to take a more direct role. Welfare schemes introduced in the prewar period, particularly those to promote decasualisation, would not be able to function effectively if liberal scales of relief were freely available. Above all, it was felt that the whole machinery of the poor law and local taxation had to be reformed. Attempts to gain control of the administration of relief in the immediate postwar period were successfully opposed by a powerful combined force of guardians and friendly societies (Gilbert 1976). The assumption of the powers and responsibilities of the Local Government Board by the Ministry of Health in 1919 did not pose a threat to poor relief, but it did enable the government, for the first time, to enforce directly the statutory obligations of the guardians.

In the confusion over social welfare and the political uncertainty of the postwar years the government could wield this new weapon with no authority. As a concomitant of the national unemployed insurance scheme, the 1911 Relief Order had proscribed the administration of outdoor relief by the guardians to unemployed except in special circumstances (p131). However the relevant clauses had dubious legality and were open to different interpretations. Furthermore, extensions of the franchise in 1918 had fostered a greater labour representation on many boards of guardians. They were more responsive than their predecessors to the increasing body of unemployed workers, and the rules governing relief were adhered to with less resolve.

By overriding approved scales of relief many boards offered relief that was far in excess of unemployed benefit administered by employment exchanges. Against this the government seemed unwilling or unable to act. For the most part, activities were confined to reasserting the principle of less eligibility. In April 1922, for example, the West Ham guardians inquired into the administration of relief. The report concluded that the maximum relief had to exceed the earnings of an independent labourer when the applicants had dependent children. The Minister of Health detected here a challenge to 'the fundamental principle of relief being lower than the normal scale of earnings', and replied:

> The Minister attaches great importance to the observation by the Board of Guardians of the principle, and in this connection enquires what are the wages at present received by wage earners of the lowest paid class in the Union, if any measures were taken to ensure that persons in receipt of relief were not placed in a better position than the independent workmen, and if so to what extent exceptions were permitted. (WHBG *Minutes* 8 June 22.)

There was one important sanction that the government possessed, however, which was to prove decisive. All increases in the scale of relief had to be approved by the Ministry of Health. If increased scales could not be met immediately from local rates, loans were negotiated from the Ministry, which could refuse to advance the funds in the event of its directives being ignored.

A series of loans had been negotiated by the West Ham guardians before the Necessitous Areas Committee (as it came to be known) approached Lloyd George. A further loan of £300,000 was granted on condition that an approved scale of relief was imposed. No such undertaking was given, but the the the money still came. A further loan of £200,000 followed early in 1923 as the debts of the guardians mounted.

Relative stability prevailed for the next two years. The Necessitous Areas Committee continued to press the Ministry of Health for national relief, but to no avail. A detailed scheme was drawn up by the West Ham Union for the equalisation of poor law expenditure throughout the country. Based on the experience of sixty-one unions, and containing comprehensive statistics on rateable values and costs of relief, it claimed to be equitable and realistic. But the new Minister of Health, Neville Chamberlain, who previously had been a major figure on the Necessitous Areas Committee, rejected the scheme since it failed to provide a satisfactory definition of a necessitous area and treated some areas in an anomalous manner.

Further loans were sought. By April 1924 the West Ham Board owed the ministry £1.25m – more than double the sum of Poplar, the next highest. Pressure had been maintained on the guardians by a seven week dock strike during July and August 1923. Relief totalling £15,000 was paid to strikers' families, an act that provoked considerable hostility from ratepaying interests. Ward, a Moderate guardian, declared at a meeting of the East Ham Ratepayers Association that

> if there had been no prospect of relief being granted there would

have been no strike... If strikes are to be called with the definite knowledge that members of Boards of Guardians who are in support of that particular movement can vote for the payment of, in some cases, more money in relief than the striker would be earning at work, a very big question is going to be opened up. (SE 15 September 23.)

Toward the end of the strike a local employer, Wiggins & Rihll, refused to pay rates as a protest against the guardians' action, and another, Vernons & Sons, paid with reluctance because the payment of relief was 'definitely prolonging the dispute and is causing enormous loss to manufacturers and other employers of labour in the Borough' (WHBG Minutes 1 October 23.)

The strike, although defeated, signalled a new wave of labour unrest in West Ham (p115). Following the November municipal elections Labour dominated the council, holding thirty-seven seats to the twenty-three held by the Alliance, and next month it won all four seats in the general election. A railway strike occurred in January 1924, and another dock strike in February. During this period communists and militant sections of labour demonstrated renewed vigour. A manifesto issued in the course of the first dock strike urged strikers to go to the guardians and cooperate with the unemployed movement. Councillor Mahon stated at a Labour Party meeting that the government was waging war against the unemployed. The solution to the question was labour representation on all local authorities, including boards of guardians. Indeed, it was thanks to a strong labour presence on the West Ham Board that strikers were not now reduced to starvation.

For many unemployed hope was now placed in the first, minority Labour government which took office toward the end of January 1924. At a Labour Party meeting local MPs spoke of the confidence they had in the government to challenge wealth and privilege, and to tackle social problems facing the country (SE 26 January 24). On the same day, speakers at a packed Communist Party meeting in Stratford Town Hall gave guarded support to the government, but urged the importance of continued industrial struggle (ibid.).

The Labour government, however, proved no more successful in dealing with the problem of unemployment. The Necessitous Areas Committee lost little time in revising the West Ham scheme for equalisation of poor law expenditure to deal with the criticisms that had been levelled by Chamberlain, and subsequently submitted it to Wheatley, the new Minister of Health. Although admitting that unemployed relief should be separated from poor relief, and the former made a national charge, he declared it was mainly a question of finance and control of expenditure (SE 1 March 24). The scheme was rejected by the cabinet.

In its short term of office the Labour government lacked the political will to tackle the problem of unemployed relief. It showed some alacrity in withdrawing the hated means test which had operated to take account of family income, but replaced it with the 'genuinely seeking work' clause.

Whether or not the government recognised the full significance of the condition, its potential effectiveness in reasserting the differentiation between deserving and undeserving was not ignored by Baldwin. By the time it was withdrawn in 1930, nearly three million claims had been disallowed. The operation of the condition, and the failure of the labour movement to appreciate its significance, was the most abiding and damaging legacy of the Labour government's activities in the sphere of the poor law (Deacon 1977).

The Labour Party in West Ham turned also to the question of representation on the guardians. Extension of the franchise in 1918 to include women had dramatically increased burgess rolls. At first labour failed to exploit this advantage. From the time of its foundation the NUWM ran or supported candidates for the Labour, Communist and Cooperative Parties, but because of lack of organisation and abstention of the unemployed in elections little progress was made (*Out of work* June 22). Now, as part of its united front policy, it worked more effectively with Labour activists not only to increase representation but also to influence the boards by persuading them to accept the mandate of the local unemployed. By 1923 Moderates and Labour on the West Ham Board were equally divided, and in the 1924 election Labour, after gaining five seats, assumed control. At a meeting of the Forest Gate Ratepayers Association prior to the election, Paul anticipated defeat:

> An awful damning apathy seemed to come over the people whenever an election came along. The only people who did work were those to whom they generally referred as 'the other side'. They deserved to succeed because of their enthusiasm. (*SE* 8 March 22.)

A report on the results in the local press remarked that the 'Labour Party had the largest band of helpers, and the zeal with which they entered the fray was remarkable' (*SE* 12 April 24).

More notable was the substantial presence of women, the proportion of whom vastly exceeded those on other local authorities. Of the fifty-two guardians in 1924, twenty-four were women, the majority of whom were part of the Labour Group. By 1926, their numbers had increased to twenty-eight. The NUWM had recognised the importance of involving women in unemployed struggles, creating a Women's Division and appointing a paid organiser, Lillian Webb. The role prescribed for women, however, was largely subordinate. As Webb wrote:

> We strongly recommend that immediate steps are taken to bring women into the unemployed movement, and Committees are urged to form women on local committees or on membership books into a separate section or group which shall have representation on and work within the general committee... The unemployed women should assist in every way possible the men when demonstrating for Work of Full Maintenance, and shall take an active part in all demonstrations... Women shall assist in making banners and tableaux, and sewing classes should be held where women can meet

and discuss the problems of the day... Women are not cognisant, as
yet, with the general aspect of the movement, and naturally do not
stand the same chance as men of being elected to higher bodies. This
will prevent a separate movement, which is not desirable. (*Out of
Work* April 22.)

It is clear, however, that women were not content to occupy such a
position. Unemployment among women was vastly underrecorded by
official statistics. Since much female employment in an area like West Ham
was part-time home work, charring or cleaning – that is, in occupations
excluded from unemployed insurance schemes – relatively few women
could register at a labour exchange when out of work. Those that were
entitled could expect harsh treatment. A report from the North and South
West Ham Committees of the NUWM recognised the nature of the problem
and asserted their determination to fight it:

At present the Committees are concentrating their efforts upon the
women who are being offered domestic service under conditions
which force them to refuse, in which case they are struck off the
payroll of the Labour Exchange, and refused relief from the Relieving Officer, which means these women are to be forced upon the
streets. The Committees are fighting this, and with these women
organised, will make a stand with their backs to the wall in this
matter. (ibid. September 22.)

Those women who avoided direct contact with the poor law because
they had had no paid employment could not escape from the effects it had
on their families. Wives and mothers bore the brunt of the distress from
unemployment. They were the ones forced to manage, to keep the family
together on inadequate relief. And with this came the daily, petty humili-
ations of survival – obtaining food with relief tickets, pawning possessions,
confronting the rent collector.

In the wider spheres of political activity women were beginning to
assert their presence in the wake of the suffragette struggles and a massive
but still restricted extension of the franchise. The Labour Party and Wom-
en's Cooperative Guild gave women a voice and sense of identity in the
interwar period. The guild, in particular, became a way of life for thousands of working-class women, providing them with the opportunity for
self education, comradeship, escape from the home and family, and
participation in a wide range of campaigns for improvement in their lives
(p45-50). Among these campaigns unemployed struggles and increased
representation on boards of guardians featured prominently.

4.8 Supersession of the guardians

The Labour majority on the council elected in 1924 seemed determined to
reform the poor law machinery. Motions on May Day holidays and
compulsory membership of a trade union for guardian employees, and a
coal allowance for the whole year – all of which had been put and lost on
previous occasions – were now carried with sizable majorities (WHBG

Minutes 17 April and 1 May 24). But there was a limit beyond which they were not prepared to venture. A deputation from the NUWM submitting increased scales of relief was informed that in view of the financial situation the board could not accede to their demands. Instead they should put them before the Minister of Health (ibid. 15 May 24). At a subsequent public meeting Killip was made to justify the decision. While conceding the validity of the demand for work or full maintenance, he expressed in familiar terms the dilemma faced:

> It was absolutely impossible to put that scale into operation under the present financial circumstances in West Ham... The Labour Party were in the majority and acted as a whole... The only way to get their demands enforced was through a national and international movement. (*SE* 24 May 24.)

By the end of 1924 it was clear to most shades of political opinion in West Ham that Labour guardians and a Labour government were no more likely to solve the problem of local unemployed relief than their predecessors. At a Labour Party meeting in August, Thorne claimed that he was never deluded by the belief that the party could do so (*SE* 30 August 24). And the local press echoed the sentiments:

> The solution of the unemployed problem is as far off today as it ever was. The Labour Government refuses to accept the share of the burden... The Guardians are powerless in the matter. They have done as well as circumstances will allow. (*SE* 20 September 24.)

Paul repeated his demand to abolish the guardians:

> Were they going to go on for ever, or were they going to take their courage in both hands and refuse to administer the 'dole' and let the government do it? Time after time they were faced with this nightmare of debt... He thought the Labour Party has courage, but they were just as weak as the others. (ibid.)

Early in 1925 the government began to force the issue. Following a deputation to the Minister of Health a further loan of £350,000 was agreed on condition that the guardians reduce the scales of relief for all adults and a scale of deductions for family earnings be adopted leading to reductions in relief. The board voted to refuse reductions, forcing a concession from the ministry that reductions would not apply to elderly couples or single adults living alone. The revised conditions were accepted at a subsequent meeting. Killip argued that it was time to vote on the cold facts:

> West Ham... could not continue indefinitely on the present basis... This money was coming from the pockets of those who could ill afford it. He was not referring when he said this to those who were seemingly called the upper middle or the middle classes, but to the great body of the working class generally... They had to carry out their duties in a bold, firm and efficient manner. (*SE* 14 February 25.)

This 'realism' accorded precisely with Moderate opinion, and gained the support of enough of the Labour vote to guarantee acceptance of the revised conditions. Killip was called a traitor by a number of the NUWM in the gallery, but was merely expressing labourist sentiment. By now the problem seemed intractable, and in the absence of government intervention ratepayers, including sections of the working class, were committed to financing poor relief, too much of which went to some of the 'biggest scroungers that could be found'. If his stand was denounced by 'leaders' of the unemployed, these were a 'mere handful of insignificant nonentities and economic fledglings'.

An application for a further loan in May was granted on condition that the board adopt economies by reducing relief and reviewing long-standing applicants. In view of the continued fall in the cost of living since the relief scales were last set, Chamberlain argued, they should be amended and many should not receive relief automatically. The board refused to accept the conditions.

The attempts by government to impose reductions on the guardians accelerated recognition among labour sections campaigning on unemployment that the terrain of struggle had shifted. Representatives of trades councils, divisional labour parties and unemployed organisations met in June to form an Active Resistance Committee with the stated aim of agitation which, if successful, would 'shake the government to its foundations' (*SE* 20 June 25). As a first step it was to organise a petition demanding that unemployed relief become a national charge and that money be advanced to the guardians to enable them to maintain present scales of relief without increasing the burden on the rates. The demand for government intervention was not new – in one form or another it had been voiced by Labour and Moderate alike – but now a political specificity was conferred upon it that previously it had lacked. It was not to the guardians that the unemployed needed to direct their attention in struggles around relief, but to the state. Thus extension of the terrain simultaneously altered the political dynamics of discourses articulated in previous struggles within the poor law, rendering some obsolete, endowing others with a new relevance.

A large meeting (estimates varied between 1500 and 12,000) took place in West Ham at the end of June 1925 to protest against the Minister of Health's attempt to impose reductions. From the platform Killip announced in radical terms a new phase of struggle:

> For the first time in the history of West Ham they had a united front. Mr. Neville Chamberlain was one of the coldest, most cynical and callous ministers he had ever known. He thought West Ham was a 'sort of fishing village' and if he could beat West Ham he could beat the lot… When the voice of the workers defied the State it would be better for the country. We are not going to allow the Board of Guardians to be used to depress wages of the people out of work… If necessary the Board would fight in the Law Courts if they had the people behind them. (*SE* 4 July 25.)

Bess Turner of the NUWM was more reticent about the significance of the moment:

The Government is not afraid of mass meetings, but afraid of organisation. If the 200,000 people in that Union area affected by the Minister's decision were organised they would find that the Government would begin to sit up and take notice. Without organisation they might have a meeting like this one every day and it would have little effect. (ibid.)

Against further demonstrations and deputations the board remained obdurate. Thorne attempted to break the deadlock. At another large meeting of the unemployed in July he viewed the prospect of direct confrontation with some alarm:

It might be that the Guardians would be able to obtain more money from the bank and that relief would cease. I hope that time would not arrive because if it did there was going to be an awful row. Physical force was no remedy at all. If they wanted a proper remedy and a lasting one, people in all parts of the country must use their votes in a proper manner. (*SE* 25 July 25.)

He immediately led a deputation from the Necessitous Areas Committee. It was received by Baldwin, the Minister of Health and the Chancellor of the Exchequer. Baldwin claimed to be ignorant of the matter, and negotiations were conducted by Chamberlain. He rejected a revised scheme for a more equitable distribution of relief on the grounds that it still contained many anomalies; instead, he agreed to establish a departmental committee to study an alternative scheme, and amend the Unemployment Insurance Acts to relieve poor law authorities experiencing abnormal unemployment.

At the following meeting of the guardians a motion by Paul to suspend relief was heavily defeated; but so, too, was a proposal to accept the government's conditions. The guardians' intransigence was seen by some to be the result not of the Labour majority which it possessed following the election of April 1924, but of a new militancy. In an interview, Ward pointed to the changed attitudes of the Labour group:

They have refused entirely to compromise on the matter, although the ratepayers' side have offered to meet the Socialist party as far as possible so that the Board might present a united front on the general question of the relief of unemployment being a national and not a local problem. The Socialists, however, remain firm and will respond to no overture, asserting that they will have the full extent of their demands. Such an attitude is entirely foreign to the usual methods of negotiating, but it seems in keeping with the new spirit of the Socialist and Labour Party. The policy of the party is actually dictated by a group of extremists who call themselves the Resistance Committee and are in fact the local Soviet. (*SE* 15 August 25.)

Amid rumours in the London press that the Minister of Health was planning to take control of the West Ham board, the final refusal to implement cuts was taken in September and the administration of relief ceased. Thorne declared that he would have nothing more to do with the matter. He had 'done his best to help the Board of Guardians, but they had bolted and barred the door' (*SE* 19 September 25). Nearly £2m had been borrowed from the ministry, of which £340,000 was repaid. As a temporary measure the ministry decided immediately to supply relief in kind at 75 per cent of the previous level.

In the following week an orderly crowd of several thousand marched to the guardians. Contingents heard that the guardians would stay firm. The Active Resistance Committee convened a conference of Labour guardians in the metropolitan area. Lansbury, Barnes and Killip attended; local MPs Thorne, Jones and Groves did not. A motion in full support of the West Ham guardians was unanimously adopted. The London Trades Council also promised support. Rainbird, secretary to the committee, suggested that the matter had now assumed a deeper political significance. The guardians were fighting to maintain the 'rights they had as elected representatives of the people'; as such, the struggle was 'not now between the Minister of Health and the guardians, but between the Government and the people' (*SE* 26 September 25).

But political support from sections of labour for the guardian's stand was beginning to crumble. A motion from the South West Ham branch of the SDF advised the guardians to accept the terms of the Minister of Health, 'having regard to the prevailing conditions' (*SE* 10 October 25). The Plaistow Labour Party resolved:

> This meeting... congratulates the Labour members of the West Ham Board of Guardians on their splendid stand for the right of local boards to determine grants to persons seeking relief. Nevertheless, in view of their now having exhausted their powers in opposing the Ministry of Health in suggesting a new scale of relief, realising the exhaustion of public funds and the probable suffering of thousands of persons in the autumn, now recommends the Board, under protest, to accept the best terms that can be obtained from the Ministry. (*SE* 12 September 25.)

An ultimatum from the Minister of Health, threatening to impeach the guardians and take responsibility for relief, was sent. Until requisite legal power could be obtained through parliament, funds would be made available to administer relief in accordance with the conditions originally proposed. On 23 October the guardians capitulated and decided to accept the conditions of a further loan. Killip and a substantial body of Labour voted with the Moderates; fourteen Labour guardians voted against. A cheque for £300,000 was dispatched.

The decision provoked immediate repercussions. Prominent Labour leaders, in particular Thorne, Jones and Killip, were howled down whenever they tried to address public meetings. When, for example, Thorne rose to speak on 'Trade unions and political action' at a meeting organised by the NUGMW, there was continual uproar. 'I am a Social Democrat', declared Thorne, 'and always have been',

but there are differences between Social Democrats and commu-

nists... You can take your course as communists and we who belong
to the ILP and SDF will take our course. We will divide our forces and
fight our own way... We shall carry on our active propaganda in the
future as we have done in the past, and I bet a thousand pounds to
a penny that in the long run we shall win the same as we have won
all along. This is only a passing incident. (*SE* 24 October 25.)

Jones and Killip were called traitors and refused a hearing.

But Labour members on the board of guardians who agreed to the
conditions of the loan clearly felt that without the wide support of the
labour movement locally, and faced with the prospect of handing the
administration of relief over to the government, they could go no further.
Blackwell, a member of the militant labour minority on the guardians,
claimed at a NUWM meeting that labour representation was not enough, for
such people did not act in the interests of the unemployed:

The sooner the unemployed men and women sought direct representation on the Board the better it would be for them... They had
secured overwhelmingly Labour majorities on many Boards, but
those Labour majorities had not in every case done what they should
have done. There had been too many retrogrades in the Labour
Party. The great tragedy of West Ham was brought about by an
invertebrate member of the Labour Party who by profession was a
parson, joining hands with a member of the Municipal Alliance who
was a publican to defeat the aims and objects the workers had in view
when they were fighting Chamberlain. (*SE* 20 February 26.)

The guardians attempted to modify scales of relief and introduce
additional relief at Christmas, but the ministry refused to sanction them,
claiming that the guardians were bound by the agreement. Matters were
brought to a head by the general strike in May 1926. Financial resources in
the West Ham Union were drained by an excess of £80,000 during the
strike; by now the board owed £2.5m and the guardians were forced to turn
to the ministry for a further loan of £425,000. This time the ministry
demanded as a condition 'drastic reductions' in relief, far outstripping
those previously sought. Either the guardians cut relief by £300,000 over
the following year, or they adopt a scale recently agreed at Greenwich
which would lead to a reduction of £200,000. Simultaneously, the government announced that not only would it refuse to give special grants to
necessitous areas, but also rejected the principle that such grants should be
given. This time the guardians refused to accede; the response from the
labour movement to their previous decision had been unexpectedly vehement, and the cuts proposed now much harsher.

Killip moved the motion, arguing that the board was approaching
bankruptcy not because of the scales of relief that had been granted, but
because of poor administration, which could be remedied:

Some of the things that have been done by West Ham Guardians –
well, the least we can do is to be ashamed of them. When you are
elected to the Guardians you don't go there to give out relief as

though you were giving away handbills. You go to operate and administer the law of the land in accordance with present circumstances... We have been landed in this position by people who have entirely abused their membership of the Board. (*SE* 5 June 26.)

If this curious statement was a desperate attempt to rescue the board by promising administrative reform, it misfired. If Chamberlain needed any justification for superseding the West Ham Board he found it here, and in subsequent parliamentary debates he exploited it to the full. The guardians were informed that it was to be replaced, once the government had obtained the necessary powers from parliament, by 'persons appointed to discharge their functions at the cost of local rates' (WHBG *Minutes* 23 June 26). This the Government did using the Board of Guardians (Default) Act, which was rapidly pushed through parliament:

Where it appears to the Minister of Health that the board of guardians for any Poor Law Union have ceased, or are acting in such a manner as will render them unable to discharge all or any of the functions exercisable by the board, the Minister may by order of the Act appoint such person or persons as he may think fit to constitute the board in substitution of the board for such a period, not exceeding twelve months, as may be specified in the order, and the persons so appointed shall be deemed for all purposes to constitute the board. (1926 Board of Guardians (Default) Act.)

To charges that the Act destroyed a fundamental principle of the constitution, namely, that affairs of local government be determined by elected representatives of local people, Chamberlain replied that, on the contrary, the Act would safeguard the principle. He had hoped to continue with the existing machinery until the planned local government reforms could be introduced, but the action of the West Ham guardians forced him to take more immediate action. It could be argued, he said, that West Ham was the victim of high unemployment, poverty and a very low assessable value, in which case national measures should be taken. But the real question was whether or not the guardians in incurring vast expenditure had acted conscientiously, and had not given relief to both the deserving and the undeserving. It seemed to him that they had taken orders from people in receipt of relief. As a result, expenditure had far exceeded potential income, and they had brought themselves to a state of bankruptcy.

Did West Ham force the government to act? Abolition of the poor law machinery was on the agenda, and had been since the report of the Royal Commission on the Poor Laws and Unemployment 1905-09 (Webb and Webb 1910). The government could have waited for the planned reforms; but the political climate of 1925-26 was propitious for confrontation with the unions and with local authorities seen to be used by Labour majorities in the pursuit of political ends. Enabling legislation for supersession of errant boards of guardians was set in motion before the general strike. That the Act constituted a fundamental challenge to local representational democracy is a measure of how determined the government was. The strike not only accelerated the process, but bolstered the confidence of the government to act when it did.

Late in July a committee of three headed by Sir Alfred Woodgate was appointed to administer poor law relief in West Ham. In an interview Woodgate said that the administration of relief 'would go on much as usual':

> We are not here to grind the faces of the poor. We are here to do justice to the poor and to the ratepayers, and if possible to make West Ham an example for others and not a bye-word... There may be possibilities of reducing expenditure, but that remains to be seen. (*SE* 24 July 26.)

Protest meetings were immediately organised. Wheatley, the former Minister of Health, declared at one that the supersession marked 'the beginning of a new stage in the struggle of the working classes'. The government had 'taken advantage of West Ham to make one of the greatest constitutional changes in the last fifty years (*SE* 24 July 26). Most active were local branches of the NUWM. They demanded that the TUC take immediate action. A committee was formed to 'fight for liberty and power... through the medium of the local council. They should not make a rate and their overseers should not levy the rate. Their slogan must be 'No say, no pay' (*SE* 21 August 26).

Support for such demands, however, was weak. Meetings were poorly attended in spite of well-organised publicity.

Councillor Kirk, an ex-guardian, was angered by this and wrote to the press:

> Chamberlain has by his forthright dealing with the West Ham guardians rendered a signal service to the local labour movement. He has revealed its public ineptitude to state a case and its complete lack of imagination to organise whatever decaying strength it still has against the reactionary forces of a capitalist government... The official Labour Party will have to work with the keenness of its old pioneering days to get a responsible citizens' agitation sweeping through West Ham like a devouring flame against the new guardians and the disenfranchisement of the people. Such miserable, petty and mean demonstrations as the one on Sunday last in the recreation ground would not then make self-respecting trade unionists and socialists blush with shame. (*SE* 31 July 26.)

In the knowledge that effective mobilisation of the unemployed was largely precluded by ever-widening splits in the labour movement, the appointed commissioners embarked on a relentless campaign to reduce expenditure. In the first three months out relief and the numbers receiving relief were cut by 45 per cent and 25 per cent respectively. Wages of staff employed in maintained institutions were reduced, and their hours increased. Repayments of relief given to the unemployed during the general strike were sought with greater determination. For Woodgate, the most gratifying part of the accounts was the reduction in the numbers receiving out relief:

> It proves that our policy, which makes it a more desirable thing to go to work than to live on out relief is fructifying. The scale given by the late board was not merely a non-incentive to work, but was actually a deterrent. (*SE* 12 March 27.)

In the three years of the regime's existence the guardians' half-yearly call was reduced from £765,950 to £462,680. Outdoor relief fell from a weekly £28,055 to £3,860, and the numbers on relief from 66,502 to 14,541 (West Ham Union 1929). Some of this reduction can be attributed to falls in the general levels of unemployment during this period; the rest was enforced at a social cost. Accusations of callous indifference to worsening social conditions were denied by Woodgate:

> If the people in great hardship let their children die because they have not enough to eat then the blame must be theirs for not bringing their cases forward... We are doing our best to encourage these people to go and find work. (*SE* 30 October 26.)

Initial resistance to the commissioners soon faded; for most of the three years they administered relief without hindrance or threat; indeed, Woodgate considered the Ministry of Health rather than the unemployed to be the main obstacle to the efficient execution of his duties. On receipt of presents as tokens of appreciation from grateful ratepayers, he recalled that in the early months he had to fight the ministry:

> Instead of giving the Government all the money which the Board thought they could save, they devoted a large share to the ratepayers. In the incredible folly of making loans to the West Ham Union, he thought the old guardians and the Ministry of Health were equal participators... By the end of the first six months he saw there would be no difficulty at all in making the finances of the Union solvent. (*SE* 18 January 30.)

The appointed guardians were abolished, along with all other boards, under the terms of the 1929 Local Government Act. Strong suggestions that the ministry was to delay the implementation of the Act in West Ham to allow the commissioners to continue their administration did not prove accurate; the finances of the Union were now healthy and with careful surveillance should remain so. Also the accountability of the commissioners remained a source of discomfort. Administration of relief was assumed by the Public Assistance Committee, a body of twelve persons appointed locally.

As unemployment intensified in the immediate postwar period, a section of the unemployed in West Ham mobilised against the most visible and public symbol of the poor law, namely, the board of guardians and the relieving officers. Articulating demands that challenged dominant discourses of the nineteenth-century poor law to a dilatory board unable to resolve perceived dilemmas, and a government forced by financial and

political crises to relax differentiation between deserving and undeserving, the unemployed wrought concessions leading to significant increases
in the scales of relief.

Subsequent extension of the terrain of struggle, and the election of a
Labour majority on the board, brought the unemployed and the guardians
into direct conflict with a government now able to act in the knowledge that
immediate postwar tremors had passed. The government decided to
repress guardians that were threatening to disrupt a poor law machinery
that was acknowledged to be defective. The Minister of Health was
granted legislative power to impeach obstructive boards; shortly after, in
a process accelerated by the general strike, West Ham guardians were
superseded by government-appointed commissioners.

Resistance to the harsh economic regime imposed by the commissioners in West Ham faded rapidly. Defeat of the general strike was telling, and
in this respect the timing of the supersession was significant. But this alone
cannot explain the sudden willingness to accede to government authority.
It is difficult to avoid the conclusion that struggles against the poor law in
West Ham were built on unsure foundations. Discourses articulated by the
organised unemployed in conflict with the guardians forfeited much of
their power when the boundaries of struggle shifted to include the state.
Within this new terrain the government reconstituted hegemony of the
poor law around principles established in 1834 with such ease that the
effectiveness of challenges to that hegemony in West Ham prior to 1926 has
to be questioned.

The constituency of unemployed engaged in struggles around the poor
law comprised principally unskilled, casual labour which, with relaxation
of restrictions on outdoor relief to the able-bodied poor, unhesitatingly
pressed their demands for relief on the relieving officers. Paul recognised
the problem soon after the onset of mass unemployment. Following a visit
to a Relief Committee he reported to the guardians that

> it was astounding. There were about 40 or 50 boys and girls from 14
> to 19 years of age... They had never asked for out-relief before; they
> had got on without it; but as soon as the Guardians' relief scheme was
> announced, they swooped down. The genuine working man was
> almost conspicuous by his absence. Only two mechanics came under
> his notice. It was necessary to look at this and see if they were not
> inflicting an injustice on the ratepayers and also creating a menace
> for the future. (*SE* 15 January 21.)

And in a retrospective account of the crisis on the eve of supersession,
the local press suggested that the early attempts of the guardians to
alleviate distress from unemployment led inevitably to the usurpation of
the poor law by people who had previously been excluded:

> There is no doubt that in 1920, in their effort to do justice to out of
> work ex-servicemen, the Guardians created a new class of relief
> recipients. The intention of that time has been enormously ex-
> tended... The Minister said there is no legal difference between the

unemployed and the other classes of Poor Law recipients, and it would seem he is determined to go back to the position that obtained before 1920. It is very probable that in such a case thousands of people would disappear from the Guardians' books. (*SE* 5 June 26.)

The body of unskilled labour could rely on little support from outside its ranks. Most skilled workers during the 1920s received benefit through labour exchanges, and as long as unemployment was intermittent, the period of benefit followed by extended or transitional benefits would last until work was found. Some were excluded after the period of benefit expired, but they were more likely to be disallowed through failure to satisfy the genuinely-seeking-work clause or attempted fraud. Those excluded became isolated, and potential protest was foreclosed (Deacon 1977). More important, a powerful stigma still attached to relief, which, unlike unemployment benefit to which they felt entitled because of the contributions paid, was seen as charity. Unemployed skilled labour, even if debarred from benefit, remained firmly embedded within dominant poor law principles and would approach the poor law only out of desperation.

These suspicions and divisions, built upon cultural boundaries and reinforced by discourses around unemployment, militated against effective working class resistance among the unemployed as a body. Nor could the unemployed command support from the labour movement; the leadership considered a national solution to be the only viable one, while the rank and file looked on the plight of the unemployed with indifference. Within the wider community, also, unemployment generated little interest. Elections for guardians, for example, had consistently lower turnouts than those for councillors (Chapter 5). This provoked criticism. Killip remarked at a Labour Party meeting in south West Ham:

> The Forest Gate Ratepayers Association were continually talking about the apathy of the working classes. The apathy of the people toward unemployment was one of the things that caused so little notice to be taken of it. They should let the people who were responsible for it see that they were beginning to take an active interest in what was the most important problem of the time. (*SE* 2 September 22.)

Only the NUWM and other socialist currents within the labour movement gave active support to the unemployed. Influential as they were in providing organisation, they remained in a small minority and could not sustain struggles against the poor law over extended periods. The diatribes of Thorne and Killip against the communists had a substantial degree of truth. In the critical period immediately after the general strike five members of the Communist Party executive, including Hannington, were in prison, and the NUWM much less capable of active intervention. Without the NUWM the unskilled unemployed, with little experience of organisation or industrial struggle, could not withstand direct assault from the government, and the resistance collapsed. Underlying Kirk's rhetoric against the failure of the labour movement to act was a clear attribution of blame for the initial crisis:

> Is muddle-headed leadership responsible for lack of courage to deal with the noxious elements creeping into the local parties for the purpose of disruption? These elements, as is well known, are pandered to by the Blackwell-Price type of parish pump revolutionaries, but the Labour Party in West Ham should be of different stuff. Whatever the mistakes the Labour Guardians made in their fight against the Government, the local unemployed leaders must take the blame. Their public utterances and private intrigues were carefully and deliberately calculated to bring the Labour Guardians into contempt… I assert that the private spite of a handful of 'so-called communists' against such men as Thorne, Jones and Killip is more responsible for the present Guardians' situation, disenfranchisement of the people, and the suffering of the wives and children of the unemployed which the 25 per cent reduction of the scale of relief has involved, than any other cause. (*SE* 31 July 26.)

Reverberations from the defeat of the unemployed in 1926 reached into the 1930s. As unemployment again climbed in West Ham, so struggles were renewed, this time against the means test and the Public Assistance Committee. But increases in relief resulted from higher levels of chronic unemployment rather than an intensification of political activity. At no time were increased scales of relief forced. Demonstrations, although occasionally provoking isolated acts of violence, were contained by the police without difficulty. They matched neither in size nor in intensity those waged against the means test in other areas of the country (Hannington 1977). Resistance to the 1933 Act which introduced the Unemployed Assistance Board was minimal.

5

THE LIMITS OF LABOURISM

Although there was a little bit of politics in me, there wasn't enough for me to be active. At that time it wasn't an interest of mine. Although I realised it was to better things, my interests lay in getting a job, getting some money and that. (Riva Stanton, tape.)

5.1 Patterns of political abstinence

By the end of 1926 it seemed that the Labour Party exercised a powerful authority over local and parliamentary politics in West Ham. So complete was this domination that West Ham suffered none of the reversals in party fortunes witnessed in the metropolis during the late 1920s and early 1930s. Its success had been based on an ability to articulate the demands of an enlarged working-class electorate. In this it was aided by an expansive cooperative movement and a number of key trade unions which began to recognise the significance of political intervention.

Potential opposition had been dismantled, largely as a result of the intractable problem of unemployment, for it was around unemployed struggles in the period leading to supersession of the guardians in 1926 that the Municipal Alliance exposed its sectionalism, and the Communist Party revealed the fragile nature of its political base among the unemployed themselves. Within the industrial sphere also communist influence was curbed; measures taken by union executives effectively undermined the base of communist activity within a trades council already damaged by a split between its political and industrial wings.

But to what extent can we see this formal labourist authority as part of a mobilisation of popular support? In other words, did the party succeed in becoming a vital component of popular culture within West Ham? Answers are not easily found to these questions, nor to those attendant questions on the reasons why labour representation occupied a specific position within working-class culture. Such concerns really demand a separate study of the political dimensions of all spheres of working-class activity, including those of work, the home and leisure in West Ham. There

TABLE 5.1 *Polls (per cent) at general elections in West Ham and selected*
London constituencies, 1918–29

	1918	1922	1923	1924	1929
Plaistow	37.8	54.7	49.9	62.1	63.2
Silvertown	42.3	49.0	45.9	56.1	60.7
Stratford	42.3	64.8	61.8	69.1	66.0
Upton	46.8	69.4	67.2	74.8	70.8
West Ham (average)	**42.2**	**59.2**	**56.2**	**65.3**	**64.7**
East Ham South	57.5	66.3	68.4	75.9	73.8
Woolwich West	60.0	70.1	68.1	79.7	76.8
Poplar, Bow	48.9	69.9	63.7	72.1	66.1
Bethnal Green SW	41.6	59.9	62.1	68.4	64.1
London (average)	**45.5**	**60.3**	**60.0**	**71.0**	**65.8**

Sources: *London Statistics* 1929-30, 33, pp16-19.
            Stratford Express, relevant years.

TABLE 5.2 *Polls (per cent) at municipal elections in West Ham and selected London*
boroughs, 1919, 1922, 1925 and 1928[a]

	1919	1922	1925	1928
West Ham (average)	**23.3**	**36.2**	**41.4**	**35.5**
Bethnal Green	23.0	30.2	38.3	35.5
Poplar	39.2	51.5	47.8	34.8
Woolwich	45.0	53.1	58.2	47.6
London (average)	**27.9**	**36.4**	**42.5**	**32.3**

Sources: As for Table 5.1
Notes: [a] Metropolitan elections were held every three years, West Ham
            annually: for comparison only the above years are relevant.

are, however, already enough clues within the main body of this work to
encourage speculation, tentative though it may be.

In spite of the success of labourism within formal political activity,
support among the working-class electorate in West Ham was restricted.
Labour activists, as we have seen, repeatedly expressed concern at the
persistent lack of support. To an extent this concern was well grounded.
Polls at general elections in West Ham and metropolitan constituencies
(Table 5.1) show that although overall averages were not significantly
different, those for the two West Ham constituencies, where Labour
control was total, were consistently lower than might have been expected.
They were, for example, lower than those of all neighbouring constituencies, including Poplar and Bethnal Green which had electorates of
similar social composition, and other Labour strongholds such as
Woolwich.

A similar picture emerges from municipal elections (Table 5.2). Average
figures were again comparable; they disguise, however, considerably
larger variations than in general elections. In 1922, for example, polls in

West Ham wards varied from 22.2 per cent in Ordnance to 54.1 per cent in Stratford New Town, matching closely lower and upper levels in the metropolis (from 23.9 per cent in Shoreditch to 53.1 per cent in Woolwich). Although polling in West Ham reflected the metropolitan experience, therefore, it was consistently below that displayed in Labour strongholds nearby. This tends to suggest that the intervention of labourism into formal politics in West Ham was restricted.

Membership of the local Labour Party is equally revealing. Detailed figures are not available before 1929, but from these and earlier surrogates such as affiliation fees we can build up a picture of branch membership during the 1920s. The 1929 *Annual Report* of the Labour Party contains data on affiliation fees paid by constituent bodies, together with the membership totals on the basis of which the fees were calculated. Many of the totals are clearly rounded, but they do provide a reasonable guide to the relative strength of local branches.

In 1929 the West Ham Labour Party, located in constituencies that had a record of unparalleled Labour success at municipal and parliamentary elections, could claim only 720 members, divided equally among Plaistow, Silvertown, Stratford and Upton branches. This was a tiny fraction of the membership of local cooperative societies and trade union branches, and small compared with that of constituencies such as East Ham North (900), East Ham South (750), Deptford (1600), Greenwich (1500), Poplar, Bow & Bromley (1200), Poplar South (1705) or Woolwich (4971), where Labour successes were rather more limited. The only metropolitan boroughs with comparable memberships were Battersea (980), Hammersmith (420) and Hackney (1065).

The affiliation fees for West Ham Labour branches throughout the 1920s had not risen above £1.10.0, suggesting that there were no significant changes in the membership. If anything membership increased gradually over this time. In 1923 West Ham Trades Council and Borough Labour Party paid £1.10.0, as did Stratford and Upton parties combined. Plaistow and Silvertown did not pay, probably because their memberships were too low.

All this suggests that involvement in the formal political sphere was low. No doubt under these circumstances it was relatively easy for small, determined groups within the party, and with a sense of political direction, to assume control of the party apparatus. Hence the domination by the South West Ham branch of the National Socialist Party over southern wards throughout the 1920s (p98). But it raises rather more questions about the nature of labourism than it answers. There is no necessary indication, for example, that labourism was an insignificant presence; it could be merely that formal political activity was a relatively minor element within its universe.

What is clear is that such activity was unevenly distributed within the borough. Detailed examination of polls on a ward basis through the 1920s reveals certain quite distinct trends, most notably, that the areas with lowest polls were those with the highest concentrations of unskilled labour. Canning Town, Ordnance, Tidal Basin, Beckton and Hudson in the south (Figure 5.1) demonstrated, with a degree of probability approaching certainty, the lowest turnouts in municipal elections. They were also the safest Labour seats, with the largest majorities when they were contested (in 1924, for example, none of the Labour candidates in these wards was opposed). Conversely, wards in the relatively wealthy areas of the borough were consistently among those with the highest polls – Forest Gate, Broadway and Upton.

Patterns of voting behaviour are extremely complex and defy easy explanation (see Forester 1976 for a brief review of the issues). I have explored some of the important factors affecting political consciousness evidenced in voting, in particular the political discourses and activities of local Labour parties, trade unions and cooperative societies. The ascent of the Labour Party in West Ham can be attributed to their success over others in articulating popular consciousness. Once we excavate beneath the aggregate surface, however, certain irregularities appear which suggest that levels of political activity among the electorate were uneven, and pose the seeming paradox that this activity was lowest in the safest Labour areas.

Some explanation of this paradox can be sought in the theory that voters are less likely to turn out where the result is predictable. There is something in this; a fairly positive correlation exists between high polls and low majorities in West Ham wards during the 1920s (Spearman rank order coefficient of 0.45 in 1922, 0.44 in 1923 and 0.56 in 1924). But there is no such correlation in individual wards over time. The coefficient for Custom House and Silvertown ward over 1922-28, for example, was –0.2.

What remains, and requires further exploration therefore, is the fact that Labour discourses in the poorer areas were, in spite of their overwhelming authority over others, unable to command wide support for formal political activity. The roots of this failure have to be sought in the social and political culture of the dominant social stratum, namely, unskilled manual labour.

5.2 Structural constraints of casualism

The unskilled, in spite of shifts in skill boundaries brought about by the emergence of semiskilled labour, had a considerable presence in West Ham (p20), and the attendant impoverishment, although not as deep as in the nineteenth-century metropolis, was still widespread. Riva Stanton moved with her mother from Bow in the East End to a Silvertown flat in 1917:

> As little as I was when I walked down Emma Street, I was appalled, really shocked. Bow was better than Silvertown. Grandfather worked in Smithfield Market, so there was no shortage of food; no one walked about without stockings. But when I went down this turning I thought 'Oh God; little tiny houses, and all the children

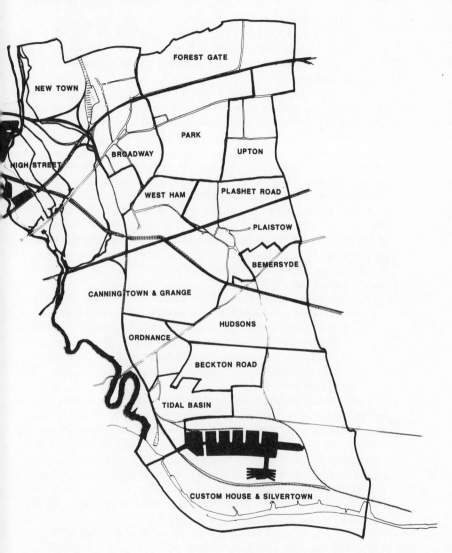

FIGURE 5.1 *West Ham wards after 1921*

looked filthy dirty and slovenly, boys with ragged trousers'.
Couldn't work it out. It left a lasting impression on me. Little as I was
I kept making comparisons with Bow and what I did there and how
we lived there. I was really shocked; it was traumatic for me.
(Stanton, tape.)

Structures of poverty placed considerable constraints on political activity. The daily routines of survival forced by irregular earnings left little
time or money for other pursuits, and had a baneful influence on hope for
the future. A study of juvenile unemployment in West Ham revealed the
enormous economic pressures on individuals to find work of any description. They had no time to think, no conception of what they were
capable of doing. For most the search for work meant long, early waits
outside factory or dock gates; even if they were lucky enough to be taken
on, many were discharged on spurious grounds when they became sixteen
because firms were reluctant to pay extra insurance or increased wages
under Trade Board regulations. When asked what they wanted to do, 90
per cent said 'anything'. Intermittent work with no prospects soon blunted
any vision of a future career (Roker and Scott 1926). A settlement worker
made the same observation:

> Having lived down in Dockland a short while I soon came to the
> conclusion that it was regularity of work – 'a regular job' – which was
> the main thing needed by the majority of its inhabitants… Boys tell
> me that it is one of the main things that knocks the stuffing out of
> them and smashes up any ideals which they might have been trying
> to build, especially when they are starting out upon married life.
> (Kennedy Cox 1939 p41.)

The prospects for female employment were no better. In wealthier parts
of the borough where there were few economic incentives for girls to work,
some were trained in commercial or teaching colleges, while the majority
gained office jobs, commuting to the city (p23). In poorer districts, girls
debarred from office work by competition from better qualified peers,
were forced into the precarious world of machining and dressmaking or,
in industrial areas, into factory work. Failing this, service or retail work
could be found. With luck, perhaps through relatives already in employment, a girl could be taken on at a local factory. For Riva Stanton, who
worked at Tate & Lyle as a sugar cutter, earning as much as £2.17.6 per
week, the job had additional attractions:

> Around Tate's was like a village. All the week I used to love to see the
> girls coming out of that factory when I come home from school. All
> them factories had their own coloured uniforms … and [the girls] all
> seemed so happy to me. I used to think, well I'm going to be one of
> them someday. What an ambition, oh my God! (Stanton, tape.)

Even in such relatively well paid jobs employment was seasonal. It
ceased altogether once a woman married, and so also did the compan-
ionship and limited degree of economic independence as wives and
mothers assumed responsibility for the maintenance of home and children

with all the attendant toil, privation and degradation. Under relatively favourable circumstances the task was onerous; in slum conditions it was overpowering. In Canning Town, for example:

> The War made things very much worse, and in recent years the overcrowding has been unspeakably ghastly. It takes different forms. In many cases there are dirty, greasy stairs, filthy paper, black ceilings, begrimed windows, ill-fitting doors, and generally in the one room tenements no proper facilities for cooking or washing, no water supply, and a terrible absence of sanitary requirements. If the housewife is an indefatigable worker most of her time and strength will be taken up with domestic duties and adjustments of furniture. (Newland 1932 p37.)

Conditions experienced by many women in impoverished households restricted any involvement in political activity. Even when the opportunity and interest were there, patriarchal ideology presented a further barrier:

> My mum didn't belong to [the Women's Cooperative Guild]. She didn't have the time to belong to anything… I mean, you think what she was doing – cooking, shopping, washing – she used to go and do a day's washing for someone for half a crown. My dad didn't do much. He sat in his armchair and gave the orders. The men weren't going to let the women get out like that, you must be joking. My dad would say 'Your place is here'. He was like a lot of men, he had what suited him. They might be socialists, but if they wanted to break the rules to suit them, they'd do it. [Mum] was a very determined woman regarding anything getting on top of her, yet my dad could brow beat her. (Stanton, tape.)

Occasionally, outstanding women emerged to play a considerable role in local politics. One such was Mrs Enever, who became a leading member of the North West Ham branch of the BSP, attended the founding conference of the Communist Party, and later set up and ran a branch of the Women's Cooperative Guild at Leyton. But even her full potential was never realised, as her son recalls:

> I wouldn't have thought my ol' man was all that bloody marvellous at helping mum. She'd have gone a lot further in the labour movement with somebody who was supportive. They wanted to run her as MP, the unemployed did, but the ol' man wasn't too supportive. Some were keen to help their wives, but they were not going to be put out in any way at all for anything. [Husbands] had either got to be meek and mild, or got to work with them… A lot of the women wanted to be active, to feel they was doing something, but they was barred. (Enever, tape.)

Mrs Clarke also, a leading member of the Stratford Women's Cooperative Guild, never attempted to serve on the council because she felt that her husband Harry, secretary of the Stratford Labour Party, needed her support (Baker, tape). It is perhaps not surprising that the women who were able to be active in this period were, like Edith Kerrison and Rebecca

Cheetham, unmarried, middle class and educated, or like Daisy Parsons, powerful enough to assert their independence.

And independent they needed to be, for public service on, say, the council demanded time in the evenings and often also in the day. Those in paid employment needed time off, and this was granted to relatively few. The GER Co. allowed employees elected to public bodies sufficient time to perform their duties without loss of pay, but this was suspended after amalgamation into the LNER Co., prompting Kirk, who had served on West Ham Council for fourteen years, to demand that expenses be paid from public funds (*Railway Rev.* 9 May 24). In general, only the self employed, union workers and the relatively well off could meet the demands of council service, or indeed regular political work, without considerable personal and financial sacrifice. These people are, for example, well represented among candidates in the 1919 election (p38), and among the membership of the North West Ham branch of the BSP (p34).

Other institutional activities which impinged on political involvement were also remote from the unskilled poor. The cooperative movement never gained a base among the poor. For the majority of its (skilled male) members, there was little point in attracting the poor; the movement was for them a business concern and any concessions to the poor could only affect dividends. The Women's Cooperative Guild, on the other hand, recognised that higher prices for standard quantities of food were an effective barrier to those who needed to find the cheapest, in smaller quantities. It had earlier opened a 'people's store' in Sunderland which sold wholesome food at cheap prices, and in small quantities, made loans to tide customers over particular financial difficulty, and provided club rooms as centres of cooperative activity (Llewellyn Davis 1904). But it was forced to close. Higher prices demanded by the dividend simply forced poor families to go elsewhere.

In complete contrast with cooperative might in north West Ham, especially around Stratford, and in neighbouring areas of East Ham and Leyton, one society existed in the south at Canning Town. Founded in 1873, it was financially insecure, eventually being taken over by the SCS in 1882, and maintained as a small outpost. Riva Stanton was taken there by a friend:

> She had these metal things; she says I got to change these for my mum. This coop, a little shop on the corner, ... was my first experience of coops. I couldn't understand it. Of course, my mother couldn't afford it. The prices was a little bit dearer than anywhere else. It wouldn't appeal to my mother – she had to go to what she thought was the cheapest and the best. (Stanton, tape.)

Trade unions tended to draw their members from the same broad constituencies. None catered specifically for the needs of labourers; and none could. Financial stability depended on regular subscriptions. The dramatic expansion of general unions during the war had been built on an ability to attract large numbers of labourers with reasonably secure employment, but with the recession and decline in female employment the unions faced severe financial problems. Overall, between 1920 and 1923 the Workers Union lost 72 per cent of its members, NAUL 65 per cent and NUGW 48 per cent (Clegg 1985 p346), although within West Ham traditions of loyalty and more stable employment amongst gas workers and council employees shored up the latter (p89). All suffered increasingly from a rapid turnover of members caused by their irregular income and a certain instrumentality to the benefits on offer.

Structural factors, therefore, operated disproportionately against the ability of the unskilled to become involved in political activity. As an explanation of political passivity, however, this is at best partial. The lived experience and consciousness of the unskilled distanced them from labourist discourses articulated by Labour leaders in West Ham. Lack of access may have promoted this, but of rather greater significance was the availability of contrasting discourses.

5.3 Political culture of the unskilled

That we cannot speak of a single, unified working class without considerable qualification is now accepted. For within this social bloc distinct strata exist, distinguished from one another by material circumstances, and a range of social and cultural affiliations. Boundaries change; over the past 150 years that between skilled and unskilled has in part been eroded, not least by the emergence of the semiskilled within the workforce. Thus the chasm that once separated the two is no longer quite so deep or wide; but it exists still.

The historiography of the British working class – whether or not individual studies recognised the fact – has been devoted almost exclusively to the strata of the skilled and semiskilled. In a sense this has been justified since it was from their ranks that trade unions, friendly societies and political parties sprang; they constituted the manifest political presence of the working class. Meanwhile the majority – the unskilled – remains largely unknown. Today we understand little more of the culture of this stratum than did social investigators of the nineteenth century.

It is from these social investigators that we must start. Mayhew recognised the singular nature of his inquiry into 'the state of the people ... in the undiscovered country of the poor', not merely because it was the first systematic investigation but also because it was based in large part on the oral testimony of the poor themselves (Mayhew 1967). His preoccupation with recording living and working conditions in extraordinary detail precluded any in-depth study of political attitudes and behaviour; what we learn is from the occasional diversion in sections on social habits. But it can be valuable.

Take, for example, his discussion of the politics of costers. Costers, it is claimed at the outset, are nearly all chartists. The ensuing discussion suggests something of the political and social base of this 'chartism'. Among coster communities there are one or two 'more intelligent' members (invariably chartists) who wield considerable influence. As one said to Mayhew:

> The costers think that working men know best, and so they have confidence in us. I like to make men discontented, and I will make them discontented while the present system continues because it's all for the middle and moneyed classes, and nothing, in the way of rights, for the poor. (ibid. I p20.)

So chartist sympathies among costers derived from an acceptance of articulate leaders in their midst who promoted a self identity not of a class, but of the poor against the rich. It was a vague, instinctive political perspective that owed more to the exigencies of daily routine than to theory. The point is made by other respondents:

> A Chartist costermonger told me that he knew numbers of costers who were keen Chartists without understanding anything about the six points. [They] have very vague notions of an aristocracy; they call the more prosperous of their own body 'aristocrats'. Their notions of an aristocracy of birth or wealth seem to be formed on their opinion of the rich, or reputed rich salesmen with whom they deal; and the result is anything but favourable to the nobility. (ibid.)

But at the heart of political consciousness was a hatred of the police:

> The notion of the police is so intimately blended with what may be called the politics of costermongers that I give them together... The hatred of a costermonger to a 'peeler' is intense, and with their opinion of the police, all the more ignorant unite that of the governing power... I am assured that in case of a political riot every 'coster' would seize his policeman. (ibid.)

Politics for the coster owed little to chartism, which in any case was by then a spent political force. It was a vague assertion of an impoverished, occupationally bounded, collective identity and livelihood against those financial and state agents who threatened them. 'Rich' salesmen restricted meagre earnings, police harassment did the same by excluding them from favourable pitches. Chartists could give voice to this discontent, but even they denied an opportunity to redress grievances in an appropriate manner:

> The costermongers frequently attended political meetings... Some of them could not understand why Chartist leaders exhorted them to peace and quietness, when they might as well fight it out with the police at once. (ibid.)

In contrast to costers, dustmen were said by Mayhew to have no political sympathies. This claim, however, is based on the observation that they have 'no clear knowledge of what "the Charter" requires', only a 'confused notion that it is something against the Government, and that the enactment of it would make them all right' (ibid. p177). What they do possess is a 'deep rooted antipathy to the police, the magistrates, and all connected with the administration of justice, looking upon them as their natural enemies', together with a fierce sense of collective identity. In this there is little to distinguish the politics of costers and dustmen or, indeed, of unskilled labour in general. For Mayhew, political discourses were those around the charter, and these were inhabited by the skilled; outside them existed the unskilled who, in spite of a tradition of resistance to state agencies, were 'unpolitical as footmen'. The divide was 'curious and striking' (ibid. III p233).

Booth also was concerned with themes of poverty and labour. His scope was socially and geographically wider than the Mayhew survey, and benefited from advances in techniques of social inquiry. However, the insights from statistical refinement were gained at the expense of ethnography; London people do not speak as loudly or as often in the pages of Booth as they do in Mayhew. As a consequence, the problem of gaining access to political culture, particularly that of the casual poor, seems even more intractable.

Booth contended that the working class of East London were politically conscious:

> Judging by the clubs there would seem to be no doubt of the political complexion of East London; and the weekly papers mostly taken – *Reynolds's* and the *Dispatch* – tell the same story. But the tone is not so much Liberal or even Radical, as Republican, outside the lines, authorized or unauthorized, of English party politics, and thus very uncertain at the ballot box. There is also a good deal of vague unorganized Socialism. (Booth 1892 Series 1, I p99.)

But precisely which working class constituency was being described? The clubs were undoubtedly part of the tradition of Radical metropolitan culture, inhabited initially by artisans, but toward the end of the century increasingly by semiskilled trade unionists who, around new unionism, were drawn to a diffuse socialism which at the time had little belief in the need for labour representation (Davis 1989; and Marriott 1984 for a discussion of this in the context of West Ham, the cradle of new unionism).

The unskilled rejected, or were rejected by, this tradition. From them, Beatrice Potter in characteristic tone claimed,

> Respectability and culture have fled... Weary of work, and sick of the emptiness of stomach and mind, the man or the woman wanders into the street. The sensual laugh, the coarse joke, the brutal fight, or the mean and petty cheating of the street bargain are the outward sights yielded by society to soothe the inward condition of overstrain or hunger. (ibid. IV p29.)

The inherent difficulties of perceiving this culture outside perceptions of middle-class observers are not resolved in the work of Stedman Jones (1972, 1974). In *Outcast London* the structural location and dynamics of casual labour are analysed with perspicacity, but it is not until the end, in a few brief pages, that we begin to understand something of its political complexion. Relying on evidence from Mayhew he concludes that the casual poor, structurally and culturally distant from an artisan elite, had no political tradition:

the most striking characteristic of the casual poor was neither their
adherence to the left, nor yet their adherence to the right, but rather
their rootless volatility... The ever pressing demands of the stomach,
the chronic uncertainty of employment, the pitiful struggle of
worker against worker at the dock gate, the arbitrary sentence of
destitution, and the equally arbitrary cascade of charity provided no
focus for any lasting growth of collective loyalty upon which a stable
class-consciousness could be based. (ibid. pp343-4.)

In his subsequent article, as part of an attempt to locate politics more
firmly within broader cultural forms, the shift in working-class politics
toward what Booth termed 'pleasure, hospitality and sport' is explored in
depth. Between 1870 and 1910, the argument runs, the metropolitan
working class was remade. Earlier struggles around radicalism were
selectively re-articulated into a distinctive, impermeable and inward-
looking culture which found its voice in trade unionism, cooperation and
eventually labour representation. It was a culture of 'consolation'; defensive and unwilling to challenge monarchy, established religion or empire,
let alone extant relations of production, it achieved its apotheosis in the
Labour Party.

Persuasive though these arguments are, and useful as they may be to an
understanding of specific forms of working-class culture such as music
hall and the origins of the Labour Party, questions remain over the broad
trajectory of change, particularly in the course of this century. The culture
described – that of clubs, trade unions and friendly societies, having roots
in secularism and radicalism – was not one familiar to the unskilled poor.
(Some forms clearly overlapped. Music hall was one, but there was a world
of difference between the respectable, palatial halls frequented by middle-
class observers, and the small halls, built as extensions to pubs, which were
little more than brothels with bawdy entertainment thrown in.) As a result
it is difficult to determine the extent to which the the casual poor were
affected by the 'remaking'. Having had only tenuous links with the older
radical tradition, any shift away from politics to pleasure and amusement
would have been almost imperceptible. If change occurred, it was in the
forms of popular cultural activity rather than across the suggested
boundaries between politics and popular culture.

The ideological universe of the unskilled has recently been explored by
Jerry White (1986) in an illuminating study of Campbell Road, Islington
between the wars. Inhabited by a lumpen, sub-proletarian community
which rejected and was rejected by the local labour market, it gained a
notorious reputation for lawlessness and violence. White excavates beneath the surface laid down by social, philanthropic and legal records
better to understand the internal economic and social relations of the
community.

From these relations a propensity for distinct but contradictory political
attitudes was constructed around the ideologies of egalitarianism, individualism, libertarianism and chauvinism. Egalitarianism sprang from a

'defensive rationalization' of the community's position outside the labour market, reinforced by collective processes of mutual aid, particularly among the women. Rejection of the labour market promoted individualism, a belief in the necessity of self interest over that of others, although not to the extent of creating economic hierarchies within the community. In this respect individualism was mediated by egalitarianism. This mediation in turn fostered libertarianism, manifest in a culture which collectively rejected dominant social codes and agencies, particularly external authorities. Finally, chauvinism emerged from the intense localism produced by outcasting. Its power did not derive from assertion of an English national pride, but rather from an assertion of a superiority over foreign people as a means of salvaging the collective identity of a displaced community.

A person occupying this contradictory ideological universe was unlikely to be committed to a political party (White p106). Only one resident was a candidate in a local election, and not one of White's respondents claimed membership of a political party. Because of the Labour Party's apparent concern with the poor, it proved the most attractive, but allegiance was vague and passive, more the result of a rejection of alternatives than active ascription to Labour's values. Furthermore, the Labour Party was a party of the skilled working class, with its own culture and identity, remote from and dismissive of the unrespectable poor. The party was strongest in South Islington wherein resided skilled workers, and gained control of Tollington ward, encompassing Campbell Road, only from 1937.

Do these arguments in any way shed light on the abstinence from formal political activity in West Ham? It is questionable whether we are dealing with the same social stratum. Poverty there was in both communities, but the decidedly lumpen countenance of Campbell Road was not characteristic of, say, Canning Town. Evidence from the local press and respondents, necessarily using a small sample, suggests that amongst Campbell Road residents male employment was dominated by street sellers and entertainers, and general labourers, with few skilled or semi-skilled workers, while females were charwomen or street sellers, with some factory employment. Canning Town residents had much higher proportions of manual labour, especially factory work and shop work, with relatively little street employment. The contrast is very much what we would expect from the more heavily industrial character of West Ham. West Ham had its share of notorious streets – Martindale Road, Malmesbury Road and Wouldham Street – with considerable lumpen elements, but even in the south where these streets were located there was not overall rejection of and by the labour market.

Politically the contrast was marked. As we have seen, throughout the interwar period there was a powerful tradition of formal labourism, manifest in the domination by the Labour Party of local politics. This domination was built around a labourist rhetoric that did articulate elements of lumpen proletarian ideology. It was egalitarian in promoting a collective self identity of a working class (an 'us'), and in urging social justice for the poor; and it was chauvinistic in asserting images both of the nation and of foreign incursions, particularly into the spheres of work and politics. But it was neither individualistic nor libertarian. The sure-footedness and continuity of labourism, and the abiding significance of trade union organisation in West Ham are testimony rather to the collective and more conformist leanings of the unskilled. There simply was nothing of the same political volatility of the Campbell Road community or its active hostility to trade unions, both of which were the products of individualism and libertarianism.

There is a more substantive epistemological problem. The ideologies identified are correctly located in material, lived realities of Campbell Road residents, but in a way which tends to suggest that they emerge 'naturally' from those realities. The emphasis is misplaced. Ideologies are actively constructed in consciousness through discursive practices. Chauvinism, for example, did not spring from changing material circumstances and class boundaries; rather it was articulated by racist and imperialist discourses during the nineteenth century, components of which took root in the lumpenproletariat (indeed the British working class as a whole) because of the propitious material conditions it experienced. It is necessary, therefore, to direct attention, as I have attempted to do in this study for other constituencies, to the precise discursive location of the unskilled.

Consider the following description of a poverty-laden existence in Canning Town:

> Illiterate, uneducated and inarticulate, uncouth and unkempt, beaten, starved, frozen, unwanted, unloved, living a less than animal existence in the filthy putrid gutters of London's East End, scratching and clawing and fighting with stray dogs and disease ridden rats for possession of scraps of rotten food thrown down by more fortunate humans, or lying in the streets after the markets had closed.

The picture given here of the daily struggle for survival is familiar to any who have read social accounts of East London. It could well have been written by Jack London, or, divested of a certain literariness, appeared in Booth or the *New survey of London life and labour*. In fact it is taken from an autobiography of a Canning Town labourer (Burr nd c1985). What is notable is not only the extent of hardship endured, but also the sense of self identity it reflects and its close resemblance to middle-class constructions of that identity.

That the unskilled poor inhabited identities which in many respects were so strongly tied to middle-class perceptions was no accident (I am indebted here to Stallybrass and White's excellent analysis of cultural imagery of the middle class, 1986). As a necessary step toward its formation in post-Renaissance European culture, the bourgeoisie gradually withdrew from popular cultural forms. In the process, many of these forms were constructed as 'low' and 'disgusting', so reinforcing the bourgeoisie's own sense of a separate and superior identity, and providing mechanisms through which a hierarchical ordering could be consolidated.

This high/low dichotomous structuring operated in the symbolic domains of the human body, the social formation, geographical space and psychic forms. Thus when the urban poor and the lumpenproletariat were rejected as a 'low Other' by a bourgeoisie actively constructing its self identity, a comprehensive symbolic repertoire was utilised to define the culture, residence, entertainment, language and body of the poor. This had a particular salience for images of the nineteenth-century city. When poor areas of the city first became known to the bourgeoisie through the efforts of various social reformers and novelists, they were viewed with disgust and fascination:

> In Chadwick, in Mayhew, in countless Victorian reformers, the slum, the labouring poor, the prostitute, the sewer, were recreated for the bourgeois study and drawing room as much as for the urban council chamber. Indeed, the reformers were central in the construction of the urban geography of the bourgeois Imaginary. As the bourgeois produced new forms of regulation and prohibition governing their own bodies, they wrote ever more loquaciously of the body of the Other – of the city's slum. (ibid. pp125 – 6.)

These symbolic constructions gained momentum in the course of the nineteenth century. Economic development within the metropolis augmented the body of casual labour on the margins of the labour market, but at the same time fuelled anxiety about its disruptive potential. The physical and moral increasingly were tied to the political and legal as the middle class sought to reinforce its own identity and align itself to the capitalist state (Hobbs 1988 pp105 – 6).

The complex litany of expulsion through which the low Other – evidenced in the slum, the fair, the cheap theatre, sexual licentiousness and crime – was constituted, simultaneously defined the respectable, the conventional bourgeois. And this was a supremely political process, for it shored up the immanent class elitism of bourgeois democratic forms.

In Stallybrass and White's study the poor retain a shadowy presence. To be fair, despite its title, challenges to hierarchical forms of political and cultural authority are not one of the principal concerns. There are suggestions, however, on ways in which the matter may be broached. These cohere around the notion of carnival.

It is largely as a result of the pioneering work of Bakhtin that carnival has recently gained currency in literary criticism and to a less extent in historiography (Bennett 1979, Clark and Holquist 1984, Eagleton 1981). Bakhtin's study of Rabelais uncovers the role of carnival in Renaissance Europe, not only as an event but also as an embodiment of a quite distinct ideological universe. Carnival in itself was not a spectacle, a festive diversion from life's rigours, rather it was a lived celebration, embracing all in a ritual governed by its own internal dynamics, subsuming the individual into the collectivity, revealing an awareness of a material, sensual and bodily community. As such it constituted not an affirmation but a threat to extant hierarchical authority.

Through carnival, folk *qua* folk are temporarily liberated from political and moral restraint imposed by official ideology to pursue alternative, utopian visions. In these visions dominant representations were transgressed – symbolically inverted or decentred, turned upside down. The king becomes fool, the fool becomes king, if only for a day. Transgression is manifest principally in bodily imagery; 'grotesque realism' provides an anatomical metaphor of and for a community as a heterogeneous and expansive community, and in which the belly and anus become the heart and mind of the new utopia.

Bakhtin recognised the significance of the carnivalesque beyond Rabelais. For him it informs and illuminates other populist visions of the world from below that seek a critical inversion of dominant ideologies. His lead has been followed, as a result of which carnival, although virtually extinct in European culture, occupies an increasingly important position as an analytical category, particularly in studies of third-world literature (Stallybrass and White 1986 p6).

Historians have been more diffident, largely because of the uncertain political specificity of carnival. Transgression is a symbolic challenge to hegemonic forms; it has never produced a platform for radical political change. With this in mind Eagleton (1981 p148) has argued that carnival is a licensed affair in which the people release tension by energetic ostentation. On the other hand, there is abundant evidence of an active suppression of the carnivalesque in popular cultural forms of late eighteenth and early nineteenth-century Britain as the middle class withdrew and attempted to redefine the boundaries of acceptable leisure, including sport (Cunningham 1980). In fact, carnival incorporates mutually contradictory elements; it is both radical and conservative, liberating and incorporating, disruptive and consolidating. It cannot be essentialised, because its political specificity is conferred by the complex political and social antagonisms of the conjuncture.

The association within orthodoxy of the carnival with the medieval has tended to avert attention from its influence on the more recent history of industrial societies. Until the late eighteenth and early nineteenth centuries popular politics and carnival were indissolubly linked. The schism between the two forced by distancing of the middle class, however, was not complete. Carnivaleque elements – perhaps in attenuated form – survived, and continued to exert an influence throughout the nineteenth and into the twentieth centuries.

The poor participated in the series of metropolitan disturbances from the Gordon riots of 1780 to the bread riots of 1855, 1861 and 1866, and the unemployed riots of 1886 (the vocabulary is significant), but this participation was instrumental and short-term, akin to Mayhew's description of the sweeps' sympathy with chartism:

> not because it would be calculated to establish a new order of things, but in the hope that, in the transition from one system to another,

there might be plenty of noise and riot, and in the vague idea that in some indefinable manner good must necessarily accrue to themselves from any change that might take place. (Cited in Stedman Jones 1972 p343.)

A similar sympathy among costers sprang from a desire to seek retribution against the police (p172). Even the 1889 Dock Strike, an event that is invariably seen as the herald of new unionism, 'bore as much resemblance to a medieval carnival as to a modern industrial strike' (ibid. p347). The contrast between it and the contemporaneous gasworkers' struggles in terms of their political rhetoric, conduct and response from the state was considerable. But then the constituencies were different (Marriott 1984).

Transgression was also enacted in 'crime'. On the margins of the labour market, and yet adjacent to the heart of finance capital, the metropolitan poor were often forced to survive by adopting entrepreneurial ethics outside the strict boundaries of the law. 'Doing the business' suggested a means of trading and dealing characteristic of a pre-industrial economy, which at the same time appropriated and actively usurped bourgeois commercial ethics and language (Hobbs 1988 p117). Through 'business' a proletarian status was affirmed which existed not in open conflict with the forces of capital but as a covert negotiation – a repartee.

In street parties, bawdy humour, fairs, street entertainment, the celebration of body over mind, sport, theatre, language and 'crime', elements of the carnivalesque survived among the metropolitan poor. When Jerry White talks of the libertarianism of Campbell Road, he touches on an ideology deeply rooted in the carnival:

> The collective rejection of the dominant social code is plainly implied in the Bunk's culture – its street theatre, involving violence, rowdiness, open gambling, some public nakedness and so on. In this culture oddness was not only tolerated it was encouraged... It was summed up in the frequent self-description of the people from the Bunk as 'rough and ready', and the internal labelling of streets like it as 'do as you please' (White 1986 p104.)

Similarly, Gillian Rose's study of Poplar in the 1920s emphasises the culture's love of performance and melodrama. Political meetings had obligatory entertainment. Those of the Poplar Labour Women's Guild, for example, used to attract about 300, who came as much for the entertainment as for political enlightenment (Rose 1988).

In West Ham elections provided many people with their first experience of political involvement. It began at an early age, and took quite specific forms. Chas Parish recalls the excitement of the occasion for children:

> At election times cars used to transport voters from their homes to the polling booth... Us kids would be allowed to ride on the back of the motor provided that we sang out suitable slogans in favour of the candidate owning the motor. Thus we would ride along the road singing:

'Vote, vote, vote for Tommy Groves
Punch old Murphy in the eye,
If it wasn't for the law
We would punch him on the jaw
And he wouln't go voting anymore'.
We were very fickle and would alter the names to suit the circum-
stances according to the owner of the motor car. (Parish nd 1983.)

In Silvertown, where people had to walk to the booths, the same mood
prevailed:

The girl across the road said to me one day 'Tomorrow we're all
going out to march, everybody's got to come'.
'What are we marching about?'
Do you know what it was for?
'Vote, vote, vote for Jack Jones
Knock old somebody in the eye...'
We walked all round the streets with this big banner – crowds of
kids, could you imagine? You wouldn't see it now would you?
(Stanton, tape.)

Elections were therefore used by the children as a vehicle for a series of
ritualised activities having much more to do with a sense of fun and
excitement than with political consciousness. They became public celebrations of collective identities, which were often reinforced by constructing 'political' opponents. The links with wider cultural practices
were evident:

We used to fight each other at election times, it was almost traditional
... the same as an Oxford and Cambridge boat race, you'd either be
a dark blue or a light blue. You had to have some opposition, so some
used to gang up and say 'We're the Tories', and they'd go round
knocking on doors, telling people to vote Tory, and we'd go round
after them telling people to vote Labour. (Robinson, tape.)

Occasionally, these rivalries were more openly hostile. Vacant stretches
of waste land became battlegrounds for election gangs.

Either one of the gangs would go up there and fix up pieces of
corrugated iron down one end of it and then down the other end the
same, and the gangs would take up their positions at each end and
throw bricks at each other all night. Gangs used to form up as Tories
just to give us something to do. It had nothing to do with the tradition
of voting Labour. It was just a matter of having some rivalry. (ibid.)

It would be easy to dismiss such activities as childish pranks, but in
important respects they represented wider cultural forms in which they
were located, and could influence future patterns of political activity. What
was striking about elections in West Ham was not only the low polls but
the contrast between these and the ways in which overtly festive elements
were incorporated. Elections meetings were frequently broken up. During
the 1922 parliamentary campaign, for example, the local press reported
that the Tory candidate Lyle was

meeting with a good deal of opposition at his meetings – a disgraceful and hooligan opposition organised by a very advanced and probably small army of extreme Socialists… The exhibition of these champions of 'freedom' do no real harm to their opponents. (*SE* 11 November 22.)

Lyle was, however, defeated and later resigned:

He had no hesitation in saying that the methods that were employed during the last election were a scandal and a disgrace to any decent body of men… They had to meet the tactics of the bludgeon, the blackguard, and the brick. These tactics resulted in such a state of affairs that up to the Thursday before the poll there was not a single meeting which they had arranged which was not broken up and the Red Flag sung. (*SE* 17 February 23.)

Each year huge crowds would gather outside Stratford Town Hall to hear the results:

A fairly large number of people assembled in the Broadway for the declaration of the poll, and most of the candidates with their friends, as well as most of the council, were present in the Town Hall. As soon as it became known that the Labour candidates had been successful, scenes of enthusiasm prevailed. Councillor Godbold saluted Mr. Groves with a hearty kiss, and later danced a 'bunny hug' with Councillor J. Jones MP who arrived at the Town Hall at about 10 o'clock. By this time the ranks of the public outside had grown very largely. The front of the Town Hall was illuminated by four big lamps, and the results announced from time to time were received with loud cheers. (*SE* 18 November 19.)

This sense of politics as spectacle and ritual helps to account for the popularity of other open air meetings, particularly those held regularly on Sunday mornings along the Barking Road. People came to see and listen to political leaders, in particular Jack Jones who was a 'marvellous orator, one of the finest speakers you ever heard in your life. He could have them falling about laughing and then crying' (Stokes, tape). But attendance was not prompted necessarily by political obligation, nor was it a source of radicalisation:

The working man will of course often listen to an extremist street corner orator, especially on Sunday mornings, but this is explained by the simple fact that the orator provided some sort of free entertainment with which to while away a dull half hour before the pubs open or the dinner is ready. (Kennedy Cox 1939 p247.)

Often a rival meeting was held by, say, the Salvation Army, which attracted just as much support: 'People were attracted by the Sunday speechifying' (Sainsbury, tape). But it was the unemployed struggles of the 1920s that provided the obvious example of carnivalesque politics. Although the leadership was largely communist inspired, the main body of marchers comprised the unskilled, amongst whom the distress caused by unemployment hit hardest. Demonstrations to the guardians gave them an

opportunity to engage in untheorised forms of open hostility to the
authoritarian apparatus of the poor law, often to the regret of the leaders:

> There was a crowd of no-gooders amongst them. They wouldn't
> have a lot of politics about them, and they didn't have much of the
> organisation amongst them... We took the Town Hall over. They'd
> go in there and play cards all day long – that element. There was a lot
> of the lumpenproletariat about – I suppose it was warmer and a bit
> more comfortable in the Town Hall than in their own home. They
> could talk there, whereas they couldn't talk in the library. (Enever,
> tape.)

Membership of political organisations, regular attendance at meetings
to debate policy and formulate strategy, steady work in electioneering,
propaganda, even voting at elections were alien to this political culture.
But at the same time it was not positioned outside the boundaries of
labourism. To say that support for the Labour Party was not active is not
the same as saying that it did not exist. The support derived from an
instinctive, traditional, commonsensical identification with the party
rather than an intellectual, ethical or moral commitment. In this sense
labourism was successful in imparting a limited political specificity to the
carnival.

Something of the nature of this identification can be grasped from Riva
Stanton's political education:

> In our way we all experienced politics. We was told if Jack Jones gets
> in, he's the Labour man, he'll look after us, we'll have better RO
> [Relieving Officer], better this, better that. I'm not saying that you
> understood it, but that it was there. (Stanton, tape.)

The identification with Labour was strengthened by the role of local
leaders. Labour leaders were remote neither geographically nor
cognitively, and so could readily be incorporated into the symbolic domain
of the unskilled:

> Tommy Groves – what an MP he was... You could get hold of Tommy
> at any time of the day or night. If he was out in the street he'd talk to
> you. If you went to his house, no matter what he was doing, he'd take
> you in, he'd listen and try to help you. Wonderful man. (ibid.)

With surprising alacrity this identification soon invested itself with the
cloak of tradition:

> People voted for Labour because it was traditional. Even today (and
> it was more so then) if you get into a group and you try to introduce
> a political discussion, you're not on, they don't want to know. This
> is the reason why. As far as they are concerned, there is no argument.
> There is no need for discussion. Labour is the party to represent
> working-class people; the working class vote Labour, finish. We
> don't want to discuss the intricacies of political dogma and that kind
> of thing, no. (Robinson, tape.)

True, West Ham had a record since the 1890s of returning labour
councillors and MPS, but given that the Labour Party did not become a

significant political force until 1906, the sense of tradition – the equation of labour and Labour – in retrospect seems premature, even if, because of previous restrictions on the franchise, voting Labour was the only voting known to many.

This was both the triumph and the failure of the Labour Party within labourism. From a working-class constituency the party gained a degree of support denied to other political organisations. Support, however, was uneven. Discourses around formal political representation had a greater purchase amongst those working-class people who inhabited the institutionalised domain of trade unionism and cooperation. Amongst those at the margins of this domain – those excluded from the material and symbolic universe of organised labour – support derived from a vague, passive, untheorised, instinctive identification with the party, rather than from active ascription to its ideals or to the need for labour representation.

The nature of this identification was fragile, and its legacy was to be cruelly demonstrated in subsequent years. A large constituency of the working class has had no abiding allegiance to the party. To the contrary, when other parties have been able to articulate its identification to alternative symbolic domains such as the nation, allegiance has shifted. Today, following ten years of uninterrupted Conservative power, doubts are raised about the ability of the Labour Party to survive. Its demise would be tragic for an influential tradition of formal political involvement; whether it would be so for labourism is another question.

NEW SURVEY OF LONDON LIFE AND LABOUR

The survey was undertaken to determine inter alia the level of poverty in the working-class population of London, and whether living conditions had improved since the comparable Booth survey of some 40 years earlier. Much of the empirical material was provided by the house sample inquiry, in which data were collected for samples of private houses, omitting lodging houses, hostels and hotels. A 1-in-50 systematic sample was used for West Ham, giving a sampling factor of 48.5. Falsification, it was claimed, was rare (see discussion of the methodology in *New survey of London life and labour*, II, 1930, *Social survey. Eastern area*).

Survey cards were completed for each family which lived as a separate, economic unit. Lodgers were described as such, subtenants listed separately. A wide range of information on socio-economic circumstances of individual family members of working age was sought. Where possible details were listed of age, occupation, weekly wage, workplace, hours of work, cost of transport, rent and birthplace.

I processed this information using a dbase plus IV data handling program. Details of 2523 individuals were included. Occupations were entered as described, and classified into one of the following: skilled manual, semiskilled manual, unskilled manual, supervisory, apprentice, retail, clerical, management, professional. Male and female were identified, unemployed listed separately. I am sensitive to the arbitrary nature of such a classification; frequently it was difficult to assign an occupation because the boundary between, say, skilled and semiskilled is not well defined. Some designated occupations incorporate a wide variety of skill levels, and we cannot ignore the cultural dimensions of skill. Hours of work and wages help in the classification, and I have attempted to be consistent. To illustrate this, some of the principal occupations are listed:

skilled	semiskilled	unskilled	retail	clerical	professional
toolsmith	driver	labourer	shop-	clerk	doctor
sugar-	hammerman	cook	keeper	civil-	teacher
boiler	postman	boot-repairer	shop-	servant	musician
plumber	machinist	seaman	assist't	typist	optician
engineer	stoker	cleaner	butcher	office-	estate agent
carpenter	solderer	domestic	draper	boy/girl	curate

skilled	semiskilled	unskilled	retail	clerical	professional
fitter	trucker	packer	traveller	secretary	architect
electri-	fireman	porter			
cian	operator	hand/mate			
mechanic	furrier	sorter			
boiler-	dress-				
maker	maker				

Workplaces were identified and assigned to West Ham, East London, London, East Ham, sea or other. Hours of work were included. Unemployed were assigned 0, irregularly employed coded separately, and where upper and lower figures were given indicating variable hours, an average taken. The same procedure was adopted for wages. Streets of residence were located in one of four areas in West Ham, corresponding to the postal districts, namely, Stratford, Forest Gate, Plaistow and Canning Town (see Figure 1.2). Details of rent are given only for the 'head' of the household so that contributions of other members of the family in employment cannot be decided. These were coded accordingly. Finally, birthplaces were classified into West Ham, East Ham, East London, London, English counties, Scotland or abroad.

In broad terms the survey is in close agreement with comparable data from the 1931 Census. This tends further to strengthen confidence in the data.

REFERENCES

Oral testimony

The research has benefited considerably from a series of interviews that I carried out with people, all of whom had vivid memories of interwar West Ham and were prepared to share them with me. They provided not only information and perspectives that I have used directly to develop arguments, but also, and less tangibly, what I can best describe as a feeling for the social and political atmosphere of the time. Extracts from transcripts are referenced by a name followed by tape, for example, (Stanton, tape). I am grateful to all who gave me their time: Fred Baker, Emily May Bartells, Jim Enever, Theo Etherington, Bob Horsley, Jim Layzell, John McLaughlin, Frank Robinson, Frank Sainsbury, Riva Stanton, Fred Stokes and George Stokes.

Primary

Place of publication is London except where stated. The second date is that of original publication.

Barton, E (nd, 1931) *Woman - in the home, the store and the state*, Manchester, Cooperative Union.

Booth, C (1892) *Life and labour of the people of London*, Longman.

British Socialist Party, North West Ham branch, *Minutes*.

British Socialist Party (later National Socialist Party, and Social Democratic Party), South West Ham branch, *Minutes*.

Burr, E (nd, 1985) *The memories and reflections of an old man of iron*, unpublished ms.

Canning Town Health Society, *Annual report*.

Clifford, M (1895) *Poor law work: suggestions and new departures*, Manchester, Cooperative Union.

Cooperative Union, *Cooperative News*.

Davison, R C (1929) *The unemployed*, Green & Co.

Department Of The Environment. Inner Cities Directorate (1983) *Urban deprivation*, HMSO.

Dock, Water and Riverside Workers' Union, *Dockers' Record*.

East Ham Echo.

Election leaflets, West Ham.

Greening, E O (1914) 'The perils of politics', *Cooperative news*, 16 May.

Hines, G (1911) 'Cooperators and political action', *Cooperative News*, 8 July.

Justice.

Labour Party, *Annual reports*.

London Cooperative Society (1941) *When we were 21*, LCS.

London County Council, *London Statistics*.

London Labour Party, *London News*.

Llewellyn Davies, M (1922) *Inaugural address; 1922 Cooperative Congress*, Manchester, Cooperative Union.
Mayhew, H (1967; 1852) *London labour and the London poor*, Cass.
National Unemployed Workers Movement, *Out of work*.
National Union Of General Workers, *Quarterly reports*.
National Union Of General Workers, *General Workers' Journal*.
National Union Of General Workers, General Council, *Minutes*.
National Union Of Railwaymen, *Proceedings and reports*.
National Union of Railwaymen, *Railway Review*.
New survey of London life and labour, 1928-32.
Parish, C (nd, 1983) *This was my life*, unpublished ms.
Plaistow Maternity Hospital, *Annual Reports*.
Saunders, C (1936) *Seasonal variations in employment*, Longman.
South West Ham Health Society, *Annual Report*.
Stratford Cooperative Society, *Magazine*.
Stratford Cooperative Society, *Quarterly Report*.
Stratford Express.
Trades Union Congress, *Annual reports*.
Transport And General Workers' Union, *The Record*.
Transport And General Workers' Union, General Executive Committee, *Minutes*.
West Ham Board Of Guardians, *Minutes*.
West Ham Council, *Minutes*.
West Ham Maternity and Child Welfare Committee, *Minutes*.
West Ham medical Officer of Health, *Annual reports*.
West Ham Municipal Alliance (1923) *'Class war' or the 'Common Good'. A warning and an appeal*, WHMA.
West Ham Municipal Alliance (nd) *The truth about the West Ham Municipal Alliance*, WHMA.
West Ham Municipal Alliance (1900) *Election manifesto*, WHMA.
West Ham Trades Council, *Annual report*.
West Ham Trades Council (1932) *Rule book*.
West Ham Trades Council And Central Labour Party (1920), *Rule book*.
Women's Cooperative Guild (1904) *Citizenship campaign*, Manchester Cooperative Union.
Women's Cooperative Guild (1915) *Maternity: letters from working women*, Manchester, Cooperative Union.

Secondary

Bailey, J (1948) 'The consumer in politics,' in Barou, N (ed).
Barnes, A (nd, 1940) *The coming of the London Cooperative Society*, LCS.
Barou, N (ed) (1948) *The cooperative movement in Labour Britain*, Gollancz.
Benwick, R et al. (eds) (1973) *Knowledge and belief in politics*, Allen & Unwin.
Bennett, T (1979) *Formalism and marxism*, Methuen.
Bonner, A (1970) *British cooperation*, Manchester, Cooperative Union.
Branson, N (1979) *Poplarism, 1919-25*, Lawrence and Wishart.
Briggs, A (1959) *Chartist studies*, Macmillan.
Briggs, A and Saville, J (eds) (1977) *Essays in labour history. III. 1918-39*, Croom Helm.
Bullock, A (1960) *The life and times of Ernest Bevin. I. Trade union leader, 1881 - 1940*, Heinemann.
Bush, J (1978) *Labour politics and society in East London during the first world war*, London University PhD.
Bush, J (1984) *Behind the lines*, Merlin.
Butler, D (1972) 'Electors and elected', in Halsey, AH (ed).
Chamberlayne, P (1978) 'The politics of participation: an enquiry into four London boroughs, 1968-74', *London Journal*, Vol 4, No 1.
Clark, K and Holquist, M (1984) *Mikhail Bakhtin*, Cambridge, Mass., Harvard

University Press.

Clegg, H A (1964) *General union in a changing society. A short history of the NUGW, 1889-1964*, Oxford, Oxford University Press.

Clegg, H A (1985) *A history of British trade unions since 1889. II. 1911 - 1933*, Oxford, Oxford University Press.

Clegg, H A, Flanders, A, and Thompson, F (1964) A *history of British trade unions since 1889. I. 1889-1920*, Oxford, Oxford University Press.

Clinton, A (1977) *The trade union rank and file: trades councils in Britain, 1900-40*, Manchester, Manchester University Press.

Coates, K. and Topham, T (1986) *Trade unions and politics*, Oxford, Blackwell.

Cole, G D H (1948a) *A history of the British working class movement*, Routledge.

Cole, G D H (1969, 1948b) A *history of the Labour Party from 1914*, Routledge.

Cronin, J E (1982) 'Coping with labour, 1918-26', in Cronin, J E and Schneer, J (eds).

Cronin, J E and Schneer, J (eds) (1982) *Social conflict and political order in modern Britain*, Croom Helm.

Croucher, R (1987) *We refuse to starve in silence; a history of the National Unemployed Workers Movement*, Lawrence and Wishart.

Cunningham, H (1980) *Leisure and the industrial revolution*, Croom Helm.

Davis, J (1989) 'Radical clubs and London politics, 1870 - 1900', in Feldman, D and Stedman Jones, G (eds).

Deacon, A (1977) 'Concession and coercion: the politics of unemployment insurance in the twenties', in Briggs, A and Saville, J (eds).

Donald, J and Hall, S (eds) (1986) *Politics and ideology*, Open University Press.

Eagleton, T (1981) *Walter Benjamin, or Towards a revolutionary criticism*, Verso.

Epstein, J and Thompson, D (eds) (1982) *The Chartist experience*, London.

Feldman, D and Stedman Jones, G (eds) (1989) *Metropolis. London. Histories and representations since 1800*, Routledge.

Forester, T (1976) *The Labour Party and the working class*, Heinemann.

Gaffin, J and Thoms, D (1983) *Caring and sharing. The centenary of the Cooperative Women's Guild*, Manchester, Cooperative Union.

Garraty, J A (1978) *Unemployment in history. Economic thought and public policy*, Harper and Row.

Gilbert, B (1976) *British social policy, 1914-39*, Batsford.

Gillespie, J (1984) *Economic and political change in the East End of London during the 1920s*, University of Cambridge PhD.

Gillespie, J (1989) 'Poplarism and proletarianism. Unemployment and Labour politics in London, 1918-34', in Feldman, D and Stedman Jones, G (eds).

Glynn, S and Booth, A (1983) Unemployment in interwar Britain: a case for re-learning the lessons of the 1930s?, *Econ. Hist. Rev. XXVI, 3*.

Gray, R (1987) 'The languages of factory reform c. 1830 - 1860', in Joyce, P (ed).

Halsey, A H (ed) (1972) *Trends in British society since 1900*, Macmillan.

Hannington, W (1977; 1936) *Unemployed struggles, 1919 - 1936*, Lawrence and Wishart.

Hannington, W (1937) *The problem of distressed areas*, Left Book Club.

Haseler, S (1980) *The tragedy of Labour*, Oxford, Blackwell.

Himmelfarb, G (1984) *The idea of poverty. England in the early industrial age*, Faber.

Hobbs, D (1988) *Doing the business. Entrepreneurship, the working class and detectives in the East End of London*, Oxford, Oxford University Press.

Howard, C (1983) 'Expectations born to death: local Labour Party expansion in the 1920s', in Winter J (ed).

Joyce, P (ed) (1987) *The historical meanings of work*, Cambridge, Cambridge University Press.

Kennedy Cox, R (1939) *Through the dock gates*, Joseph.

Kingsford, P (1982) *The hunger marches in Britain, 1920 - 1940*, Lawrence and Wishart.

Laclau, E (1982) *Politics and ideology in Marxist theory*, Verso.

Langan M and Schwartz B (eds) (1985) *Crises in the British state, 1880 - 1930*,

Hutchinson.

Llewellyn Davies, M (1904) *The Women's Cooperative Guild, 1883 -1904,* Manchester, Cooperative Union.

Lovell, J (1982)'Trade unions and the development of independent labour politics, 1889-1906', in Pimlott, B and Cook, C (eds).

Macintyre, S (1980) A *proletarian science. Marxism in Britain, 1917–1933,* Cambridge, Cambridge University Press.

Maguire, P (1987) 'Cooperation and crisis: government, cooperation and politics, 1917-22' Paper presented to the History Workshop Conference, Newcastle.

Marriott, J W (1984) *London over the border; a study of West Ham during rapid growth 1870-1910,* University of Cambridge PhD.

Marriott, J W (1988) 'West Ham: London's industrial centre and gateway to the world. I. Industrialization, 1840-1910', *London Journal* Vol 13 No 2.

Marriott, J W (1989) 'West Ham: London's industrial centre and gateway to the world. II. Stabilization and decline, 1910-1939' *London Journal* Vol l4 No1.

Martin, R (1969) *Communism and British trade unions, 1924-33. A study of the National Minority Movement,* Oxford, Oxford University Press.

Martin, R (1980) *Trades Union Congress: the growth of a pressure group, 1868 - 1976,* Oxford, Oxford University Press.

McClelland, K (1987)'Time to work, time to live: some aspects of work and the reformation of class in Britain, 1850-1880' in Joyce, P (ed).

McKenzie, R and Silver, A (1968) *Angels in marble. Working class Conservatives in urban England,* Heinemann.

McKibbin, R (1974) *The evolution of the Labour Party, 1910-24,* Oxford, Oxford University Press.

Miliband, R (1973; 1961) *Parliamentary socialism: a study in the politics of labour,* Merlin.

Mitchell, M (1985) 'The effects of unemployment on the social condition of women and children in the 1930s' *History Workshop Journal,* No19.

Mitchell, B R and Dean, P (1962) *Abstract of British historical statistics,* Cambridge, Cambridge University Press.

Nairn, T (1965)'The nature of the Labour Party' in New Left Review (ed).

New Left Review (ed) (1965) *Toward socialism,* Fontana.

Newland, F W (1932) *Newland of Claremont and Canning Town,* Epworth Press.

Nicholas, K (1986) *The social effects of unemployment on Teeside, 1919-39,* Manchester, Manchester University Press.

Panitch, L (1986) 'Ideology and integration: the case of the British Labour Party' in Panitch, L (ed).

Panitch, L (ed) (1986) *Working class politics in crisis,* Verso.

Pankhurst, E S (1987; 1932) *The home front,* Cresset.

Pimlott, B and Cook, C (eds) (1982) *Trade unions in British politics,* Routledge.

Roker, P and Crawford Scott, H (1926) 'Juvenile unemployment in West Ham' *Economica* March.

Rose, G (1988) 'Locality, politics and culture: Poplar in the 1920s', *Environment and planning D. Society and space,* (6), pp151-68.

Rowan, C (1985) 'Child welfare and the working-class family', in Langan, M and Schwarz, B (eds).

Rubinstein, J (1982) in Pimlott, B and Cook, C (eds).

Savage, M (1987) *The dynamics of working class politics. The labour movement in Preston, 1880-1940,* Cambridge, Cambridge University Press.

Saville, J (1973) 'The ideology of labourism', in Benewick et al. (eds).

Schwarz B (1986) 'Conservatism, nationalism and imperialism', in Donald J and Hall S (eds).

Schwarz, B and Durham, M (1985) 'A safe and sane labourism: socialism and the state 1910-24', in Langham, M and Schwarz, B (eds).

Sharp, E (1933) *Buyers and builders. A jubilee sketch of the Women's Cooperative Guild, 1883-1933,* Manchester, Cooperative Union.

Stallybrass, P and White, A (1986) *The politics and poetics of transgression*, Methuen.

Stevenson, J (1982) in Pimlott, B and Cook, C (eds).

Stedman Jones, G (1972) *Outcast London*, Oxford, Clarendon Press.

Stedman Jones G (1974) 'Working-class culture and working-class politics in London, 1870-1900', *J. Soc. Hist.* (7) 4.

Stedman Jones, G (1982) 'Rethinking Chartism' in Epstein, J and Thompson, D (eds).

Thompson, P (1967) *Socialists, Liberals and Labour; the struggle for London, 1887 - 1914*, Routledge.

Waites, B (1987) A *class society at war. England 1914 - 1918*, Berg.

Webb, S and Webb, B (1922) *The consumers' cooperative movement*, Longman.

Webb, S and Webb, B (1910) *English Poor Law policy*, Longman.

White, J (1986) *The worst street in North London. Campbell Bunk, Islington, between the wars*, Routledge

Whiteside, N (1987) 'Counting the costs: sickness and disability among the working people in an era of industrial recession, 1920-39', *Econ. Hist. Rev.* XL, 2

Williams, K (1981) *From pauperism to poverty*, Routledge.

Winter, J (ed) (1983) *The working class in modern British history; essays in honour of Henry Pelling*, Cambridge, Cambridge University Press.

Wrigley, C (1982) 'Trade unions and politics in the first world war', in Pimlott, B and Cook, C (eds).

Whiteside, N (1979) 'Welfare insurance and casual labour; a study of administrative intervention in industrial employment, 1906-26', *Econ. Hist. Rev. XXXII*.

INDEX